Gem Magic

Gem Magic

THE WONDER OF YOUR BIRTHSTONE

Cornelia M. Parkinson

Fawcett Columbine ✧ *New York*

A Fawcett Columbine Book
Published by Ballantine Books
Copyright © 1988 by Cornelia M. Parkinson, Inc.
Illustrations copyright © 1988 by David Lindroth

Grateful acknowledgment is made to the following for permission to reprint
previously published material:

Doubleday and Company, Inc.: excerpts from the poem "The Gypsy Trail" by
Rudyard Kipling from *Rudyard Kipling's Verse: Definitive Edition* by Elsie Kipling
Bambridge and Caroline Kipling. Reprinted by permission of Doubleday and
Company, Inc.

Viking Penguin, Inc.: excerpt from the poem "The Creation" from *God's Trom-
bone* by James Weldon Johnson. Copyright 1927 by The Viking Press, Inc.
Copyright renewed 1955 by Grace Nail Johnson. All rights reserved. Reprinted
by permission of Viking Penguin, Inc.

Library of Congress Catalog Card Number: 87-91168

ISBN: 0-449-90275-7

Cover design by James R. Harris
Photo by Don Banks

Text design by Mary A. Wirth

Manufactured in the United States of America
First Edition: February 1988
10 9 8 7 6 5 4 3 2 1

To Parky, with love through the ages

Contents

CONTENTS · ix

Acknowledgments

My love and gratitude go to Eileen Nauman, writer, lecturer, teacher, astrologer, psychic, numerologist, and adventurer in all higher realms of awareness. In her presence the concept of this book came to me. (I'd like to give her more credit, but at the time I got the flash she was grading papers and didn't look up for an hour. By then the basic outline had become clear to me.) Her psychic interpretations of the numerals of each birthstone shed exciting new light on the energies and legends of the gems. Thanks for your cheerful contribution, Eileen.

My appreciation also goes to all those psychics, philosophers, poets, dreamers, dowsers, explorers, pharmacists, chroniclers, soothsayers, Jews, Egyptians, Persians, Indians, lapidaries, scientists, prehistoric amulet makers, alchemists, ancient rulers, historians, artisans, Christian mystics, craftsmen, physicians, bishops, astrologers, saints, miners, scholars, jewelers, scryers, healers, and others, like me, who have loved gemstones enough to investigate their properties both practical and unprovable, and who passed their findings down through the centuries. They have all had their influence, and it is reflected in these pages. Believe what you will, and consider the rest.

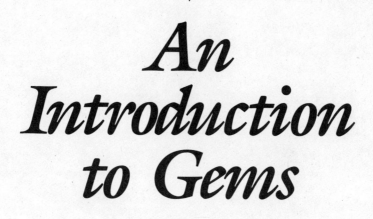

An Introduction to Gems

"There are more things in heaven and earth, Horatio,
Than are dreamt of in your philosophy."

WILLIAM SHAKESPEARE, <u>HAMLET</u> I.v.

---✧---

Yes, there is magic in your birthstone! A magic that goes back centuries in time before the birth of Christ, a magic that was well known not only to sorcerers and seers, but also to the man (and woman) in the streets of ancient Mesopotamia, Egypt, India, and Babylonia. This mystical power of gems was invoked to prevent drunkenness, cure impotency, foretell danger, heal wounds, and relieve eyestrain.

In this handbook on birthstones and other gems, I'll tell you all about them. I'll introduce you first to some of the general characteristics and powers that have been attributed to gemstones, relating a few legends and archaeological discoveries to whet your appetite for the stories about *your* birthstone. Then I'll briefly discuss the formation of gems and some of their physical distinctions. Finally, in the chapter for each stone, you'll find out what your birthstone looks like, where it comes from, and exactly what magical powers each gem is said to have.

Read the introduction first, to get an overview of gemstones. Then don't wait any longer—turn right to the chapter for your birthstone and read all the fascinating details.

✧

ANCIENT USES

Man has ascribed to gems mystical, even miraculous powers, and woven folklore, legends, and religion about them. He has sought opals and diamonds in the suffocating depths of the earth and dug for lapis lazuli on bitter, snow-swept mountaintops. He has coveted gems of great beauty and value, killed for them, died for them. In the most romantic and important events of his life, he has assigned gems a vital role.

Before money was devised, gems and jewelry were a convenient, portable medium of exchange. Even today, people, fleeing a country where their lives are endangered, able to take only a few things with them, will try to have the family jewels among their possessions.

In ancient times, one gem was used to facilitate childbirth, another to make rain or to make the sun shine. There were even sacred stones in which to deposit cut hair, to prevent evil ones from using the hair to make a charm. This belief lingered for hundreds of years, for at the turn of the twentieth century, every lady had a china "hair receiver" with a hole in the lid, in which to deposit the hairs that came out when she brushed or combed her long locks.

Powdered and drunk in a potion, a sapphire could cure sore eyes or dysentery or heart disease. Bullets of garnet had a greater power of killing the enemy. If inscribed with symbols, one gem might provide a powerful defense against injury or fraud, another would attract honors and adulation, yet a third reconcile enemies.

Gems have symbolized the saints, colors, planets, days of the week, and numbers. In the language of the ancient Mexicans, blood was called *chalchiuhatl*, meaning water of precious stones, for just as blood was vital to life, precious stones were the most costly things known.

Gemstones were revered even in Biblical times. In Exodus, chapter 28, we read of the holy garments of Aaron, first head of the Hebrew priesthood. One of his garments was a breastplate, made of gold, blue, purple, and scarlet fabric and fine twined linen. The breastplate was square, about nine inches on each side, bearing twelve stones, each stone engraved with a different name, one for each of the Twelve Tribes of Israel. The stones were placed in four horizontal rows of three stones each. Under the breastplate, and fastened to it, the High Priest wore an apron-like garment called an ephod. Upon its shoulder pieces were two onyx stones, set in gold filigree. In a pouch under the frame of the breastplate, he wore the Urim and Thummim, stones used in casting sacred lots and in divining God's Will.

The Sumerians, the Egyptians, and other early civilizations buried fine gems along with their noble dead. Even prehistoric peoples did this, for in archaeologically excavated graves and barrows have been found treasures of amber, jet, turquoise, lapis lazuli, garnet, quartz, and shell, as well as mica, gold, silver and copper items of adornment. Things treasured by the living person, and items that would help him in the afterworld, were buried with him when he died.

Many American Indian tribes place stones on a grave as a token of respect and remembrance. Each time someone passes the grave, he lays another stone on the pile. In Connecticut, what seems to be an ancient Indian grave has been preserved in the side yard of a modern house. The pile of stones, some quite large, is about ten feet high.

In pawn, great gems have demonstrated the power to finance countries as well as their wars. Henry III of France wore the fifty-four-carat Sancy diamond as a decoration on the cap that hid his baldness. After his death, in 1589, the gem was pawned to hire twelve thousand Swiss mercenaries to fight for his successor, Henry of Navarre. The campaign was successful; the diamond was redeemed. Then, because France was bankrupt, the stone was sold to King James I of England for 60,000 *ecus*.

In a different conflict in 1645, Queen Henrietta Maria of England was able to pawn some of her family's gems, plus some of the lesser crown jewels of England, to raise money for the battles in which her husband, King Charles I, was embroiled.

So strong is the power and attraction of gems that parents sometimes give their children a gemstone name. Jasper is a gem as well as a male name. Pearl and Beryl are names for either males or females; for girl children the names Ruby, Opal, Topaz, Jacinth, and Garnet are familiar. In Sri Lanka today—the land known as the Isle of Gems—many people are given the name of a gemstone. In that country gemstones, besides being a principal source of wealth, are also held in high spiritual regard.

Several centuries ago, the Greek writer Theophrastus declared that gems had gender, the dark stones being male and the lighter ones female. He said that some diamonds, exposed to light and then taken into the dark, became phosphorescent. He even wrote of certain diamonds which, in the dark, cloned themselves. Now *that's* magic!

✧

GEMSTONES AS CHARMS

It was man who called stones precious, who assigned them mystical value centuries before the Wise Men brought their gifts of gold to the Infant Jesus. Was it a flash of divine insight, or the slower process of observation and deduction, that led human beings to perceive this esoteric quality in stones? They saw beauty in the sunrise; but the sun became blinding by midday. There was color in leaves and flowers, until they withered. Water sparkled, but it could not be worn for long. Of all the natural wonders of the earth, only the stones endured. They must indeed be magical; and those who possess magical things can sometimes put to work the magic in them.

So some prehistoric man got the idea of the amulet or talisman, a powerful good-luck charm, to wear about his person. And parts of these amulets have endured the ravages of time.

In a grave in Russia, established to be twenty-four thousand years old, a Cro-Magnon male was buried in a tunic adorned with over three thousand ivory beads. A boy and a girl were buried together with spears of ivory, eight thousand ivory beads, and numerous rings and anklets, probably proclaiming their rank.

A Mesolithic culture, the Natufians, lived from about 10,000 to 8,000 B.C. in Palestine, in caves and open-air sites in the central coastal plain and the Judean hills. The men wore fan-shaped headdresses of shell and necklaces of shell, bone, and fish vertebrae. Some of their burial sites were excavated beginning in 1929. There the amulets were found of men who hunted, fished, and established permanent settlements ten thousand years ago.

The remains of a Bronze Age man were found last century in an archeological dig in Bohemia. Scattered close around him were beads of garnet which had been pierced as for use in a necklace. A similar story is told of another dig, where the beads were amber. As early as 3500 B.C., in Crete, stone beads were cut and bored for wearing.

Another, much more elaborate find was made in a tomb in Egypt. This man had also lived about 3500 B.C. Around his neck lay a necklace of beads made from carnelian, shell, garnet, and amethyst, with a turquoise pendant amulet about half an inch long, carved in the shape of an ibex. The hundreds of exquisite examples of early Egyptian jewelry speak eloquently of the skill of their goldsmiths and jewelers.

Kings and queens in ancient Egypt made everyday use of chairs, couches, thrones, and chariots overlaid with sheets of gold and lavishly ornamented with precious stones. Turquoise was used widely. Vases of lapis lazuli, headdresses, rings, necklaces, bracelets, and girdles of gold set with turquoise and other gems were among the possessions excavated from the tombs of the wealthy and the rulers. Most of the jewelry items found in Egyptian tombs were especially made for burial with the individual, to outfit him or her for the life that followed death.

Perhaps the most notable burial of gemstone-studded tributes with a dead sovereign is that of Tutankhamen, the young king who ruled Egypt about 3,300 years ago. His sumptuous tomb was discovered in 1922, crammed with rings, bracelets, amulets, diadems, collars, and breastplates wrought of gold and set with precious gems. Some of these enduringly beautiful treasures toured the United States in an unprecedented display; books have been written about them, complete with color photographs. They may be viewed in the Egyptian National Museum.

Centuries after King Tut, Charlemagne, the wise and good ruler of the French around A.D. 800, forbade the burial of precious things with the dead, on the grounds that the practice took too much wealth out of circulation. Does that sound familiar? Evidently we haven't changed much in over a thousand years.

In those early times men, rather than women, wore gems. About the time that the Biblical David reigned as King (1000–961 B.C.), the then-scarce iron was being used for men's bracelets and anklets. Perhaps the gems served as adornment, but more importantly they were worn for protection against evil.

We still use amulets and talismans, even though we may not think of them as such, or place as much faith in them as people did who lived closer to nature. Our amulets are all familiar pieces of jewelry. Necklaces, for example: those set with brilliant or colorful stones distract the observer's gaze away from the wearer's face, and so ward off the Evil Eye. Brooches or pins serve the same purpose, with additional protective power conferred by a correctly chosen gemstone set in the brooch. Specially chosen talismanic shapes—the ankh, the mandala, the scarab, the yin and yang, the thunderbird—hundreds of symbols created of precious metals and gems can be found in modern jewelry. Some people believe that rings—wedding rings particularly—are the strongest amulet of all.

Gemstones were used as early as 3800 B.C. in sacred works of art. A tablet found at Telloh records the capture of a Babylonian city and the burning of several temples. "Silver and precious stones were carried away therefrom," the tablet states. The Bible mentions precious stones as personal ornaments; kings wore them in their crowns, and priests in their garments.

✦

GEMSTONES OF GODS, GODDESSES, EMPERORS, AND KINGS

In India, since the earliest times, men and women have worn and revered precious stones and jewels. The writers of classic Sanskrit poetry, relating the lives of the mythological heroes and the demigods and their consorts, outlined in exact detail the adornment of these heroic figures with jewels and precious metals. The *Ramayana*, written in the third century B.C., describes the glorious majesty of the god Shiva (the Destroyer), and includes a long list of ornaments of the period. Rama, an incarnation of Vishnu (the Preserver), wore wedding-day necklaces of pearls and flowers, and a crown of pearls from which ornaments dangled to his chest. His bride Sita wore jeweled butterflies in her black hair, golden bells on her ankles, and the landscape in between head and feet was brilliant with the precious stones she wore.

The Bhagavad-Gita, a Sanskrit epic tale of Krishna, describes necklaces, bracelets, earrings, diadems, rings, and bells worn by the males and females of the story; and around the neck of the hero's horse there is a chain set with jewels. Another record, this one a two-thousand-year-old play, describes a jeweler's shop, listing the gemstones to be found there; tells of the several kinds of gold used, and notes that flowers are the basis of the ornamental motifs, as they are in India even today.

An ancient Indian *sutra*, a sort of guidebook for living, gives fixed rituals for each of the many religious ceremonies that govern daily life. Ornaments of jewelry to be worn are named, each designated as having a particular religious significance. Beauty and wealth, therefore, come after the moral significance of the jewel. The only personal property owned by wives—their jewelry—is still stringently protected by an ancient law.

Between the eighth and the second centuries B.C., according to inscriptions found on the premises, Buddhist monks intermittently dwelt in caves they cut into stone in a desolate region in India near Aurangabad. In 1817, British soldiers on maneuvers discovered these Ajanta Caves, as well as unimaginable treasure of the highest artistic skill. On the cave walls and ceilings were painted frescoes depicting the lives of gods, goddesses, and legendary heroes. All the stories of Buddha's life, all his incarnations, his friends and disciples, are there in incredibly rich and glowing color, ornamentation, and detail; mythological heroes, gods and animals, river goddesses, celestial dancers and musicians and angels move, embrace, and all but sing.

In a three-hundred-year period, truly inspired artists and goldsmiths had portrayed these marvelous scenes which had been written of centuries before. The wonderful bodies of the heroes and heroines are nude, adorned only in necklaces, pendants, bracelets, ankle hoops, girdles, and turbans wrought of fine gold and encrusted with rubies, emeralds, pearls, and other gemstones. In addition, the artists had skillfully used gold and gems, pearls and precious ornamentation on the facades, the doors, and the columns, turning caves into fantastic palaces occupied by the stunningly beautiful beings of myths and legends.

The oldest talisman of India, whose use began well before the Christian Era, is the *naoratna*. This is a gold piece set with nine precious stones, each possessing its own metaphysical power, each corresponding to a heavenly body, each exchanging radiations with all the other stones in the talisman. The *naoratna* was said to protect against inauspicious zodiacal influences. It was worn—flamboyantly, with large uncut stones—by Mogul monarchs. Hindu beliefs in the radiant influences of stones and minerals influenced their lives from birth onward. Everyone wore talismans and amulets, even children, whose amulet was a carnelian engraved with a text from the Koran.

Royal thrones were encrusted as thickly with precious stones as pebbles on a beach. One throne, that of the Mogul Emperor Shah Jehan of India, laid all others out in its shade. At the beginning of his reign (1628–1658), Shah Jehan formed the thought of a sumptuous throne that would summarize—for all who saw it—his sacred majesty, his power, his wealth. The goldsmiths of Delhi executed the Shah's wishes in every detail; and in like manner their completed work was described by several famous European traveler/writers who saw it. This was the fabulous Peacock Throne.

To begin with, you couldn't just walk up like a tourist and gawk at this fantastic sight. It was splendidly situated in the center of the royal tent, which you entered only at the invitation of the Shah. The tent was immense, held up by some forty columns, all plated with gold or silver. Brilliantly colored silks and brocades formed the inner walls. With reverence and trepidation you approached the Shah on his throne, walking through the fields of flowers that were depicted on the one hundred carpets that covered the ground.

At the requisite distance away from the silver steps that led up to the throne, you stopped in awe. The silk-and-jewel-bedecked splendor of the Shah himself was eclipsed by the magnificence of his throne, which was covered with enameled gold, and encrusted with diamonds edge to edge. A canopy, supported by columns set with hundreds of emeralds, represented the night sky, with stars of diamonds, pearls, sapphires, and rubies. Behind the throne were two resplendent sacred peacocks with their tail plumage spread. They were made of gold set with pearls; a likeness of the mystical eyespot in each tail feather was formed of artfully placed emeralds and sapphires. From the breast of each peacock hung a great pendant ruby and a pear-shaped pearl.

Above the throne hung an enormous sun, a wondrous sardonyx of golden orange red, as well as a bow and quiver set with many jewels. Suspended in front was an enormous diamond, whose sparkling beauty could mesmerize the Shah into forgetting the yawn-inducing daily tasks of being a monarch.

Magic in gems? This is only the beginning.

The skills of Jewish and other Semite goldsmiths and jewelers developed concurrently with those of India, and long before the time of Christ. They fashioned wires of gold and silver into lacy ornaments, often studded with gemstones, and made all the usual additional objects of precious metals and precious stones. Other ancient Jewish jewelry, found at archeological digs in Palestine, includes the treasures of a prince of Megiddo, about the fifteenth century B.C. Under the floor of a palace room, hidden away from invaders, were a gold-mesh chain, an electrum* ring with a scarab setting, some lapis lazuli cylinder seals, a heavy gold bowl, beads of granulated gold, gold-trimmed cosmetic jars, and a ceremonial whetstone with two gold caps. In the Orient, jewelry items and gems, with their ready portability, formed the bulk of royal or even family wealth.

Because of constant looting and the levying of tribute by conquerors, most of the jewels of the Biblical period have been lost. However, some exist, such as the golden jewelry of Hyksos, excavated at Tell-el-'Ajjul, and may be seen in museums in Beirut and Jerusalem. The sarcophagus and jewels of King Ahiram of Byblos are displayed at the National Museum of Lebanon in Beirut. Jewelry objects include his solid gold and enamel bracelets, scarabs, pins, statuettes, silver-soled sandals, and scepter. A broad, shallow "Queen Esther" golden cup was recovered in the palace city of Shushan. The silver bowl of Artaxerxes I, who reigned in Persia 464–424 B.C. is in the Metropolitan Museum of Art.

It is not my intention here to say a great deal about the precious metals, even though without them our jewelry would be much less imaginative and useful. Gold and silver have been used in jewelry, ornaments, artistic objects, religious figures, household vessels, and plates for thousands of years. Early in the reign of King David, iron was also a precious metal.

Iron is not much used now in jewelry, but before 1200 B.C. it was considered as valuable and decorative as gold and silver. The first known iron of the Middle East was from meteors and contained small amounts of nickel. The Egyptian name and the cuneiform ideogram for iron characterized it as a metal of heaven.

The prosperous reigns of King David and his son King Solomon were due mainly to industrial developments of the Iron Age. The Philistines had a monopoly on manufacture of this precious metal until David conquered them and made iron available for common

* A natural pale yellow alloy of gold and silver.

use in Israel. The raw material was plentiful from the Wadi Arabah all the way south to the Red Sea. Archeologist Nelson Glueck discovered sites that had been in use for centuries for refining this ore to be used in axeheads, hatchets, vessels for the tabernacles, chariots, chains, graving tools, idols, and bars of prison gates.

✧

THE HOLY GRAIL

The Angel Satan, when he rebelled against God, wore a great precious stone, long said to be an emerald or a ruby, in his crest. In the titantic struggle between the fallen angels and the Heavenly Host, the Archangel Michael struck Satan down. The enormous gem, cleansed by space, fell to earth. Much, much later it was discovered by an early people, who used their considerable artistic skills to create from it a majestic chalice.*

King Solomon acquired the chalice, and from him it was handed down to his descendant, Jesus Christ. It was this chalice, the Holy Grail, that Jesus is said to have used at the Last Supper to originate the Sacrament of Communion. When Christ was on the cross, Joseph of Arimathea used the chalice to collect his sacred blood. Imprisoned, Joseph was sustained by the Grail. In A.D. 37 he took it and other sacred relics to Glastonbury in Britain, where it was enshrined for some time.

The Holy Grail was taken to Spain and thence to northeast Asia, to the kingdom of Kuruz. Ghengis Khan killed the last king of that country; the chalice was taken to Antioch. From that time on, nothing is known of the chalice from which Jesus Christ drank.

The famous Chalice of Antioch, which can be seen in New York's Metropolitan Museum of Art, is of silver with carved open-

---

* Now, with the general increase in spiritual awareness and the recognition of the high purpose of moldavite, an extraterrestrial stone, some gem dealers are beginning to speculate that the stone in Satan's crest was a moldavite. It is thought that the Holy Grail may also have been made from moldavite. Moldavite is a charcoal-green stone of meteoritic origin, having the potential of providing direct access to higher dimensions of energies. Consider the connections of the Grail to the Highest Dimension, and its extraterrestrial origin makes good sense.

work, bearing symbolic designs and the figures of twelve men. Though a valuable example of very early Christian art, its date of origin is controversial. This chalice might possibly have housed the Grail, but if that occurred, it is believed to have been four or more centuries after Christ.

✧

THE SCENT OF GEMSTONES

If you have ever sniffed a geode* or struck two flint rocks together and smelled their sulphury odor, you will agree that rocks have a scent. It is said that in reducing gemstones to powder, an agreeable fragrance is released. A physician's account of this phenomenon appeared in 1757. He wanted a number of gemstones so finely pulverized that they would not grate between the teeth and that a layer of the powder could scarcely be seen. He hired his lodger, a medical student, to spend a month pulverizing emeralds, rubies, sapphires, pearls, and jacinths. After about three weeks the student's room (which was large) was fragrant with a pleasant and lingering perfume. Since nothing else in the room could have produced it, the physician believed that it came from the powdering of stones.

✧

GEMSTONE THERAPY

There *is* something magical about stones. Why else would people have placed so much faith in their curative and protective powers throughout the long centuries? The therapeutic use of stones began probably as long ago as the first headache. In ancient times it was believed that the parts of the body were each controlled or governed by a particular stone, metal, and planet. Therefore, to be effective, the gem used had to correspond to the ailing part.

As late as 1757, it was possible to go into a chemist's shop in

---

* A nodule of stone, from lemon size to sometimes larger than a basketball, having a cavity lined with crystals or mineral matter.

London and buy powdered ruby, emerald, rock crystal, or lapis lazuli, to be used much as we use aspirin, Tums, or Ben-Gay today. In pharmacies in India even now, one can buy *Bhasmas*, which are the ashes of specific gems to be administered as medication under the principles of Ayurvedic medicine. Also available are ready-made gem medicines in other forms.

Gemstones have been used in India as medicine from time immemorial. Ayurveda, a three-thousand-year-old system of healing, uses the ashes of diamond, sapphire, ruby, emerald, pearl, coral, and moonstone, plus other gemstones, either separately or in combinations, to treat all types of medical conditions. The stones, which are reduced to ash, may be gem quality, clear, transparent, flawless, perfectly cut and polished—provided the patient is wealthy enough to afford that. Those available through pharmacies more frequently began as *Nagina*, or second-class gems, round or odd shaped, which were polished only and then burned to ash. *Bhasmas* prepared from the second class of stones are considered high-class medications.

Another school of healing which uses gemstones is known simply as Gem Therapy. This successful present-day method, which was developed in India in the 1940s by Dr. Benoytosh Bhattacharyya, uses the vibrations of the colors from gems to treat various ailments and diseases. It is similar to Ayurvedic medicine in that the aim is to restore the cosmic color balance to the human system and thus heal it.

The cosmic colors are violet, indigo, blue, green, yellow, orange, and red—the colors of the Seven Rays of the rainbow, a natural phenomenon that has become the symbol of the New Age. The theory behind Gem Therapy is that every tangible thing consists of rays and radiation; all things are created, maintained, and eventually destroyed by rays; and when the human body becomes unbalanced—that is, unable to assimilate a particular ray or rays—then illness sets in. By restoring the body's color balance, health is restored.

The color vibrations for Gem Therapy are obtained by placing the proper gemstone in absolute alcohol, and keeping the closed container away from light for seven days and seven nights while the alcohol absorbs the vibrations. Then the container is shaken and the Mother Tincture poured into another vial containing blank medicinal globules. Further gentle shaking medicates the globules, which the patient then takes in the manner of a prescription.

The vibrations of a single gem are used, sometimes supplemented with the First Mixture and the Second Mixture. The First Mixture will contain up to five gems; the Second is a nine-gem combination. (The gemstones continue to vibrate, and are used to make new tinctures again and again. The patient is advised not to take the tincture undiluted.) The major advantages of this therapy are that it is inexpensive, benign, has no side effects, and is orally administered. Some remarkably swift improvements and subsequent complete recoveries from serious illness have been reported.

In Teletherapy, an allied medical use of gemstones, the cosmic colors are dynamic rather than static, as they are in Gem Therapy. The methods are equally effective. The colors the individual needs are generated by the correct gems set on disks, which are either electrically rotated or vibrated at specific high frequencies. The target is the patient's photograph or his name on a slip of paper. The colors released by the gems travel from the photograph or the name telepathically to the individual.

In Radionics, a healing method used since the beginning of this century, a machine is used to diagnose and prescribe for the individual. The vibrations from the correct gemstones (plus other minerals, etc.) are then electromagnetically transferred to the medicating vehicle, which can be water or milk-sugar pills. The remedy may be taken either orally or by absorption through the skin. Alternatively, it may be sent electromagnetically via the ether to the patient.

A currently popular way to get your vibes from crystals is to drink "gem and tonic"—water from a glass in which a gemstone is sitting. The gem vibrations are transmitted to the one drinking the water. (If the gem is small, it might be prudent to devise a strainer.)

A direct method of absorbing the vibrations from gemstones is used by the great and respected Kokichi Mikimoto. This gentleman, who pioneered the culturing of pearls and gained for them acceptance as jewels, made a remarkable statement when he was ninety-four years old. He said, "I owe my fine health and long life to the two pearls I have swallowed every morning of my life since I was twenty."

Many gemstones work their healing magic through the chakras. The chakras are energy points in the astral body, that aura of light which surrounds the physical body and its etheric double. Rather than going into a full explanation of the numerous chakras, which is the subject of several other books currently available, I'll give brief descriptions of the seven major chakras.

Chakra (shock-ra) is a Sanskrit word for wheel. To a psychic the chakras of spiritually undeveloped people appear as static circles about one and one-half inches across. As the person develops, the chakras open, assuming color, radiance, and whirling movement.

Chakras are not physical; they are of the spiritual realm. They are connected to an energy channel that runs up and down the aura along the spine. Their function is to amplify or diminish the various psychic abilities and spiritual attributes that are associated with them. They are of major importance in healing the interconnected body, mind, and spirit. Energy directed toward a particular chakra in the astral body will act on that part of the physical body as well. However, through trauma or stress these energy points may become blocked, damaged, or misaligned with the energy channel of the astral body. Physical and/or psychological problems will be the result. To rebalance the flow of energy, it is very helpful to treat and realign the chakras.

There are seven major chakras.

The first, the base or root chakra, is located at the base of the spine in men, and between the ovaries in women. It is concerned with individual survival and perpetuation of the human species.

The second, the spleen chakra, is just below the navel. Through this chakra we recognize and are sensitive to the emotions of others. Also, this center is concerned with sexual energy, sending and receiving it.

The third, or solar plexus, chakra is the body's distribution point for psychic energies. It's your gut-level-feeling center, the hangout for butterflies in the stomach.

The fourth, the heart chakra, is your highest spiritual center, the center of oneness with all, of love and compassion.

The fifth, or throat, chakra, located at the hollow of your throat, is your communications chakra. If you can't speak out or speak up, it gets you right here with coughs, colds, and thyroid troubles.

The sixth, or third eye, chakra, is between the eyebrows and just above them. This is your center of clairvoyance, visualization, and telepathy.

The seventh, the crown chakra, is at the top back of the head. This is the chakra of intuition and pure knowledge. When you are meditating, it is this center through which you receive universal energy and direct it to the other chakras. When you have a hunch about something—or absolute knowledge—it comes through the crown chakra.

With these brief explanations of the function of each chakra, you can see the importance of keeping your chakras properly open and aligned, in order to produce the optimum flow of energies into and out of the body, mind, and spirit.

✧
PREPARING YOUR OWN GEM ELIXIRS

Only recently has it become possible to buy therapeutic preparations of gems and precious metals in the United States. Several companies now manufacture these elixirs, bottled with droppers and labeled with suggested purposes, dosages, and gem derivations. They are available at some New Age stores. Or if you prefer, you can make your own.

Gemstone elixirs contain the vibrations, the essence of the stone, and are very close to the pure life force. The mineral kingdom is attuned to the etheric forces; it coordinates and harmonizes the human being's physical and etheric bodies to bring healing, wholeness, and spiritual unfoldment. Now, in these days when we are on the leading edge of the Age of Aquarius and more and more people are becoming spiritually aware, it is important to maintain proper balance in our health physically, chemically, mentally, emotionally, and spiritually. The vibrations from the gemstones we wear, or from those we take therapeutically, can help us in this necessary work.

The chapter for each gemstone includes a list of the maladies the particular gemstone helps to heal, whether it is worn or taken as an elixir.

Here is a simplified way to prepare your own elixirs from gemstones. The stone or crystal (except for a few very soft ones which do not enter into consideration here) is not harmed, nor are its vibrations lowered. Only the etheric values are transferred from the stone into the water; there is no leaching out of physical properties. After use the gem can be cleansed in sea salt and/or powdered quartz and used again and again. The gemstone or crystal should be stored in natural material, such as a wooden box, or wrapped in cotton, linen, or silk.

Some major criteria are that the gem mineral be of good quality, and that it be uncut and unpolished, with no chemicals on it, and no inclusions of other minerals in it. If some of the matrix (the base mineral on which the mineral grew) is still attached, this is beneficial in attuning the mineral to earth energies. Proper metaphysical methods (described below) should be used to cleanse the gem and the utensils. Distilled water is used in the processes. Before actually making the elixir, set the mineral in the sun, and hold a quartz crystal or star sapphire while you take several minutes to calm, clear, and focus your mind.

Utensils used for preparing the first elixir may be cleansed and used again and again. Store all the items apart from household utensils, reserving them for this purpose only. To make an elixir, you will need the following:

1. An enamel, glass, stainless steel, or copper utensil large enough to hold items 2, 3, and 4 for the purpose of boiling them in water.
2. A new bowl that will hold two cups or more of water. The bowl may be of quartz, of clear uncolored glass with no designs on it, of copper, or of stainless steel. Plastic should not be used, nor should aluminum because of its toxicity.
3. New storage bottles or jars, preferably blue glass because of its ability to promote healing. Clear glass will do. All will require lids. You will need a pint container and one or more one- or two-ounce containers for each gem elixir you are making.
4. Glass or stainless steel funnel is optional.

5. Sea salt, one pound or more, to cover your gemstone. Sea salt draws toxicity from other objects to itself. Health food stores carry this.
6. A clean towel of natural materials such as cotton or linen.
7. A gallon or more of distilled water, to be used for the elixir and also for boiling and cleansing the utensils.
8. The gemstone or stones (preferably in crystal form) from which you wish to make the gem elixir.
9. A sunny day, preferably a cloudless morning.

Prepare the gemstone by placing it in a secure position where the rising sun will shed its light on the stone. Leave it there for two hours minimum, two weeks maximum. Moonstone, pearl, and quartz should be placed under the moon when it is at its highest point. All stones can be placed under both sun and moon. The rays of these heavenly bodies activate the vibrations in the stone, purifying and enhancing them.

The stone or crystal may be further purified by covering it for a half-hour with a mixture of two parts sea salt, one part powdered quartz. Then rinse the stone well under distilled water, and dry. Or, at the absolute least, shake the gem to cleanse it and amplify its properties.

Next cleanse your utensils. Boil distilled water in item 1 for ten minutes to cleanse it. If you have a pyramid, place items 2, 3, and 4 under it for one-half to two hours. In any case, boil these items ten minutes in the large utensil and dry them on the towel.

Now you can begin to make the elixir. Having sunned the gemstone or crystal while you have quieted yourself, you are ready to start. Center your gemstone in a prepared bowl and cover with twelve or more ounces of water. Place the bowl in the sun on a board, a cotton or linen towel, a log, or the grass. It may be covered with a piece of plain glass. Leave it for two hours. The vibrations from the gemstone enter the water to form the elixir. The elixir looks just like water.

Pour the completed elixir into the large storage jar. You may want to use a funnel for pouring it into the small bottles. Label each bottle with the name of the gemstone.

An alternative way of preparing elixir is to boil the stone. The boiling expands the molecules of the stone so that it releases its

energy into the water. First cleanse the mineral in sea salt or powdered quartz for a half-hour. Boil the stone in a clean glass or
stainless-steel bowl for ten minutes. To reap the beneficial effects
of the sun or moon, do this work at sunrise, at high noon, or, for
the moon-connected stones, at sunset.

This liquid is called mother essence. From it you take seven
drops and put it into your large storage jar with about twelve
ounces of distilled water. You may use the mother essence in this
way to make as many jars of elixir as you have mother essence for.
To stabilize elixir made by boiling, place it under a pyramid overnight.

The dosage is three to seven drops three or four times each day
for two weeks. Shake the bottle first, to amplify the mixture. Take
your dose on an empty stomach upon rising, before meals, and at
bedtime. After two weeks, stop for a week to observe the changes,
then if necessary resume the dosage on the same on-off cycle, until
the condition no longer exists.

Except with chronic conditions, don't take the gem elixirs con-
tinuously. Even though you know how they are prepared, they
are quite powerful—and effective.

Note: If you are serious about pursuing this aspect of gems,
study the two books by Gurudas listed in the bibliography. There
you will find a wealth of specific information.

✧

THE ORIGIN OF GEMSTONES AND CRYSTAL SYSTEMS OF MINERALS

Where do gems come from? What are they made of? Do they
grow in nature, or are they something science has cooked up?
What makes one merely a rock and another of gem quality?

Genuine gemstones are among the natural wonders of earth.
Except for pearl, all the birthstone gems are minerals. Minerals
form as crystals. The crystals of certain minerals, when of fine quality, are used as gems. Although some minerals grow these crystals
in abundance, only a small proportion of them will be of gem
quality.

The crystals of minerals are identified by their form, which in turn is classified according to a rather intricate system having to do with the axes within the crystal. The structure of the molecules of the mineral is reflected in its crystal form, which reveals mathematical relationships among the axes. Crystals have two or three axes, generally at right angles to each other.

For example, study a quartz crystal just as it grew, with its sharply planed sides and its point made up of geometric forms. A crystal always has several sides, which are defined by natural flat surfaces. Crystals are obedient to certain rules of growth, established by directional patterns within. No matter how large a crystal gets, its pattern remains the same.

Crystals will show distortions, inclusions, and other interferences in their development. For example, a crystal may form around an object, commonly other crystals; yet the growth pattern remains standard for that mineral. Certain stones, such as emerald and ruby, typically have inclusions. But as a rule, unless the inclusions are interesting, it's the perfectly formed crystals that have the potential of becoming gemstones.

In the hexagonal system, for example, there are four axes, one axis at right angles to the other three, which are arranged at 120-degree angles to one another. The gem crystals which belong to the hexagonal classification include benitoite, aquamarine, emerald, beryl, ruby, sapphire, quartz, and tourmaline.

Diamond, garnet, lapis lazuli, and spinel belong to the cubic crystal system. These crystals look like two pyramids with their flat bases fitted together. Zircon crystals are tetragonal, whereas crystals of peridot are orthorhombic.

Those birthstones and other gems which are not of mineral origin are pearl, amber, jet, and coral. Pearls are an oyster's way of saying "ouch!" when a bit of grit slips inside the shell to stay. The oyster surrounds the grit with layer after layer of nacre (mother of pearl), thus forming the lovely, lustrous pearl.

Amber is the fossilized resin of certain ancient trees. This resin, which flowed from the trees, was subject to heat and pressure over millions of years, and transformed into a hard, transparent yellowish-brownish substance rather like plastic.

Jet is a fossilized coal, or brown lignite. Jet is black, and is easily chipped or cracked.

Precious coral is a plant that grows in the sea. It, like the pearl, is composed of the mineral aragonite. Its color ranges from white to pink to red.

Some gemstones are harder than others.

Softness in a stone is identified by its position on the Mohs Scale (a comparison of hardness among minerals), which uses a rating of 1 to 10. The higher the number, the harder the substance. However, the numbers have nothing to do with percentage points. It is inaccurate to say that diamond, which rates a 10, is three times as hard as pearl, which is only 3.5 to 4; or that diamond is 30 percent harder than amethyst, which is rated 7. Diamond, the hardest substance on earth, is *many* times harder than pearl, *many* times harder than amethyst.

The major thing to remember about the softer stones is that they will get scratched or lose tiny chips from the edges more easily than the harder ones. In your jewel box, this means simply that some of your gemstones may become scratched by harder gems. Diamond, the hardest of all known substances, will scratch anything—literally. Ruby and sapphire are next in hardness; then topaz, alexandrite, aquamarine and emerald, zircon, tourmaline, the quartz gems, garnet, peridot, moonstone, turquoise. Most delicate of all are opal and pearl. A particular gemstone may be scratched by any stone I have listed before it, and will scratch any listed after it.

✧

MINING GEMSTONES

Sri Lanka (formerly Ceylon), where many gems are mined, is frequently referred to as the "gem island." One of its ancient names was Serendib or Serendipe, root of the word *serendipity*, which means happy coincidence. Here the legend of the holiness of gemstones lives on in religious observances. The miners are usually Buddhists. Before a mine is opened, they will consult an astrologer and religious leader for the most favorable date, the most favorable hour, to begin exploring for gems. Once mining has begun, frequent prayers and religious offerings are made in honor of the sacred stones.

In some parts of Sri Lanka the gem-bearing gravel is below the surface, perhaps as much as thirty feet. Here a shaft must be sunk and shored up. The gravel and accompanying ground-water are raised by rather primitive means in buckets, or pumped out with small pumps.

In the rivers, mining is done with rakes. This long-handled implement is called a *mamoti*. The gravel is scraped from the river bottom and the watery slurry swirled around in fiber baskets to remove the mud and sand. The heavier gemstones sink and are sorted from the basket by hand. In the same basketful of gem soil may be found topazes, amethysts, garnets, carnelians, and occasionally a diamond.

Throughout the world, small-scale gem mining operations are far more common than large-scale mechanized ones. It pays to bring in heavy equipment and mechanize a mine only where the returns are known to be fabulous, such as in diamond mining. A great percentage of the world's gems are mined with hand tools by small-scale or part-time workers. In the prolific mines of Brazil, mechanization is minimal; the wages of workers are low, and the stones are still harvested in plenty. In gem-rich Sri Lanka, despite the contrary attempts of ambitious men, tradition has kept the modes of operation the same as they have been for centuries: hands take the gems from the soil. For these people, whose reverence for gems is a part of their inmost being, and who are divinely influenced by the power of the stones, that is the way for it to be.

The basics of gem mining apply to all gemstones. Once the stones are recovered from the ground in which they appear, they are washed, sieved, and sorted, graded, sold, cut, sold again, mounted, and sold yet again.

In diamond mining, for example, diamond pipes and some alluvial deposits (washed down from the mountains and deposited on the beds of streams) can only be exploited properly by mechanization. First the topsoil, the gem-bearing yellow ground, is scraped off with road-grading equipment and taken to a processing plant. Then the unproductive rock surrounding the pipe is cleaned away. This reveals the kimberlite or blue ground, the peridotite rock in which the diamonds are embedded. Here the underground mining begins.

Shafts are dug down, safely below the pit left from removal of the yellow ground. Underground caves and passages (drifts) are blasted out. The drifts are connected with the mine shafts. Caves are connected with drifts by conical openings through which the excavated rock falls into the drifts and is scraped into hoppers which fill trucks. The trucks, on electric tramways, take the rock to be crushed. All the material is handled mechanically.

In mechanized open-cast mining, the sandy topsoil is removed and then the gem gravel is vacuumed out of the holes. Vacuuming is also used, and is economically feasible, in recovering diamonds from the seabed.

The crushed rock, containing gravel, kimberlite, and loose diamonds, is washed, passed through screens, then through separators using specific gravity. In one separator, the rock is whirled in a high-density liquid; this forces lighter waste material to the top of the liquid and diamonds to the bottom. What is left is washed over moving belts coated with grease. Clean diamonds (those free of mud) can't be wetted, nor can grease, so the diamonds stick to the grease while other stones are washed off it. Alternatively, the stones are passed under X rays, and the diamonds identified by their fluorescence.

Mined gems are placed with a cutter who will treat the crystal with reverence, and a merchant who, if he touches the gem with his hand, will bring it good luck.

✧

TURNING STONES INTO GEMS

Cutting the raw gem crystals to bring out their beauty has a parallel in the farmer who, after careful tilling and tending of his field, had a bountiful harvest of wheat. The preacher, looking at it, commented on what a beautiful field the Lord had given him. The farmer replied, "You should have seen it when the Lord had it all by Himself."

In gem crystals the potential is there, only waiting for us to find it and set it free. Yet if the potential is not there, all man's skill in cutting and polishing cannot produce a gemstone with color, brilliance, or fire.

In ancient times, the first thing done to improve gemstones was to polish or brighten them up. Lapidaries (stonecutters) of India polished diamonds with diamond powder, buffing off the outside coating and polishing the natural facets of the crystal before mounting them point up.

The earliest gem-cutting technique was to round the top (cabochon cut) to let in extra light. The next step was to cut one facet (flat spot) on the top, and small random facets to remove or disguise inclusions. By 1520, diamonds were being rose-cut with six facets. Cutting progressed to the thirty-six-facet rose cut, the fifty-eight-facet old mine or old European cut, and then the fifty-eight-facet modern brilliant cut. With the additional facets, gemstones could take in more light and reflect it back; they could twinkle, sparkle, dazzle, in a flashing rainbow of colors.

There are numerous names for the cutting patterns used on gems, but all the cuts fall into one of the three categories: *càbochon* (mounded); *brilliant* (with numerous symmetrical facets plus a flat table on top and a flat culet on the bottom); and *emerald* or *step cut* (having a large table and culet and stepped facets around it).

Cutting patterns include the round brilliant and the oval cut, a modification of it. The marquise is pointed at both ends. The pear is pointed at one end and rounded at the other. The emerald or step cut, usually a rectangle, is attractive in large stones. The baguette cut (a long narrow rectangle) is used in small stones which form designs or accentuate larger stones. The heart, kite, and square cuts are also used. Proper cut brings out all the color, fire, brilliance, and clarity of any gemstone.

Even early man sought to increase those qualities—by carving and engraving pagan symbols on the stone itself. When—after centuries of amuletic use of stones—the Catholic Church forbade such practices, the ancient carved symbols soon became transformed into religious ones more acceptable, "Jupiter" turning into "Moses" because someone *said* so.

The early Christians used a variety of religious symbols on engraved gems, many of which have been recovered from tombs in the catacombs under the Roman Appian Way. A favored figure found on these gems is that of the Good Shepherd. Other designs include the fish, the dove, the ship, the lyre, the anchor, and the Lamb of God.

Gemstone Cuts

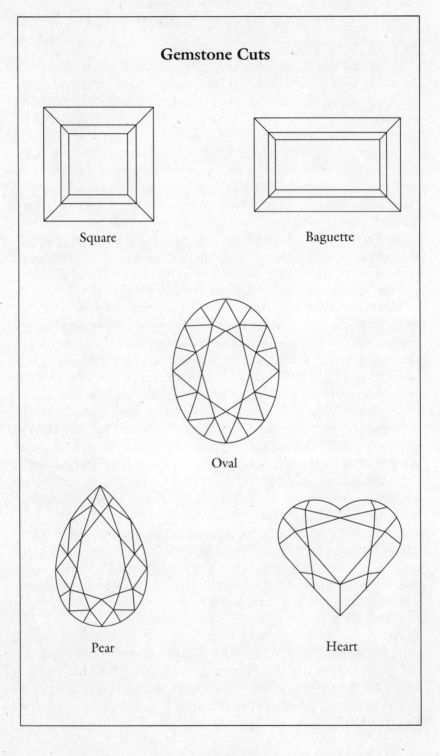

Square

Baguette

Oval

Pear

Heart

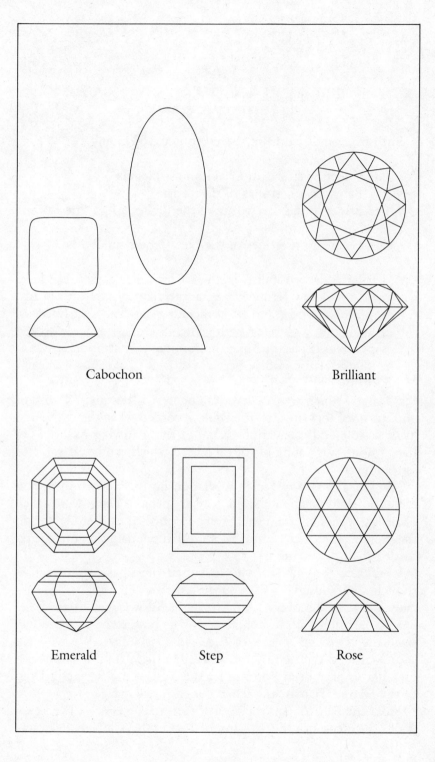

Cabochon

Brilliant

Emerald

Step

Rose

✧

FROM PLANETARY STONES
TO BIRTHSTONES

Birthstones evolved from several sources, including

- The planetary stones of Chaldean astrologers
- The Babylonians' stones of the zodiac
- The stones of the Breastplate of the Biblical High Priest of the Jews
- The Foundation Stones of the New Jerusalem

A strong fifth possibility is the divine Hindu city Devaraka which, like the New Jerusalem, is said to have blazed with pearls, rubies, and diamonds, and had emerald pillars and courtyards of rubies. Its highway glittered with gems; its crossroads were decked with sapphires. It gleamed like the summer sun at noonday.

The stones of the zodiac began with the Chaldeans of ancient Mesopotamia. The Chaldeans were astrologers and worshippers of the planets, which they believed influence the destinies of all. For ten centuries they studied the stars, recorded what they saw, and made astrological calculations. One of the gratifying offshoots of their studies was a long historical record which is of great value to astronomers.

The Chaldeans believed in a relationship between heaven and earth. So they assigned a stone to each planet. These were called planetary stones. Certain traits were ascribed to each stone—or do the stones possess these qualities, and the Chaldeans merely recorded their observations?

It was the Babylonians who first used the signs of the zodiac, though some observers have suggested that the signs were originally a psychic discovery from Universal Knowledge. In any case, modern astrological symbology seems to be greatly tamed down since the terrifying images of those long-ago days. We who are accustomed to the signs Virgo and Libra might find it rather disquieting to have been born under the Sign of the Ravening Dog, or the Sign of Tiamat, the female origin of all evil.

From the Babylonians the zodiac went to the Greeks, the Egyptians, the Persians, the Indians of India, the Chinese. Changes were continually made in order to adapt the zodiac to the beliefs of the particular country, but one thing remained constant: there was always a relationship between the stones and the zodiac.

The twelve stones of the zodiac have varied a bit from one century and one country to another. But according to one early authority, the stones under Aries, Leo, and Sagittarius (the three fire signs) are all hot and dry. Those under Taurus, Virgo, and Capricorn (the earth signs) are all cold and dry. Under Gemini, Libra, and Aquarius (the air signs) they are hot and humid; and under Cancer, Scorpio, and Pisces (the water signs) they are cold and humid.

The Breastplate of the first High Priest of the Jews was of great importance. The High Priest was Aaron, elder brother of Moses. He held this office for forty years, sometime around 1400 or 1300 B.C. In Exodus, chapter 28, we read that the holy garments were to be made for both glory and beauty. They included the breast-piece, a waistcoat or vest, a robe, a coat, a turban, and a girdle. The breastplate was to be of skilled workmanship, about nine inches square. On it, set in gold filigree, were twelve precious stones, each engraved with the name of one of the Twelve Tribes of Israel. Thus the High Priest carried on his heart the names of the Children of Israel. When the priest wore the breastplate, the gemstones on it amplified his consciousness and discernment, so that he communicated directly with universal planes to receive revelation or prophecy.

The Urim and Thummim, also known as Oracle and Truth, were worn in a pouch under the frame of the breastplate. These were double-terminated quartz crystals, one clear, one smoky. One was held in each hand; the clear crystal aided in seeing the future while the dark one revealed the past. The clear quartz, a yin or feminine energy, was used for discharging energy. Dark quartz, yang or masculine, was used for receiving energy. Sometimes these crystals were cast for divination, like dice or I Ching coins. They were also used as a focus for meditation to stimulate visions.

As you'll see when looking at the table of the gems of the Breastplate (page 255), even some of their names have an ancient sound. The twelve stones recurred time and again in regalia of early times (the insignia of royalty, the crown jewels), and thus the original symbolism of each stone was perpetuated.

✦

THE INTRODUCTION OF BIRTHSTONES

The concept of birthstones began in the first century A.D. In former times the year was divided into twelve zodiacal periods, each represented by a gemstone. But when the Roman calendar of months came into use, the zodiacal periods each began on the twentieth to twenty-fourth day of the previous month and ended on the nineteenth to twenty-third day of the month under discussion, as they still do today. At that time the writer Flavius Josephus made a connection between the twelve stones of the zodiac, the twelve stones of the High Priest's breastplate, and the twelve months of the year. He stated that each month (and each zodiacal period) had a specific stone, which was especially powerful for persons born in that month or period.

Then, in the fifth century, Saint Jerome wrote much the same thing. But nobody seemed to be wearing his or her natal stone. People felt more urgency to wear or use a stone that would cure their afflictions rather than one that merely sent out good vibrations.

It was a Roman custom to wear all twelve stones, the appropriate one during each period. The wealthy enjoyed a fad of wearing several of them at once, causing a contemporary chronicler to write of rings "up to the fingernails." (How fashions do recycle!) The stones in these rings were small. Much later, people wore the stone signifying the month of their birth.

Credit for the popularization of birthstones has been given to the Jews who immigrated into Poland in the 1700s. Learned Jewish men have written much about the gems of the breastplate, for the High Priest was a Jew. Jews who own gems have always taken them along wherever they went. It seems logical that the fashion of wearing birthstones would originate with this people whose interest in jewelry began thousands of years ago.

Birthstones have varied through the millennia; however, six of the breastplate stones are also official birthstones in current usage: topaz, carbuncle (ruby), emerald, sapphire, diamond, and amethyst.

Some birthstones have been the same always. Amethyst, for example, has been the February choice for the Jews, Romans, Arabs, Polish, Russians, Italians—and even Saint Isidore, the Bishop of Seville in A.D. 600—up through the centuries to the present. Topaz for November has the same record. Aquamarine, now the alternate stone for March, was for long decades the favored stone for October.

A modern list of birthstones is an amalgamation of Biblical lore, tradition, variety, psychic perception, astrological knowledge, ancient beliefs and customs, and outright practicality of the times.

When the American National Retail Jewelers Association was compiling this official list in 1912, they considered all the aspects of birthstones. At that time there were several lists, and that confused everybody. Some birthstones had proved unsuitable, or unobtainable, or were not attractive according to modern tastes. But tradition, once established, has great power of association. So with these things in mind, they made the best list they could. Since then two additions have been made, alexandrite and citrine. And blue zircon has replaced lapis lazuli (which at present is reasonably available). All other stones have remained.

Today the American National Retail Jewelers Association and the American Gem Society recommend the list which appears in the Table of Birthstones on page 252. They have adopted nineteen birthstones, which includes seven alternates. March has a birthstone and an alternate. June has a birthstone and two alternates.

Other months having one birthstone and one alternate are August, October, November, and December.

✧

WORDS USED IN THE TRADE

To qualify as a gemstone, a stone must possess three important characteristics: *beauty, durability, and rarity*. The stones called *precious* have these qualities in the highest degree.

Most precious stones are *transparent*, that is, as clear as glass. They have the ability to transmit light. "Light above all things," said Francis Bacon, "rejoices the spirit of man." Examples of transparent stones are diamond, aquamarine, and amethyst.

If the stone is not quite so clear but will transmit light weakly, it is called *translucent*. Examples of translucent stones are opal, moonstone, and alexandrite.

A stone which cannot be seen through at all is *opaque*. Opaque stones include turquoise, sardonyx, and bloodstone. In all translucent and opaque stones, color and surface luster are highly important.

It is not true that all sapphires are blue, all diamonds have the rainbow shining over them, or that all garnets are dark red. Many of the minerals which produce gem crystals do so in several colors. Some famous diamonds are deep blue, such as the Hope Diamond; they may also be shades of pink, yellow, or brown. Garnets range from a deep rich green, called demantoid, through yellow to red. The mineral corundum, from which come ruby and sapphire, bears not only transparent red and blue, but green, yellow, orange, and violet stones. Tourmaline crystals, always unpredictable, might be rose pink at one end, yellow in the center, and a dark green at the other end.

Quartz, the most common mineral in the world, is a prolific producer of durable gemstones. Its wardrobe is endless in hue and pattern. Quartz gems may be transparent (amethyst), translucent (chrysophrase), or opaque (agate); they may be striped, streaked, banded, or mottled. As part of their distinctive patterning, they may include ferns or moss. From quartz we get sand (as at the seashore) but we also get amethyst, bloodstone, jasper, citrine, cairngorm, rock crystal, rose quartz, agate, and cat's-eye.

Some of the characteristics by which an expert judges a gemstone are luster, color, brilliance, fire, clarity, and, of course, cut. *Luster* describes the appearance of the stone's surface. It can be adamantine (hard but fine, diamondlike); pearly; vitreous (glassy, as in quartz stones); silky (a satiny sheen).

Color in almost all gemstones is caused by impurities (usually non-gem-forming minerals) which combine with the parent gem-forming mineral. The truly pure stones are colorless. Opaque stones, such as lapis lazuli and turquoise, depend heavily on color for their popularity. The transparent stones, while beautiful in color, have additional features.

Brilliance describes the amount of ambient light reflected back from a stone, which gives it a sparkling look.

Fire, or dispersion, is achieved by the zigzag path of light entering one facet, bouncing off another, and exiting through a third; this breaks up the light into the rainbow colors of the spectrum. Some stones show no fire, but dichroism, only two colors of the spectrum. Gems displaying dichroism include kunzite, which shows lavender and bluish flashes; amethyst, showing red and violet; and chrysolite, with its fires of green and yellow.

Clarity indicates freedom from internal or external blemishes or inclusions. Some stones, such as emerald, are characterized by inclusions; but in most gemstones they are not preferable. The author has a 12-carat kunzite of fine lavender-pink color and brilliance with plainly visible inclusions of silvery-gold rutile needles looking like fine metallic threads brought to a point. In this stone, the inclusions add to its unusual attractiveness.

Some stones can show more than one color, depending on which side of the crystal you look through. This phenomenon is called trichroism when three colors show, or dichroism when only two colors show. When this occurs, the internal structure of the gemstone is acting as a filter, allowing only certain spectrum colors to pass through. When all colors are transmitted, the gem appears white or colorless. If a stone allows only red to pass through it, then the stone will look red. If certain colors are transmitted only in a particular direction, this phenomenon is called pleochroism.

✧

THE IMPORTANCE OF NUMEROLOGY

In 1747 the poet William Collins wrote of "numbers warmly pure and sweetly strong." We number our days, measure our height and girth, weigh our meat, count our calories, and watch the clock and the calendar. We are told that even the hairs of our heads are numbered; but who can number the sands of the sea, the drops of rain, the days of eternity? We tend to think that round numbers are always false. We like the idea of luck being in odd numbers.

But the numbers Collins referred to go far deeper in significance than our everyday use of them as a medium of measurement. The higher consciousness responds to number; psychologist Carl Jung stated that the numbers were not invented, but rather discovered. Human beings, in other words, were drawn to the high level on which the symbol already existed. Pythagoras, the Greek philosopher of the sixth century B.C., founded a religious brotherhood, one of whose beliefs was that the essence of all things was number, and that all relationships could be expressed numerically. The Pythagoreans discovered the numerical relationship of tones in music, and in geometry. It was Pythagoras who worked out a system of numerology based on the numbers 1 through 9.

The New Age healer, speaker, teacher and metaphysician Lynn Buess states his belief that numerology existed in Atlantis, and likely earlier in Lemuria. He connects numerology to the culture of the ancient Hindus and to the Arabic system of numbers we use today. The Cabala and numerology are intertwined; numerology forms the basis of symbolism in the Bible. The Egyptians, Phoenicians, Sumerians, and Chinese—all of whom have traditions of mystical wisdom—used written numbers. By inference then, these early peoples had an esoteric knowledge about numbers that exceeded the taking of inventories or creating of calendars.

But how does numerology affect us today?

Numerology affects us in the same way that numbers, and their relationship to every thing, have always affected every thing. Each number has its own vibrational characteristics. Everything—from atom and molecule to the entire universe—consists of vibrations. All that we do is in response to vibrational patterns or in creation of them.

Each letter of the alphabet has a numerological value. A is 1, B is 2, C is 3, on up through I, which is 9. J begins at 1, K is 2 and so on. S is 1, T is 2, U is 3; Z is 8. You can make a chart by writing 1 through 9 on a line and leaving space between the numbers. Under 1 put A; under 2 put B, and so on. You can check what you have done by seeing if A, J, and S are under 1. This concept will be much clearer to you if you do it on paper.

Each number has three aspects: the *assertive*, the *passive*, and the *harmonious*. Usually one aspect is emphasized more than the other two. There are three Master Numbers: 11, 22, and 33, all of which may indicate the potential for leadership and mystical powers, and therefore the necessity for accepting greater responsibilities.

Although numerology is primarily applied to an individual's

birth date, life number, and so forth, we'll apply it here only to gem names. Take the word *garnet*, for example. Placing the vowel numbers (a, e, i, o, u, or 1, 5, 9, 6, 3) at the top and the consonant numbers at the bottom, and adding each horizontal line separately, you will use the numerological values for each letter as follows:

$$
\begin{array}{ccccc}
1 & & 5 & & 6 \\
\text{g a r n e t} & = & - \\
7 & 9\;5 & 2 & 23
\end{array}
$$

Reduce each number to a single digit by again adding horizontally. Thus 23 becomes 5. The word *garnet* adds up to 6 over 5, totaling 11. This further reduces to 2, giving garnet the dual number 11/2.

The number 6 represents responsibility and service (which can be used either assertively, passively, or harmoniously, remember). The number 5 is a flexible number, talented, friendly, uncertain, restless, seeking out new experience without always assimilating the lessons of the old. The total of the two, 11, is a Master Number, having the trifold attributes of zeal, impracticality, overreaction, sensitivity, mystical giftedness, the expression of higher consciousness, and creativity. This number belongs to pie-in-the-sky types, who need to keep one foot on earth at all times. Boiled down to a 2, the number is vacillating, arbitrary, gentle, or adaptable—or some aspect of these characteristics.

I offer here a brief overview of the harmonious attributes of each of the numbers, by no means complete:

1 denotes ideas, desires, will, beginnings—a masculine number.
2 stands for working together, adaptability, warmth, diplomacy—a feminine number.
3 relates to creativity, self-expression, abundance, intuition.
4 is authority, discipline, tenacity, earthiness.
5 stands for freedom, progressiveness, curiosity, the mercurial personality.
6 is conventionally responsible, idealistic, practical.

7 is a magic number, or can be. It is the number of soul growth. Sevens are wise though skeptical, discerning, aloof.

8 denotes realism, energy, ambition, materialism, security-mindedness.

9 is the number of altruism, of service to the universe, of perfectionism and strong character.

When you are using the foregoing interpretations, for example, to read character through a person's name, bear in mind the assertive, passive, and harmonious aspects of each characteristic, and you'll see how well the numbers fit.

The numerology readings Eileen Nauman has done for each gemstone are a combination of numerological interpretations, channeling of spirit, and intuitive knowledge.

For much fuller explanations of numerology, refer to the books listed in the bibliography.

✧

SELECTING YOUR GEMSTONES

You should always comparison-shop for gemstones. Look, for example, at a selection of topazes, or opals. Which color appeals to you most? Which seems to have the highest brilliance? Which stone has the most pleasing cut? Which is the best value? Most probably you'll pick the one you like, the one you feel most at one with. Sometimes the very first one you see is the one you will wind up with; if it is the stone for you, it will still be in the jeweler's shop when you return.

It is a good idea to look at a lot of gems of the kind you want eventually to buy, so that your eyes will recognize the look of your stone; also so that you'll know what qualities you *don't* want in that particular gem. I must point out that staring at forty or fifty peridots won't make you an expert on peridots or any other gem; but you'll begin to learn what to look for and what you like. Go to two or three jewelers, at least, and make notes of price, carat weight, and how well you like the color and cut. You may want to buy the stone and have it mounted later. If the gem is already in a mounting and you want a different one, the jeweler will make the change for you, sometimes at no additional cost.

When choosing your birthstone, or any gem, *know your jeweler*. If this is not possible, I strongly advise that you comparison-shop at the stores of Registered Jewelers of the American Gem Society. This is a phrase that all such jewelers use in their advertising and which is displayed prominently in certificate form inside the store and usually on the sign outside. Registered Jewelers (or the more advanced Certified Gemologists) of the American Gem Society have taken intensive training in knowledge of gemstones, have passed stringent tests of their knowledge, and will use instruments in gemstone inspection. They must constantly meet the exacting professional standards of a national organization.

Registered Jewelers and Certified Gemologists of the AGS are pledged to protect the buying public and to maintain high business standards and practices among AGS membership. In a member store, you'll get accurate information on the comparative qualities of the gemstones in a selection. If, for example, the stone you like is flawed, the Registered Jeweler will point this out to you, and will explain what such flaws in this particular gem will mean in terms of durability, beauty, value, and other factors of gemstone ownership and use.

Other places to buy gemstones are rock shops, gem and mineral shows, antique shops, and pawn shops. If you have diligently comparison-shopped, you'll have some means of deciding whether or not the prices you see are higher or lower than those of a Registered Jeweler for a stone you like. Often, at rock shops, a Registered Jeweler will be available. At gem and mineral shows there is frequently a much larger selection than most jewelers carry; and the prices will be favorable. Comparison-shopping will be greatly to your advantage here. A magnifying glass will help you to spot gross flaws not visible to the unaided eye, as well as wavering color.

Warning: if you buy at any place except that of an AGS member, you'll have to be a good judge of the seller's truth as well as of his/her gemstones. The seller may mislead you as to the identity of the stone. (I paid $50 at Uncle Sam's Pawnshop for a beautiful, flashing postage-stamp-sized "white zircon set with six diamonds." Uncle Sam himself wrote it on the receipt. When I had a Certified Gemologist appraise it, he identified the stones as synthetic spinel—nevertheless, his appraisal set its value at $150; I'm still pleased with it, and until now, nobody knew but me and the gemologist.)

The seller may not tell you everything about your stone. It may be

- Heat-treated or dyed to create its present color
- Imitation (glass or paste, made to resemble the actual stone)
- Synthetic (man-made, with almost exactly the same physical and optical properties as the genuine article)
- A pale stone lent color and brilliance by a foil backing
- A doublet or a triplet (two or three slices of stone skillfully glued together to form an attractive piece)

Such stones can be quite satisfactory *if you buy them for what they are*.

Practically any transparent gemstone of reasonable clarity, color, and brilliance, when nicely mounted and kept clean of soap and grease deposits, will give its owner a great deal of pleasure. The same applies to translucent and opaque stones.

Within limits, you may find as much satisfaction with a less expensive stone *simply because it is your stone*. Out of a collection, your stone leaps up at you like a happy puppy, and all but licks your face in gladness to be with you. And when you finally cave in and buy it—rather than that handsome thoroughbred you liked but couldn't afford—you will have years of enjoyable ownership as you and your gemstone continue to discover how much you have in common.

You may be born to a particular stone, say opal, but can't stand the things and wouldn't wear them if you had them. You'd rather have emeralds. My suggestion is to shop for emeralds, read about them, feel them in your fingers—and follow your instinct. The same intuition that points out *your stone* to you will guide you in deciding between your birthstone and another gem that you have a yen (or perhaps several hundred yen) for. Don't wear a stone you dislike; you and the stone are telling each other something. It's far better to feel happy and comfortable with your gems.

If you are born at such a time that your month birthstone is one gem and your zodiacal stone is another, then you may make the choice. Again, it is the relationship between you and the stone that is important, not some arbitrary rule that dictates what you shall wear.

Often when we think of gemstones, we visualize them in rings. This need not be so, for either men or women. Gems can be mounted in necklaces, brooches, bracelets, earrings, tie jewelry, lapel pins, and so on. Many collectors prefer to enjoy their gems unmounted, appropriately and safely displayed in their homes or offices—or perhaps locked away for a rainy day.

Whatever your birthstone, whatever your favorite gems, may you wear them in good health and good fortune. They may not cure your afflictions, or protect you from danger, or turn you from a mouse into a tiger . . . but . . . *your stone* might.

The
Birthstones

◇

Garnet

ZODIACAL STONE FOR

CAPRICORN

(December 22–January 20)

Cornelia kept her in talk till her children came from school. "And these," said Cornelia, "are my jewels."

—ROBERT BURTON (QUOTING SENECA)

Numerologically, garnet is an 11, a Master Number. This reduces to a 2, giving it the dual number 11/2, the same as sapphire.

You who are drawn to this precious stone are looking for something different—a stone that makes a statement about your individuality rather than your sameness. Your taste will be liberal, rather than conservative. The overall warmth or color of the stone will trigger a chord deep within you.

You'll want to flaunt the gem's differentness. You may have it mounted in a larger than usual setting, or wear it in an unexpected way.

The sentimental value of garnet will be great, since you will either receive it as part of an inheritance, or you will pass it on to another deserving family member later in your life. This stone stays in families for generations, and is appreciated for its traditions and warm memories rather than as a gem that is "in."

Garnet is a stone for a sensitive, shy individual, and is strongly drawn to females. It conveys warmth on an unseen vibratory level, passing on a soothing energy to those who would embrace its gentle qualities.

✧

PHYSICAL PROPERTIES

Only when garnet is clear and transparent is it precious garnet, suitable as a gemstone. Think of garnet and what comes to mind? A dismal red? But think of garnet as gooseberry green—orange—deep red—brown-red—black—or grass green. This lively stone is any of those colors, depending on its locale of origin. A stone with more brilliance than emerald, it is found in gem gravels in the United States, South Africa, Tanzania, and Zaire.

Garnet is a silicate mineral, formed of silicon and oxygen, with random amounts of calcium, magnesium, iron, and aluminum, which govern its colors.

There are several subvarieties of garnet: pyrope, almandine, rhodolite, spessartite, grossularite, and demantoid. Each has its distinctive color, caused by its particular chemical composition.

Pyrope garnet is red, a warm glowing shade with pulsations of scarlet, crimson, and purple in its depths. Seen under a microscope, pyrope garnet often shows long needle-like crystal inclusions. Pyrope was a popular stone for many centuries, worn on the wrists, throats, shoulders, and brows of Egyptians, Greeks, Romans, Anglo-Saxons, and medieval ladies.

Almandite or *almandine* garnet is brownish red to reddish violet. Its name comes from Alabanda in Asia Minor, where it was extensively found, and there polished for gem use. Pliny the Elder, that famous Roman observer and chronicler of A.D. 23–79, gave it the description *carbunculus alabandicus*. This is the "carbuncle" of ancient days, alternatively thought to be ruby. The carbuncle was the third stone, top row, in the breastplate of Aaron, the first High Priest of the Jews.

Almandine garnet microscopically shows a fine crisscross pattern and inclusions of zircon crystals.

Rhodolite is a rare form of garnet, halfway between pyrope and almandine in its rose-red or rose-purple color.

Spessartite or *spessartine*, also rare, forms in shades of brown or reddish brown. One of its colors is an assertive orange which, when cut with many facets, makes an extraordinarily distinctive gemstone.

Grossularite, or gooseberry garnet, is opaque. Its colors range from dull red-brown *hessonite* (also known as hyacinth garnet or cinnamon stone) to a sparkling coppery-gold to yellow to light green. In the Transvaal are found a jade green, a gooseberry green sporting black dots, and a raspberry red grossularite. The color within hessonite is unevenly distributed in a wavelength pattern. Under a microscope, it shows this rolling wavelike effect.

In 1969 in Africa there was discovered a brilliant new stone, a clear green grossular garnet. Officials at Tiffany's decided to prospect for deposits of this stone, with the hope of introducing it to the public. Bear in mind that a stone which is too rare is of interest only to collectors; in order to qualify as a gem, there must be enough gem-quality material to create jewelry and thus stimulate public demand. After some time, deposits were found near Tsavo National Park. The gemstone was called *Tsavorite*. Looking into its brilliant deep green is as soothing and pleasant as gazing toward the sun through leaves.

Demantoid (from Dutch *demant*, meaning diamond) garnet is a fine transparent medium to dark green whose considerable fire has been measured as exceeding that of diamond. Its beauty seems to draw the light to it, where it moves and sparkles within the heart of the stone. Demantoid, unfortunately, is rare, occurring only in the Congo and the Ural Mountains. The distinctive inclusion of this stone is a feathery horsetail, which proves it as genuine demantoid.

Garnet is one of three gems which sometimes have natural stars within the stone, sapphires and rubies (which are sister stones from the same mineral, corundum) being the other two. These stones are known as *asterias*. Rubies and sapphires have six-pointed stars, whereas garnets usually have four. This star is visible when light shines on it, so that when either the light or the stone is moved, the star moves too. This radiant effect is caused by microscopically small hollow tubes which have formed within the crystalline structure of the stone. Another cause of this asterism is the mineral rutile, which forms in thin needles in a star pattern within the crystal, and reflects light as a six-pointed star.

The three crossbars that give the star effect represent faith, hope, and destiny.

Once in a great while, when a garnet is cabochon cut, a star will be revealed. Garnet stars are four-rayed because the crystal system of garnet is four-sided. *Very* rarely a six-rayed star will occur in garnet.

It is also unusual to see large garnets. Museums in Vienna and Dresden own exceptional specimens. The king of Saxony was reputed to have had a garnet weighing 468 carats.

· · ·

◆

SHOPPING FOR GARNETS

When you are shopping for garnets, look for transparency and liveliness or clarity of color. The stone can be brilliant cut, step cut, or cabochon, depending on its placement in the mounting. A poorly cut, or flawed, stone can look feverish and gloomy. Properly presented, garnet can be bright as a stoplight, dancing with companion hues of heliotrope, flashing with gold.

◆

CHARACTERISTICS AND ATTRIBUTES

Garnet symbolizes constancy, fidelity, and friendship. If worn around the neck, garnet has virtues against melancholy. A garnet amulet will protect a traveler from accident. The stone is said to turn dark when danger approaches, resuming its original brilliance when the peril has passed. In Asia, bullets made of garnet were used to draw more blood from an enemy's wound. Accounts of our wars against the Indians of the American Southwest also mention the Indians' use of garnet bullets.

This gemstone is associated with the sun, and the fixed star Heart of Lion at 23 degrees Leo. Though one authority says it is a gem of summer, another places it with January. It is the gem of the apostles Andrew and Simon, called Peter. As a carbuncle it is the talisman gem for the guardian angel Amriel, who is a prince of the order of Thrones and chief officer of the twelfth hour of the night. Pope Gregory allied carbuncle with the Archangels, the next to highest of the hierarchy of the Heavenly Host. The name Amriel is found inscribed on an Oriental Hebrew charm for warding off evil.

Sometimes the garnet is known as the gem of Persian princes, for in that country the stone was often carved with the likeness of the ruler. A garnet with the form of a lion engraved on it will protect and preserve health, bring the wearer honors, and guard him from ambush. Intention in use of garnet is important. While the gem can cause profuse bleeding in an enemy, in the hands of a healer it has the opposite power: to control hemorrhage. In India and Persia, garnet was used as a talisman against the possibility of being poisoned—not a bad idea in hot countries without refrigeration.

Garnet also protects one from being struck by lightning. In the Middle Ages the red gemstone was a remedy for inflammatory diseases and boils. According to the principle by which "like cures like" (red disease, red stone; or what it could cause, it could also cure) it was used in the type of treatment called homeopathy. This law of therapeutics was discovered by Hippocrates but was not used much because knowledge of drugs in that day was limited. Currently its validity is recognized by orthodox medicine in the practice of inoculation and vaccination. Homeopathy, revived in 1796, is still being used successfully today. Sometimes a stone of opposite color, such as blue, was resorted to instead of the homeopathic remedy.

Wearing garnet promotes honesty in oneself, and trustworthiness. It is the gem of integration and regeneration. It is the master regulator of the seven vital body chakras (energy centers), which govern all aspects of being. It keeps energies flowing, like the contents of a pot being stirred and then allowed to simmer and blend together. The vibrations of garnet amplify and bring into balance all the processes of regeneration.

✧
HEALING MAGIC

As with all gemstones, garnet's vibrations may be passed on to a person either through wearing the stone, through Ayurvedic methods, Teletherapy, or Radionics; or by taking the elixir.

Here follows a partial list of the body organs or areas, physical and emotional maladies, and psychological ailments for which garnet elixir may be used.

Hessonite garnet—liver, bones, skin; emotional balance, nightmares, psychosomatic ills; stimulates self-healing and attunes one to nature and earth energies. It balances the feet chakras.
Pyrope or rhodolite garnet—skin, skeletal system, lungs, intes-

tines, capillaries; detoxifies the system, treats genetic diseases and environmental pollutants; astral, emotional, and etheric bodies.

Spessartine garnet—kidneys, liver, thyroid; herpes, anemia or hemorrhaging, nausea, venereal diseases. Use in meditation, raising consciousness, and spiritual illumination; for the throat, heart, and base chakras and the spiritual and emotional bodies.

Taking garnet elixir: Use eight drops in a bath. As an external application, mix it with peanut oil and olive oil. Great effectiveness is obtained through massaging it over the solar plexus or under the arms.

✧
GARNET DREAMS

If you dream of throwing a garnet, especially a red pyrope, it means you are trying to attract someone's love. Dreaming of wearing a brown spessartine means that you're a rather quiet person, but with a steady inner fire. If you're wearing a green Tsavorite, you will find a happy new love in the springtime. If the stone is large and deep green, your new love will come in late spring.

Should you dream of losing a garnet necklace of any color, this means that a series of trying events in your life are now past, and you are able to proceed with these lessons behind you. Seeing a rose-purple rhodolite in dreams indicates that you'll soon be feeling healthier. A dream of holding a yellow grossularite means that you hold the future in your own hands. Garnet of any color set in a filigree mounting is a message of love from your ancestors.

Dreaming of seeing an orange garnet is exceptionally lucky. If it is in a shop window, you'll have to wait and work awhile before your luck arrives. Seen in a friend's jewel box, this spessartine garnet indicates a possible past-life connection between the two of you. Dreams of an orange garnet in your own jewel collection mean vitality and harmony in a new undertaking.

• • •

✧

GARNETS THROUGH HISTORY

Garnets have held a position of respect and admiration from the time of the ancient Egyptians through Queen Victoria's reign. In ancient times the stone was cut cabochon, because the technology for cutting facets on gemstones did not come to the world until the fifteenth century.

Plentiful in Bohemia in gem quality, garnet was used even in prehistoric times. A lake dweller of the Bronze Age was found by modern archaeologists with garnets scattered around him. The stones had been pierced as for a necklace, probably an amulet. It seems that the man was important—perhaps a warrior or a medicine man—because of the amuletic use of red.

In ancient Greece, garnets set in gold were worn on the wrists or used to fasten garments at the shoulder or to decorate a pure and noble brow. The Greeks favored deep-red pyrope and purple-tinged almandine in (to our taste) uneasy company with dark carnelian. The Romans used garnet, ruby, and glass in their rings, bracelets, and pins. The Anglo-Saxons treasured it and used it splendidly. From the earliest times, goldsmiths and jewelers have set garnet in helmets, buckles, brooches, stomachers, rings, earrings and necklaces.

Starting before and gaining impetus after the fall of the Roman Empire, the Migration Period lasted a few hundred years. The Huns, the Franks, the Avars, and the Merovingians—migrating hordes of warlike peoples—swept across Europe and central Asia, seeking out lands they could capture. It was blood they shed, and blood they proudly wore in the form of blood-red pyrope garnets—in significant jewelry, constantly worn. These were magnificently mounted in gold, the gemstones slivered on their natural cleavage line and inlaid onto the precious metal with a jewelers' art whose perfection cannot be equaled even with modern technology. In the British Museum, the rich Sutton Hoo collection includes an important seventh-century king's or warrior's jewelry items: purse-lid, shoulder clasps, buckles, and more. All are created of gold, with intricately interlocked designs and unsurpassed punchwork, finely executed, and superbly, sumptuously, spectacularly set with garnets.

This manner of inlay is called cloisonné (cloi-son-nay), meaning that the metal of the mounting is subdivided by little raised partitions of metal called *cloisons*. Into these little enclosures was set cement, with the garnets exactly fitted inside the metal boundaries. Another type of cloisonné, used from ancient times to today, fills the spaces between the thin metal strips with colored enamels to make designs of flowers, birds, and so forth.

The reign of Britain's Queen Victoria saw an increase in the general wealth. With it came increased popularity of gemstones, in both the aristocracy and the middle class. Garnets, being showy and inexpensive, were the fashionable gems of the period.

Pyrope garnet "parures" were particularly popular. These were sets of matched jeweled ornaments which might include combs, bracelets, stomachers, necklaces, and earrings. Stomachers were mainly women's jewelry: boastful, ostentatious, heavily embroidered or jeweled garments that might reach from collarbone to thighs.

Red stones in general signified the nobility. According to Giacinto Gimma, a writer of 1730, red stones worn by a woman indicated pride, obstinacy, or haughtiness. Worn by a man they stood for command, lordship, and vengeance. Interestingly, the given name Garnet is hardly ever used for a man.

Garnet originates in the Latin word *granatus*, meaning seed. It is so called because it appears in very tiny seedlike crystals thickly sprinkled in matrix (mineral-bearing earth). Usually these crystals can't be used for gem purposes.

In French, the stone is called *grenat*. In German, Spanish, and Italian it becomes *granat, granate*, and *granato*, respectively.

Garnet once commanded a high price. It and the gemstone spinel were confused with ruby. During the Middle Ages stones of the same color were classed under one heading. A red stone was a ruby, *n'est-ce pas?* Before the discovery of facet cutting, stones were cut *en cabochon*, as mounds, and all the red ones were called carbuncles.

The word carbuncle comes from the Latin *carbunculus*, meaning a little coal. Medically, carbuncles are mounded skin inflammations, painfully common in the days before antibiotics. They were treated in the twelfth and thirteenth centuries by applying blue sapphire to the red swelling.

In the fourteenth century, an emperor of China had a carbuncle from Ceylon fitted as a ball in his cap. The stone cost 100,000 strings of cash and weighed one ounce.

An ancient test of the genuineness of garnet required that the possessor of the stone strip off his clothes, still wearing the garnet, and have his body smeared with honey. Then he was to lie down in the vicinity of flies or wasps. Should his stone be imitation, he would be royally bugged. If no insects came to him, it was proof that the gemstone was genuine. However, after he took off his garnet, if the insects clustered on him, it was further proof of the stone's genuineness. (Perhaps blue sapphire was used to treat the bites.)

The Bohemian King Wenceslas, about whom a Christmas carol was written, is the patron saint of Czechoslovakia. He lived from A.D. 907 to 929. The crown jewels of his time glittered with pyropes found in his country.

In the fourteenth century, the interiors of many Bohemian churches were decorated with garnets. Excellent examples of this work are the jeweled chapels of the ancient royal castle of Karlstein and the Cathedral of Saint Vitus in Prague.

In modern industry, garnet is an important abrasive. Garnet paper and cloth (sold at your friendly neighborhood hardware store) are used for fine-finishing articles made of wood, leather, or rubber. Small garnets are still occasionally used as jewels at the wear points in watch movements.

BIRTHSTONE FOR FEBRUARY

❖

ZODIACAL STONE FOR

AQUARIUS

(January 21–February 19)

I'll tell you how the sun rose—
A ribbon at a time,
The steeples swam in amethyst,
The news like squirrels ran.

—EMILY DICKINSON
PART II, NATURE LXXIII

---◇---

Numerologically, amethyst is a 3.

People drawn to this vibrant red-violet gem are of a caring and warm nature, given to the strong tenets of family, children and community, responsibility and caring. Amethyst is bought with the idea that it will become a family heirloom and be passed down through the generations.

If amethyst is your birthstone, you are an individual who enjoys showing off the beauty of such a gem. Indeed, with your creativity and childlike spontaneity, the vivid color of this gem simply captivates you.

You view this as a "fun" gem, neither too expensive nor too cheap, a gem that is equally at ease with blue jeans or at the opera. You like a gem that is laid-back and versatile, not one that requires an armed guard to accompany it.

Amethyst breeds loyalty in its wearer. Probably you'll wear it on a daily basis, like a favorite piece of costume jewelry. Wherever you go, your amethyst will go also, experiencing many new adventures in your world of wonders.

You will always have amethyst around you. You may purchase a geode or two filled with the softly sparkling crystals, keeping one in your office and another in your home. No place that expresses your personality should be without some amethyst. The aura around the gem is sharply creative, with a nervous, bouncy edge to it: your kind of energy. With the numbers backing it, amethyst is a stone of great healing capability, protecting the purchaser or wearer.

This gem finds a home with someone who loves it unequivocally and wears it often.

. . .

✧
PHYSICAL PROPERTIES

Amethyst is a quartz gem, one of nature's happiest surprises from out of her most abundant mineral. Its crystals are purple, ranging from a shy, foggy-gray orchid color to a sociably aware purple-brushed-with-rose to a robust reddish purple. Generally the pale shades are not cut as gemstones now, although they were popular in Roman and Greek times.

Exposed to strong sunlight over time, amethysts will fade. This is an unfortunate natural characteristic of the stone. Heat treating can kill the color altogether. Certain amethysts can be heat-treated and transformed to the misty but vibrant yellow gemstone called citrine, or to a brownish red. The violet-red stones from Madagascar, upon being heated, change into white quartz of a different crystal structure. These stones will melt at 1,710 degrees Centigrade.

Though now it does not rank as highly as emerald, ruby, sapphire, or diamond, mainly because it is a relatively "softer" stone, in earlier times amethyst was mounted in jewelry and in regalia as a peer stone with these others.

The most sought-after shade is the deep purple-red. Frequently stones of this shade are flawed, have feathery inclusions, or are unevenly colored. Fine amethysts used to be scarce, until they were found in gem quality in South America.

Amethyst is the only purple gemstone found in quantity. Some sapphires are violet; so occasionally are amber and andalusite, but all are rare. Gem-quality amethyst is not abundant, even though plenty of crystals form. It is found in Brazil, Uruguay, Sri Lanka, South Africa, Mexico, Madagascar, Russia, Australia, North America, Spain, France, Hungary, and Italy.

✧
SHOPPING FOR AMETHYSTS

When you are shopping for amethyst, look first for the color that most pleases your eye. Perhaps you will prefer a slightly lighter shade than the ideal deep purple. Since this is a dark stone, mounted in a ring or necklace it will stand out against light skin, but may blend right into dark skin. So try on several to see how the particular color complements your skin tones. When choosing cut, you'll want to take into consideration the shape and size of your hands, neck, or whatever body part you plan to wear it on. Or if you're looking at some other piece of amethyst jewelry, such as a pin, look at it against the special outfit you'd most like to wear it with. Though it's hard to beat a good big step-cut amethyst ring for authority and sheer dash, the variations on this cut and the brilliant cut offer choices for everyone.

✧

CHARACTERISTICS AND ATTRIBUTES

One of the early zodiacal stones was amethyst. In Arab tradition, it was the stone for Aquarius, as it is today. Amethyst represents transformation, helping the system accept and assimilate new knowledge stemming from adjustments on the path to higher awareness. It is a purifier and amplifier of healing and spiritual energies.

A stone of great nobility, amethyst holds within itself the vibrations of love, understanding, and tenderness. It can change discord into peace and contentment, bring pleasure out of pain. It has the ability to change the molecular structure of matter, and to bring health and well-being to the entire planet. Amethyst can bring into harmony one's mental, physical, emotional, and spiritual realms.

Sunlight focused through amethyst enhances the energies that come to the physical body from the spiritual realm. The light of the moon focused through amethyst is beneficial to the mental, emotional, and spiritual aspects of the individual.

Amethyst is even capable of responding physically to vibrations of love. Recently the author was visiting a friend, Beth, who owns a piece of an amethyst-bearing geode. A geode is a hollow stone sphere which, when broken open, proves to be lined with mineral crystals. Beth's geode looks like a jagged slice of light gray melon filled with transparent pale violet crystals. It is perfectly balanced on a narrow flat section of itself. Sitting quite near it, I was relating a highly spiritual experience, one which had given me great joy. Without being touched, activated only by the sound of my voice, the geode began to rock to and fro, as gleeful as a child in a swing. When silence fell, it came dreamily to a halt. We in the room were awed, as if the universe had smiled.

Amethyst is the twelfth foundation stone of the Holy City; the third stone in the third row on the High Priest's breastplate; it was the stone of the tribe of Dan, which stood for judgment. It represents justice, courage, authority, and perfection. It inspires virtues and high ideals.

Amethyst controls evil thoughts and calms evil passions; boosts intelligence; preserves the wearer from contagious diseases, from gout and nightmares; protects the warrior in battle and brings him victory. Should your amethyst be engraved with a bear, it will chase away demons (particularly those little men with the hammers on the morning after.)

In humble souls, amethyst signifies the constant thought of the heavenly kingdom. It was said to be the favorite stone of Saint Valentine. It has been set into rings for the Pope and into the crowns of most Christian kings. The Jews believed that the amethyst could bring visions and dreams.

Amethyst is the talismanic gem for the apostles Matthias and Judas, and for Adnachiel, who is guardian angel of the month of November and ruler over the sign of Sagittarius. It is the stone of the planets Mars and Jupiter, and of the fixed star Scorpion at 3 degrees Sagittarius.*

The writer Reichelti, in 1676, expressed the opinion that the hardness of precious stones enabled them to retain their celestial virtues long after they are mined. The celestial virtues are the stones' stored-up energy from the stars and planets. Reichelti stated that each stone is sensitive to the emanations from a particular planet, star, or group of stars. This also explains the increased power of a stone engraved with the correct symbol to tie it to its own heavenly body.

Amethyst is a gem of springtime, of Wednesday and of eight

* Stone associations differ according to the period, the country, or the authority quoted.

o'clock in the morning. It is the talismanic gem for Saturday, whose child must work for a living. It is the gemstone for a seventh wedding anniversary.

✧

HEALING MAGIC

To receive the soothing and healing vibrations of amethyst, you may wear it anywhere on your body. For faster results, the elixir is quicker.

Here follows a partial list of the body organs or areas, physical and emotional maladies, and psychological ailments for which amethyst elixir may be used.

It is especially good for imbalances of the blood and the nervous and endocrine systems. It treats either diabetes or hypoglycemia through the pancreas, pituitary, thymus, and thyroid. It strengthens red corpuscles. It increases overall vitality in the physical, emotional, mental, and spiritual bodies. This gem elixir is valuable in the treatment of eye problems and headaches, physical coordination, dyslexia, and nutritional deficiencies.

Amethyst clears and balances the mental and emotional faculties and gives courage. In improving one's self-esteem it helps one attune to nature, earth, society, and deity. It is useful in centering oneself, controlling unruly passions, and achieving maturity. It aids in opening the third eye and works with the base and throat chakras to put communication and discernment on a new, sturdier foundation.

To use amethyst elixir: Take it when your stomach is empty. Start with three drops four times daily for three days. Then take five drops; by the end of a week, take seven drops as a dose. Take the elixir for two weeks, then stop for a week, then take it for another two weeks, until the condition you are treating improves.

In your bathwater, seven drops are good for cleansing the subtle bodies that are a part of our being. As a third-eye opener, lotus oil mixed with seven drops of amethyst elixir is to be rubbed between the brows and slightly above. It's best to do this once each morning.

✧
AMETHYST DREAMS

Seeing an amethyst ring or brooch in a dream foretells a serene married life. To dream of losing an amethyst indicates trouble in your love affairs: you may be slighted, or even suffer a broken engagement. You will know contentment with your income (possibly through your business dealings) if you dream of amethyst lying on the ground. This lovely gem seen against white means that peace of mind and contentment will come to you through unexpected good news.

Hold an amethyst crystal in your dreams, and you will know the meaning of creativity in more areas of your life. Making a dream gift of amethyst to another means that you are forgiving a wrong you thought that person did to you. A string of amethysts indicates freedom, carefreeness, a releasing of worries.

Buy an amethyst for yourself in a dream, and this indicates that you are raising your spiritual awareness. If you dream of receiving an amethyst, you will have good fortune in all your endeavors.

✧
AMETHYSTS THROUGH HISTORY

Amethyst is such a satisfying word to say; it comes from the lips and the tongue sounding like jewels, and fine wines, and sweet kisses in the pungent autumn sunlight. The French call it *amethyste*, the Italians *ametista*. But, the Greek word for amethyst is *amethystos*, meaning remedy for drunkenness; or *amethyein*, to be immune from it. Drunkenness can result from an excess of alcoholic beverages—or any other excess. Drunk with power, drunk on dreams, are familiar expressions. Amethyst, with its capabilities of restoring balance, can bring back into harmony those who are drunk on any heady mixture. In ancient Greek and Roman times, this power was taken literally, and at orgies it was *usitatus* (customary) to imbibe from an amethyst goblet if one wished to avoid morning-after pain. Another traditional use of amethyst is in ecclesiastical rings, particularly for bishops. Here it would seem that the intention is to prevent the ecclesiastical authority from going to the bishop's head.

The Chaldeans carved this lovely gemstone to make seals. Seals are often cut *intaglio*, meaning that the design is cut below the surface, rather than raised, as with a cameo. Romans used it in signets. The Egyptians and Greeks loved amethyst, utilizing even the streaked or light orchidy-colored crystals. The fashion of engraving amethyst for seals and pendants has disappeared, along with the craftsmen skilled in doing it.

Among the Latuka, Bari, and Laluba tribesmen living along the upper Nile River in Egypt, the medicine men are generally the chiefs. They are elevated to that position primarily because they have the power of making rain. Rain is vital in this area, for a dry season means famine and death. The rain-making chiefs are nobody's fools; they build their villages on the slopes of a high hill, aware that the hills attract clouds. They back up their abilities with rain-stones: amethyst, aventurine, and rock crystal. When rain is desired, the chief puts the rain-stones in water. Muttering incantations, he takes a peeled cane in his hand and uses it as a pointer to tell the clouds which way to float. When the rain begins to pour, it is hard for us to say how much of the credit is due to amethyst.

In the days when amethyst was most costly, the nobility used it in greatest quantity. Well into the 1600s, amethysts were equal in value and desirability with diamonds. From the Chaldeans through the nineteenth century, amethyst maintained its post in fashion, and was particularly popular during the Classical and Renaissance eras. In the Russian treasury at the time of Tsar Alexis were twenty thrones, each one for a different ritual or season. In 1660 he received one that was set with 1,223 amethysts and 876 diamonds. Queen Charlotte, in the 1700s, had a magnificent amethyst necklace, then valued at two thousand pounds.

The Shah of Persia gave a throne to Ivan IV of Russia; it was set with 15 amethysts, 1,325 rubies and zircons, 539 turquoises (a favorite stone of Persia), plus pearls, peridot, and sapphires. Obviously it was felt that the amethysts could hold their own even though relatively few in number.

◇

Bloodstone or Heliotrope

ZODIACAL STONE FOR

PISCES

(February 20–March 20)

How many a thing which we cast to the ground,
When others pick it up becomes a gem?

—GEORGE MEREDITH
"MODERN LOVE," XLI

$\diamondsuit$

Bloodstone is a numeral 4.

Only a select few will be drawn to this unusual gem. But those who are will feel a specific vibration when they pick up bloodstone and hold it in the palm of their hand. This gem is for the discerning: people who are analytical or logical, experts in a chosen field or vocation. This is a gem that, like the expertise it accompanies, will be passed down from one generation to the next.

If you are practical and down-to-earth, you will like bloodstone, whether or not it is your birthstone. You will not be deterred by the plain, sturdy qualities of the gem in comparison with its more brilliant and transparent cousins. No, this stone invites faithfulness, patience, and organization.

There is a grounding energy to bloodstone that will keep the wearer steady despite the turmoil nearby. This gem has a powerful vibration of Mother Earth, and lends that energy to the man or woman who feels drawn to its special aura.

$\diamondsuit$

PHYSICAL PROPERTIES

The gem for those born in March is bloodstone. Confusingly, it is also called heliotrope. Some know it as plasma. It is one of the varieties of quartz labeled chalcedony. The chalcedonies are smooth and waxy, generally translucent to opaque. Their markings are highly varied, sometimes having layers of different colors, sometimes streaked or marbeled.

Bloodstone is a deep green chalcedony with evenly distributed small spots of red jasper (formed by iron oxide) which give the stone its name. The spots may also be yellow or white. If the spots are large, or form stripes, the stone is not considered gem quality.

Bloodstone, like other chalcedonies, has no visible crystalline structure. Its composition is more fibrous. Microscopic examination reveals a mass of tiny individual crystals. Its surface is capable of taking a fine, high polish.

The name chalcedony comes from the ancient city of Chalcedon in Asia Minor, where large deposits of the mineral have been found. It is now found in the East Indies, Germany, and Egypt.

✧

SHOPPING FOR BLOODSTONES

When you're shopping for this unusual gemstone, you'll be looking for depth of green and red, for definiteness in the spots, and for careful cutting. You may prefer bloodstone with yellow or white spots. For the sake of quality, avoid stones which seem streaky or blurry . . . unless, of course, the stone recognizes you and establishes an immediate relationship. In that case, follow your instincts. Do be on the lookout for symmetry of cut. Lay the stone down and turn it in all directions to check one side against the other. To display its colors to advantage, bloodstone is cut cabochon, or flat table-cut with a beveled edge.

✧

CHARACTERISTICS AND ATTRIBUTES

Planetary connections of bloodstone are with Jupiter, Mercury, and Saturn; it is anciently associated with the zodiacal sign of Cancer and the god Mercury.

It has been written that there is no greater object than a bloodstone, that anyone who carries one with him will be given anything he asks for. Whoever holds the stone and pronounces the name engraved on it will find all doors open to him, will be freed of any bonds, and will have all obstacles removed from his path.

It is said that when bloodstone is placed in water, it gives the water a reddish tint and when that water is struck by the sun, the reflections are red. In ancient times bloodstone, often called helio-trope, was important in ritual magic.

During magical use of bloodstone or heliotrope (which means sun-turn), the reflection of the sun in the stone itself turns blood red. When the herb heliotrope is applied to the stone heliotrope, the gem dazzles the perception of the beholder, so that the one wearing or handling the stone becomes invisible.

A bloodstone engraved with a bat gives the wearer power over demons and helps with incantations.

It was believed that with the use of bloodstone one could cause storms of rain, wind, thunder, and lightning.

The Babylonians used the power in bloodstone as a weapon to destroy their enemies. Roman warriors carried amulets of it to apply directly to battle wounds to stop their bleeding.

A more earthy and personal application of this stone lies in its ability to stop bleeding from hemorrhoids. Some have found a remedy for this by always wearing a ring set with bloodstone.

It is said to make its wearer fortunate and rich. A Roman writer stated that "the virtue of the heliotrope is to procure safety and long life to the possessor of it."

According to one interpretation, bloodstone was the birthstone for Aries, March 21 to April 20. An old bit of doggerel reads:

Who on this world of ours his eyes
In Aries opens shall be wise
If always on his hand there lies
A bloodstone.

As a March birthstone, this gem was preferred by the Romans, Arabs, and Poles.

✧

HEALING MAGIC

The symbolism of color has played an important part in the use of stones for particular diseases. The red stones, such as blood-stone, ruby, garnet, spinel, carnelian, were all thought to be effi-cacious remedies for hemorrhages and inflammatory diseases.

A recorded instance of the use of bloodstone to control a hemorrhage concerned the painter Luca Signorelli, who lived from 1441 to 1523. He was placing a painting of his in a church when his companion, Giorgio Vasari, began to bleed violently. Signorelli took a bloodstone amulet from his pocket and put it between Vasari's shoulder blades. The hemorrhage is said to have stopped immediately.

Bloodstone was cut heart-shaped and worn as an amulet by the Egyptians, Babylonians, Arabs, and some American Indians. A Franciscan friar, a missionary to the Mexican Indians, wrote in 1576 that he saved the lives of many natives who were at the point of death from hemorrhage caused by plague. His remedy? A heart-shaped bloodstone amulet cooled in water and given to the patient to hold in his right hand. The Spaniards, seeing the efficacy of the Indian practice, were quick to adopt it for themselves.

Another story concerns a red-faced man who had frequent nosebleeds. A woman friend gave him a bloodstone to wear about his neck. So long as he wore the stone, he was free from nosebleeds. When he took off the stone, they began again.

A woman was unconscious from loss of blood, and still bleeding, when an acquaintance placed a bloodstone upon her. The flow stopped immediately.

In the Middle Ages physicians used bloodstone not only for stopping bleeding, but also in treating blood poisoning and for healing wounds. It was sometimes used to prevent lightning from striking one, or thunder from causing fright. It could also stop— or start—the rain. Bloodstone made its wearer brave and strong, and granted power of prophecy.

Bloodstone's ability to stanch bleeding can be explained by the fact that the iron oxide in the stone is an effective coagulator used in modern surgery.

In the hands of a master healer, bloodstone is capable of sending out vibrations that stimulate the individual's own energy for perfect healing.

As with all gemstones, bloodstone's vibrations may be passed on to a person either through wearing the stone, through Ayurvedic methods, Teletherapy, or Radionics, or by taking the elixir.

Here follows a partial list of the body organs or areas, physical and emotional maladies, and psychological ailments for which bloodstone elixir may be used.

It seems especially efficacious in disorders of the blood, digestion, and reproductive organs. Those with problems of tumors, leukemia, the heart, stomach and abdomen, bone marrow, and general low vitality benefit from this elixir.

It is helpful in uplifting consciousness and setting spiritual goals. It promotes bravery, mental balance, and clarity. It works effectively with the base and heart chakras.

Eight drops of elixir in the bath increases circulation.

An oil elixir, for external application, can be made by mixing the elixir with jojoba and olive oils. (See "Preparing Your Own Gem Elixirs," page 17.) Set this in the sun for four hours. Apply to the forehead, base of the spine, and the thymus area. This will stimulate circulation.

✧

BLOODSTONE DREAMS

If you dream that someone hands you a bloodstone to examine, the two of you will grow in brotherhood. Should someone trace three lines on your forehead with a bloodstone, you will discover an important truth. After dreaming of picking up a bloodstone, you'll be given new strength. Dreams of wearing this gem in an oval shape portend coming delight.

A bloodstone set in gold predicts that harmony will enter your life. If you dream of buying uncut bloodstone, you may enter into correspondence with one who shares your interests. When you dream of being given this unusual gemstone, it indicates that your heart is open to others.

✧

BLOODSTONES THROUGH HISTORY

There has always been a recognition, even in Christianity, of the symbolism and mystical powers of gems. The earliest Christian usage was for engraved gem amulets which, to the initiated, denoted one of Christ's followers. By medieval times the articles of the altar bore seven gemstones. Each kind in its particular place symbolized one of the seven gifts of the Holy Spirit, and was associated with a heavenly body. Stones were placed on the crucifix, the chalice, the candlesticks, the baptismal font, or the vessels for holy oils. The incense burners, the icons, the rosaries, and the priests' vestments were all adorned with gemstones. In addition to diamond (or rock crystal) sapphire, ruby, topaz, emerald, and amethyst, there was chalcedony. Chalcedony stood for fear of God and was associated with the moon. Bloodstone is of the chalcedony family, and in Christian tradition represents Christ's blood, shed for us on the Cross. This legend holds that Christ, wounded by the spear of Longinus the centurion, bled drops onto green jasper and so formed bloodstone.

As a matter of historical record, the special properties of bloodstone were put to use before Christ's time. Called heliotrope, it was used extensively in magical rites. Pliny used bloodstone as a mirror to watch the eclipse of the sun. It was an ancient belief that a bloodstone, engraved with the figure of a scorpion at the time when the sun was entering the sign of Scorpio, prevented the formation of bladder stones.

The Egyptians wore thumb rings of bloodstone. Nechepsos, an Egyptian king, wore it to improve his digestion; his stone was a talisman engraved with a dragon surrounded by rays. Roman soldiers wore it to attract success and renown, and as protection against bleeding from wounds.

After the Crucifixion, the stone did seem to take on increased powers. It was used as a charm against the bites of spiders, scorpions, and snakes, and had virtue in the treatment of ague. Pregnant women wore amulets of bloodstone to prevent miscarriage and edema. Creative persons in all fields wore it to enhance their talents. The Chinese preferred this dark green gem set in gold.

Amulets portraying Christ have been cut from this stone. There is, in a private art collection in Paris, a bust of Christ which has been sculpted from a large piece of bloodstone. It is skillfully done so that the small red spots resemble drops of blood flowing down his hair and face from his crown of thorns.

ALTERNATE BIRTHSTONE FOR MARCH

❖

Aquamarine

ALTERNATE ZODIACAL STONE FOR

PISCES

(February 20–March 20)

I am the daughter of Earth and Water
And the nursling of the sky. . . .

—PERCY BYSSHE SHELLEY
"THE CLOUD"

$\diamond$

Aquamarine is a 1, the numeral of beginnings.

The person whose birthstone it is, or who would purchase this gem, is a real go-getter in the world. Its buyer will own the stone because of its value as a gem now and in the future. After all, you may sell it at a later date for an even better, bigger price! People who like this brilliant stone know what they want out of life and are willing to work hard to achieve it. It is a power gem for men and women who work well in positions of authority—the government, law, big business, politics.

What aquamarine bestows on its wearer are added sensitivity and awareness of emotions and feelings of oneself and others. And as a naturally ebullient individual, you need this balancing characteristic. Women are strongly attracted to this gem—but only assertive, confident ones who are willing to pay the price to own its beauty. Vigorous, enterprising people will purchase aquamarine. They will buy it because the stone is one of a kind, or because of its intense color and clarity.

If it is your birthstone, you will flaunt it for just the right occasion, and will do so with the idea of impressing those around you with your good—and expensive—taste!

The aura around aquamarine is for world-beaters: those who want to be first in an endeavor or pave a new way. This is a gem for the strong and resolute, not the meek and mild. The more clarity the stone possesses, the more energy can be transmuted through it, bestowing courage and confidence on those who dare to wear it.

. . .

✧
PHYSICAL PROPERTIES

For March the alternate birthstone, and a very feminine gem, is the light-footed and lovely aquamarine. This transparent blue to sea-green stone was said by Pliny to be invisible in seawater, hence its name.

It is one of several offspring of the beryl family. Beryl is an important gemstone mineral. Other beryl stones are the rich green emerald, the rose-pink morganite, the golden heliodor, the colorless goshenite, and beryls in tints of yellow, green, and gold. Beryl crystals can grow huge, weighing several tons each, but these monsters are seldom of gem quality.

However, quite large crystals that are gem quality do form. In the National Gem Collection of the Smithsonian Institution is a flawless cut beryl weighing 2,054 carats, of a compellingly beautiful yellow-green color. Other beryls in this same collection weigh 1,363 carats, 1,000, 914, and 578 carats.

Aquamarines and other beryls are found in gem deposits all over the world. It is mined in the United States, India, and Russia. The principal deposits are in Bahia, Espírito Santo, and Minas Gerais, all in Brazil. Here gems may be recovered by open-pit mining, where the mineral occurs near the surface and is simply dug up the same way that gravel is quarried, the laborers using pickaxes and crowbars to loosen the surrounding rock. In deeper mines, vertical shafts are dug and horizontal tunnels are made. Safety conditions are casual, if not actually sleazy; for example, workers go down the shafts on insubstantial-looking ladders made of vines. Once there, they use powerful jets of water to loosen up the gem gravels. This gravel is gathered with shovels and rakes and washed in nearby streams. Stones of gem quality are cut in Rio de Janeiro, Brazil, or in Idar-Oberstein, Germany.

Unlike their sister stone the emerald, aquamarines are usually free from inclusions. Their one occasional flaw—for which they are easily forgiven because of its beauty—is a perfect little crystal snowflake. There are no synthetic aquamarines available. A synthetic stone called aquamarine would actually be a synthetic spinel.

· · ·

✧
SHOPPING FOR AQUAMARINES

In considering aquamarines of equal carat weight and clarity, remember that the more intense the shade, the more desirable it is; and true blue without any green is most desirable of all. The blue can vary from a deep, almost sapphire blue to a sky blue with no green in it. The aquamarine with a hint of green still has the "sea quality"—clear, cool, sparkling.

It's hard to go wrong with aquamarine in any of the faceted cuts, for it is beautiful in all shapes.

✧
CHARACTERISTICS AND ATTRIBUTES

Among artists of the Renaissance, green aquamarine (they called it the "sweet-tempered stone") was a favorite for engraving, being tough enough yet not too hard for working with. Unlike the other beryl stones, which nearly always have cloudy or discolored portions, the light green aquamarine is often large, free of flaws, and consistent in color throughout the crystal.

The sea-green aquamarine signifies moderation and control of the passions, and the perfect operation of prophecy.

In the seventeenth century this gemstone was used for prophesying. A ring set with a beryl stone was suspended over a bowl of water with the alphabet marked around its edge. The ring was whirled gently; by pausing at certain letters, it spelled out the answers to questions.

Aquamarines had power over evil spirits. A man with one in his mouth might safely call a demon out of hell to answer questions. If you own an aquamarine, you may stay always young and happy.

Because of its association with water, aquamarines are good luck for persons traveling by water. They also protect the wearer from poison.

When properly engraved with a hoopoe bird contemplating a tarragon herb, a beryl gem confers on the owner the power to invoke water spirits and talk with them, as well as to call up the mighty dead who will answer questions.

Beryl is the gemstone of Vulcan, god of fire and craftsmanship, especially metalworking.

Pope Gregory the Great associated beryl with the Powers, who are fourth from highest in the angelic hierarchy. Pope Gregory believed that the Powers had charge of checking forces which might act contrary to God's will.

Beryl represents the tribe of Asher, one of the Twelve Tribes of Israel. It was the eighth foundation stone of the Holy City, and one of the stones worn by the wealthy merchant-king of Tyre. It is the gem of Saint Thomas, the special apostle for the month of June, because it represents the sea and the air, and Thomas made long journeys by sea to spread the Word. It was once the natal stone for October. It is the talismanic gem for December's guardian angel Humiel, who also governs Capricorn.

Beryl stones are influenced by the planets Venus and Mars, and by the fixed star Sirius at 10 degrees Cancer.

✧

HEALING MAGIC

As with all gemstones, the vibrations of aquamarine may be passed on to a person either through wearing the stone; through Ayurvedic methods, Telepathy, or Radionics; or by taking the elixir.

Here follows a partial list of the body organs or areas, physical and emotional maladies, and psychological ailments for which aquamarine elixir may be used.

This clear gemstone leans toward conditions which ask for clarity: eye problems, disorientation, and the ability to express yourself. It strengthens the body's immune system, as well as the neck and jaw, teeth, throat, stomach, abdomen, liver, kidneys, and spleen. Use for problems of the vertebrae and the skeletal system. It raises the consciousness and helps attune to one's higher self. It is associated with the spleen and throat chakras, the etheric and mental bodies.

Use aquamarine elixir externally, a few drops in oil for massage. To amplify its powers, add seven drops of turquoise to the mixture.

✦
AQUAMARINE DREAMS

If you dream of seeing an aquamarine, it presages a happy love life for you. If you lose one, it's a warning about one to whom you might give your affections.

It is always a fortunate omen to give or receive an aquamarine in a dream. But if you dream of buying one, you'll have to answer for some undercover maneuvers. A dream display of these gemstones signifies social activities: little dinners, the theater, lights and laughter, all the glitter and gaiety of the party world.

Should you dream of an aquamarine in water, you will know abundance of all good things. If you wear an aquamarine ring in your dreams, it indicates your willingness to help others. Dreaming of an aquamarine pendant on a silver chain shows that you have a clever sense of humor. Aquamarines made into a design (such as a mandala, a triangle, or a butterfly) predict new friends for you, and happiness in store.

Aquamarine in other languages is almost exactly the same: *aquamarin, aquamarina, agua marina*. Until the Romans gave it this name, it was known as the blue beryl.

✦
AQUAMARINES AND BERYL
THROUGH HISTORY

Jews and jewelry go back to their beginnings together. Most Hebrews of ancient Palestine had a few jewels, either imported or native stones. These gems were cut and polished and mounted, but faceting was unknown for many more centuries. Mentions of gemstones and jewels, and comparisons with them, and gifts of them, are scattered throughout the Bible. Genesis 24 records a betrothal gift to Rebekah and her family. In Revelations 21 the New Jerusalem is described in terms befitting jewels.

King David, as a result of his conquests, became possessor of the jeweled crown of King Ammon. Two centuries after David, Joash had such a crown placed on his head. King Solomon had a throne trimmed with gold and ivory; the Queen of Sheba brought him gold and precious stones as gifts. For thousands of years Jews have been skilled jewelers and goldsmiths; today they still ply their trade in the marketplaces of Jerusalem and Damascus . . . and in the Big Apple.

The Diamond District of New York City—in midtown Manhattan, Forty-seventh Street between Fifth and Sixth Avenues—is business home to hundreds of Orthodox Jews who are jewelers. In this single block hundreds of jewelers, crammed side by side in tiny street-level booths, sell diamonds, colored gemstones, and precious metals. Above these stores are offices secured with private guards, triple doors, and closed-circuit television. Here cutters, polishers, dealers, brokers, and importers carry on their work—a bit of ancient Palestine in the New World.

A turn of the century scholar and writer on gems who was foremost a famous gemologist, George Frederick Kunz of Tiffany's, suggested, after due consideration of the evidence, that aquamarines were worn in the breastplate of the High Priest of the Second Temple. (Kunz wrote several books on gems and gemstones, which are now available in paperback. He owned the world's largest library of books and manuscripts on gemstones; some of his manuscripts were centuries old.) The breastplate he referred to, made perhaps in the fifth century before Christ, replaced the breastplate of the first High Priest, which was made about fourteen or thirteen hundred years before the birth of Christ.

Besides the beryl, which was the eleventh stone of the second breastplate, and which Kunz believed was an aquamarine, the High Priest wore on his shoulders two stones, each engraved with the names of six of the tribes. Possibly because aquamarine was known to be "sweet-tempered" with engravers, Kunz felt these were aquamarines also.

The highly developed spiritual entity Gurudas, who gives information through trance channel Kevin Ryerson, has confirmed that the first breastplate was carried away as spoils when the Jews were taken in to captivity in Babylon. The second breastplate, after several hundred years of being shifted around in Rome, Constantinople, and Jerusalem, was captured by Persians or Muslims in the sixth or seventh century A.D., after which it dropped from human knowledge. According to Gurudas, both breastplates are preserved intact, and archeological discoveries concerning them will probably be made before 1990.

BIRTHSTONE FOR APRIL

Diamond

ZODIACAL STONE FOR

ARIES

(March 21–April 20)

Lost, yesterday, somewhere between sunrise and sunset, two golden hours, each set with sixty diamond minutes. No reward is offered, for they are gone forever.

—HORACE MANN, EDUCATOR

Diamond is a Master Numeral 33, which reduces to a 6, giving it the dual number 33/6. No other birthstone has this Master Numeral; so this is another of the many ways in which the diamond is unique.

Diamond appeals to almost everyone on a universal vibration. It is in demand worldwide, always recognized for its unparalleled qualities of beauty. In its own chosen way, diamond becomes a part of nearly every family or country. Because of its master number vibration, diamond has the capability of saving or breaking countries; of helping to win or lose wars; of binding together families or lovers, or separating them.

Diamond is for the discerning who have an eye for perfection. If diamond is your birthstone, yet you do not feel drawn to it, don't wear it. In fact, never wear a stone you're not at ease with, for the powers within the stone are wrong for you.

For those who feel comfortable with it, there is a mystical vibration in diamond that harmonizes with your emotions when you wear it, and lifts you up to its own high level.

✧

PHYSICAL PROPERTIES

Lucky is April's child who is given her birthstone, for it is the diamond. Pliny the Elder, who lived from A.D. 23 to 79, called a diamond the most valuable thing in the world. Diamonds are one of today's most reliable investments, for their beauty never diminishes, while their value often increases over the years.

Though the color of diamond is thought of as being somewhere between a rainbow and a flash of lightning, it occurs naturally in colorless, blue white, and shades of yellow, green, pink, red, blue, gray, and black. Spiritually, all the colors of diamond are the most highly refined quality of that color. A pink diamond, for example, would be the ultimate, the perfect color of pink.

Known in Pliny's time as *adamas* or *adamant*, meaning unyielding, diamond is many, many times harder than gold, platinum, or steel, or any other gemstone. There is no harder substance on earth. Only diamond will cut diamond—and the famous black diamonds of Bahia are so hard they cannot be cut at all.

Diamonds were formed millions of years before man walked this planet, formed by unbelievable heat and pressure in molten rock deep in the core of the earth. Volcanic action pushed this material outward, through natural tubes, or pipes, to the surface. As the rock cooled and solidified, it became kimberlite, or blue ground. What had been lumps of pure carbon emerged transformed into diamonds.

In twenty-three tons of blue ground there may be found about 1 carat (one-fifth of a gram) of rough gem-quality diamond. Yet in twenty centuries of diamond mining, approximately 12 *million* carats have been produced!

The scientific properties of diamond are unusual. If your diamond rings are in a fire, their gold mountings may melt into a puddle, but the diamonds themselves will be unscathed. They can be burned only under stringent laboratory conditions: the diamond must be suspended in a jar of pure oxygen, and heat from 1,400 to 1,600 degrees Fahrenheit must be applied.

Diamond is the least compressible of all materials. After all, it is already compressed about as far as it can go. Subjected to intense heat, it expands least of all materials. It cannot be dissolved in most acids or alkalis.

Diamonds unsuitable as gems are used extensively in industry as abrasives, as glass cutters, in diamond-set saws and other tools; it is set into drill bits for oil prospecting, mining, and structural engineering work. Manufacturing diamond for industrial uses is an industry itself.

Under the microscope, every gem and piece of jewelry has its own distinguishing molecular characteristics. In 1938 Scotland Yard reported a method of "fingerprinting" a gemstone, especially the costly diamond. Using special ten- or thirty-power cameras, microscopic photographs are taken of the gem's internal crystal structure. No two are exactly alike. So even if it is recut, a particular diamond may still be identified by the "fingerprints" of its internal structure.

Diamond deposits are found in Africa, India, Brazil, Borneo, Russia, Australia, and Arkansas. Practically all the large, old, and famous diamonds have come from India. Currently, most gem-quality diamonds come from South Africa.

In the 1860s diamonds were being prospected for and mined by hand in South Africa, much as the California gold of twenty years before had been. In 1867 a stone found in South Africa was identified as a 21-carat diamond. It sold—amid much publicity—for 500 pounds. A model of it was exhibited at the Paris *Exposition Universelle de 1867*. Then another diamond was found, valued at 150 to 200 pounds. Suddenly South African farmers, tradesmen, civil servants, and others of all ranks were prospecting for diamonds on the banks and in the shallows of rivers. In 1869 the Star of South Africa, 83½ carats, came to light. Prospectors began to arrive from all over the world, including some who had been miners in the California Gold Rush.

Claims were dug in the low hills surrounding the Vaal River. Tent camps, established by the South African colonists who had come earlier, were orderly, the surroundings attractive, and hope brightened every day.

In July 1871, on a hill near the farmhouse of the two brothers De Beers, was discovered a volcanic fissure or pipe in which were concentrated great quantities of diamonds. Excitement abounded—the news spread swiftly. In those "dry diggings" the gems could be extracted using a pickaxe and shovel. The camps were consolidated, the tents upgraded by houses of wood and iron. The town of Kimberley, and the De Beers Consolidated Mining Company, had been established.

The Kimberley Diamond Mine reached 1,200 feet in depth as an open mine. Shafts were carried to 4,000 feet below the surface. That mine was abandoned in 1915. Today it is an immense crater filled with water.

Alluvial gravels of South Africa are rich in diamonds, of which an astonishingly large percentage is gem quality. There, in the early years of this century, diamonds were *gathered* by rows of workers on their hands and knees, picking up stones from the surface. Sounds like a dream, doesn't it.

✧

SHOPPING FOR DIAMONDS

When you are shopping for a diamond, any reliable jeweler will tell you that the value of the stone is determined by the four Cs: color, clarity, cutting, and carat weight.

The finest quality diamonds are crystal-clear and without color in the *body* of the stone. This may be judged by use of a colorimeter, an electronic instrument for measuring the precise body color of a diamond; or it may be color graded against a master set of diamonds of known color grade. The much-abused term blue-white actually applies to diamonds which do have a trace of blue in the color; these are rare and very valuable.

Clarity refers to the relative absence of flaws or inclusions in or on the stone. The jeweler determines this by use of a diamond-scope. Grades of clarity, starting with highest quality, are: Flawless; Very, Very Slightly Imperfect; Very Slightly Imperfect; Slightly Imperfect; and Imperfect. Anyone can see the inclusion or flaw in an Imperfect diamond.

Cutting accuracy is *essential* to the beauty of diamonds. The extraordinary power of the diamond to refract and reflect intense flashes of prismatic light rays is one of its major claims to beauty. It must be cut with scientifically correct proportions, to precise angles, and with each facet highly polished. A stone cut with too wide a top facet, or too thick in the body, will be cheated of its true fire and brilliance.

A carat is subdivided into 100 points; so a ½-carat diamond weights 50 points. There are 141¾ carats to an ounce. Carat weight of a diamond is not a complete indication of its value. The other three C's must first be considered. When two stones are equal in clarity, color, and cut, the heavier stone will be of greater value.

•   •   •

✧
CHARACTERISTICS AND ATTRIBUTES

If you own a diamond, or it is your birthstone, its unconquerable hardness will bring you victory, constancy in lovers, and serenity in your life. It will repel poison, nightmares, witchcraft, madness, strife, and pestilence. It will drive away ghosts and prevent calamities. If you work with wild beasts, your diamond will make them tame.

Diamond is a gem of winter, but the rare green diamond signifies spring. It is the shining alternate gem of the weekend days—Saturday and Sunday, representing the high hour of noon. It signifies the seventy-fifth wedding anniversary. In Arab tradition, it was alternate gem for Taurus. A seventeenth-century book assigned diamond to the planet Mars. It has also been attributed to Jupiter and the fixed star Caput Algol, at 18 degrees Taurus.

The Chaldeans attributed diamond to the sun. Master of the mineral kingdom, diamond symbolizes the central sun of our solar system, a force immutable and constant that signifies the fulfillment of the divine law that order plus harmony equals equilibrium in all aspects of our lives.

If you have parted with a dear one, wearing diamond will revive that person's love for you.

It is said that the devil, who typifies darkness, is the enemy of diamond, the very archetype of sovereign virtue and light, because the gem consistently resists his spells.

A fourteenth-century manuscript advanced the belief that diamond is sometimes consumed or melted when it thunders.

Diamond is associated with the angel Israfel. Israfel is the angel of resurrection and song, who will blow the trumpet on Judgment Day. An Islamic tradition is that Israfel was companion to Mohammed for three years, initiating him in the work of a prophet.

In 1730 Giacinto Gimma wrote that black stones—of which he specifically mentioned diamond—stand for Saturn and Saturday. Worn by a man the stone indicates gravity, good sense, constancy, and fortitude. Gimma—who was lamentably chauvinistic—said that if an unmarried woman wore diamond, she was fickle and foolish; but if married, she showed perseverance in all things including love.

Diamond itself signified envy and mourning, and was a bit on the sinister side. Gimma said its animal was the hog, and in people it signified the age of decrepitude. He assigned it the numeral 8—which in our modern numerology system signifies finance.

Among the Jews, Romans, Russians, and Arabs, sapphire was the birthstone for April; only the Polish chose diamond. From the fifteenth-century until the twentieth, diamond was the primary stone and sapphire the alternate. Now diamond, superbly alone, represents this month of renewal and hope.

Spiritually, diamond has attributes that cover the whole spectrum of energy; it has the power to help nearly all conditions. The continuing search for eternal meanings is amplified by this gem. The balancing of inner qualities, and the openness of one's being to spiritual guidance, are speeded up by the wearing of diamond. Its energy raises all physical energy to a higher level.

Diamond is the sixth stone in the Breastplate of the High Priest; also the stone of the Israelite tribe of Zebulon.

The Talmud mentions a diamond worn by the High Priest, which was used to reveal the guilt or innocence of persons accused of a crime. If the stone dimmed, the accused was guilty. But if it shone more brightly, it declared the person's innocence. A similar test was employed to determine adultery.

In Buddhist writings, as well as those of the early Christians, are found references to precious stones as representing religious virtues. A third-century manuscript lists the attributes of diamond, saying that the king should also have these attributes. The manuscript says that diamond is pure throughout; it cannot be alloyed with any other substances; it is associated with only the most costly of gems. So should the king be pure in his means of livelihood; he should not mix with wicked men as friends; and he should seek only the highest in excellence. In this decade, a popular love song asks the listener that the singer be "a diamond in your eyes."

In the Hindu writings the Bhagavat Puranas, the divine Krishna went to abide in the Holy City of Devaraka. (Krishna was the eighth incarnation of Vishnu, one of the three major deities of Hinduism.) Various gods and genuises came to visit:

> Some descended from the sky, some from their cars; and alighting underneath the banyan tree, looked on Devaraka,

the matchless. The city was square . . . decked in pearls, rubies, diamonds, and other gems. The city was high; it was ornamented with gems; and it was furnished with cupolas of rubies and diamonds, with emerald pillars and with courtyards of rubies. It contained endless temples. It had crossroads decked with sapphires, and highways blazing with gems. It blazed like the meridian sun in summer.

The Hindu Holy City was alight with colors, like a meadow of precious wildflowers.

◇

HEALING MAGIC

In the hands of a properly attuned spiritual healer, diamond becomes a gem through which powerful healing energies can be focused to help the wearer or others the healer may feel directed to help. It is an intensifier and amplifier of other stones. It can draw toxicity out of the body, and amplify the discharge of toxicity from the system.

As applied in Bhattacharyya's Gem Therapy, diamond is a concentrate of the cosmic color indigo. It is used as a single gem in part of the therapy for convulsions, diabetes, eclampsia, epilepsy, fistulas, menopause, nephritis, psoriasis, ringworm, and sterility; and as an ingredient in nearly every gem mixture to treat most ailments.

Diamond dust, even in medieval times, was known to be deadly if it was swallowed. It was said, however, that if you managed to live through that event, you would be gifted with exceptional courage. This expensive dust, because of its radiation capabilities, can leach out one's life force.

As with all gemstones, diamond's vibrations may be passed on to a person, either through wearing the stone; through Ayurvedic methods, Teletherapy, or Radionics; or by taking the elixir.

Here follows a partial list of the body organs or areas, physical and emotional maladies, and psychological ailments for which diamond elixir may be used.

It treats autism, dyslexia, epilepsy, tuberculosis; facilitates detoxification; aids the muscle and nervous system; helps with physical coordination; improves production of the endorphins; strengthens the pineal and pituitary glands and the testicles. This elixir improves such psychological symptoms as jealousy, insecurity, and low self-esteem; it eases stress and balances the personality. It restores vitality, and acts as an aphrodisiac in sexual conflicts.

Spiritually, diamond elixir aids in clairvoyance and attunes one to the higher self. It applies especially to the third eye and the sex chakras, and works on all subtle bodies, especially the etheric and mental bodies.

Place the elixir or the gemstone on the finger, top of the head, the base of the brain, or the temple; then meditate. Diamond alters and corrects the muscle structure in the jaw and the shoulder blades. It arrests the progress of most diseases.

✧

DIAMOND DREAMS

If a maiden dreams of being given diamonds in any form of setting, it signifies that she will marry a gentleman of high position and great wealth. A bachelor who dreams of giving diamonds to his sweetheart should select his mate carefully. If you dream of wearing diamond earrings, expect a disagreeable experience with a friend.

Seeing diamonds in a dream, if you are not rich enough to own them, foretells a luxurious income. But if you do own them, a dream of seeing diamonds warns you to be careful with your own. A dream of owning diamonds indicates great honor and recognition from those in authority.

Dreams of wearing a diamond bracelet indicate that you are destined to be with your mate for life. Wearing diamond rings in a dream is a sign of patience and adaptability. Dreaming of a diamond necklace means that you appreciate all forms of beauty. To dream of having your diamonds taken from you means that you are surrendering all false pretenses.

✧
DIAMONDS THROUGH HISTORY

Diamonds were found occasionally before the Christian era. Hindu tradition says that the Koh-i-noor, possibly the world's oldest known, was found four to five thousand years ago. It was the discovery of diamond fields near Golconda, India, between 600 and 500 B.C. that started this magnificent stone on its way to sovereignty in the gem kingdom. Every Oriental potentate wanted his own private supply of this unique gemstone. (Before the area was exhausted, $675 million in gems had been mined. At today's prices that figure would be considerably larger.)

Gradually, here and there, merchants and traders introduced diamonds into Europe. By Pliny's time a few Romans were wearing them. Set uncut into rings, with one crystal point up and one down, Roman diamonds bore little resemblance to the dazzling beauties of today. A diamond in the rough, uncut, unpolished, is neither brilliant nor beautiful, but instead looks like frosted plastic. Not until 1456 was the art of cutting symmetrical facets invented, and the brilliance of diamond set free.

Rough diamond's popularity in spite of its lack of pizzazz suggests that there was recognition of diamond's spiritual value and intrinsic worth, rather than its good looks (especially when compared with the then available cut and polished colored stones) that drew people to it.

The brilliant, romantic diamond has long been the stone for engagement rings, being thought capable of softening anger, strengthening love, and promoting harmony in marriage. In 1574 Jean de La Taille wrote that diamond drives away "the terror that comes by night." The playwright Anita Loos, in 1925, said frankly that diamonds are a girl's best friend.

The thought of diamonds brings one to the thought of rings. Some of the earliest rings carried personal seals, which were used in clerical work, to authenticate inventories, letters, documents of all kinds. No doubt as a convenience, the seals were mounted in a form which could be carried on the finger. Today's school and signet rings are descendants of seal rings.

Rings are usually made in a circular shape. The circle means completeness; beginning and end and beginning; wholeness; trust; the circle of love and friendship.

In Caesar's time, a young woman was given an iron ring as an earnest of intentions upon the drawing up of the marriage contract. At the wedding ceremony she received a gold ring. But then the wedding ring was worn only on special occasions.

The first engagement rings were given by royalty. The first known diamond engagement ring was given in 1477 to Mary of Burgundy by her fiancé, the Archduke Maximilian of Austria. This seems to have begun a long tradition.

✧

SOME FABLED DIAMONDS OF HISTORY

The Koh-i-noor

Around all the famous jewels of history there lingers an aura of romance, mystery, and intrigue. Big diamonds mean international adventure, a king's or a country's ransom one can hold cupped in the hand. A large gemstone is so incredible a prize that its very existence arouses covetousness in the heart. The truly magnificent diamonds have all counted their worth in human lives.

The Koh-i-noor, presently mounted in the crown made for the coronation of Queen Elizabeth (now the Queen Mother), has a centuries-long tradition of bringing ruin to its male possessor and doom to his kingdom. In the nearly five thousand years since its discovery in the Godavari River in India, the 186-carat gem has never been sold, but has acquired new owners through theft, trickery, conquest, and murder.

Its recorded history began in 1304. After generations of belonging to the rulers of Malwa, the stone became spoils of victory for the conquering Sultan Ala-ed-Din. In 1526 when Sultan Baber, founder of the Mogul Dynasty, conquered India, he took possession of the stone. For two hundred years the stone stayed in the treasury of the Mogul rulers at Delhi. It was said to have been set into one of the eyes of the famous Peacock Throne of Shah Jehan, descendant of Sultan Baber and builder of the Taj Mahal.

In 1719 Nadir Shah captured the mogul kingdom. He wanted that diamond. One of the harem girls whispered its whereabouts to him, and so at a public ceremony, where there could be no courteous refusal, Nadir Shah suggested a goodwill exchange of turbans with the deposed monarch. In his tent afterward, Nadir Shah unbound the turban, and as the big diamond fell gleaming into sight, he gasped, "Koh-i-noor!" meaning mountain of light. Triumphantly he took the gem home to Persia. A few years later he was assassinated.

One black deed followed another in the next century of the Koh-i-noor's history. Torture, imprisonment, blinding, death— these were the fates of its innumerable hapless owners. Then in 1849 the British annexed the Punjab—and its "stone of destiny," the Koh-i-noor.

Queen Victoria had it recut for greater brilliance, and wore it in a brooch. No king of England has ever worn it. Now weighing 108 carats, it was last reset in the crown for the wife of George VI, Queen Elizabeth. The diamond for possession of which men cheated, stole, and murdered, is now leading the sedate life in a stronghold in Waterloo Barracks, in the Tower of London, where it may be viewed along with other British crown jewels.

The Stars of Africa

The largest diamond ever found was as big as a man's fist, weighed a pound and a third—and was a fragment broken off a larger stone! It was found by Frederick Wells, surface manager of the Premier Mine in the Transvaal. Making his rounds one January day in 1905, Wells caught a gleam in the "blue ground" above his head. He dug with his pocketknife, broke a blade, and completed the excavation with his fingernails. Even when the magnificent prize was in his hands, he could scarcely believe it was real. A diamond the size of a half-grapefruit? Weighing 3,106 carats? Wells's company believed it was real; they gave him a $10,000 bonus and named the outsized gem the Cullinan, for Sir Thomas M. Cullinan, President of the Premier Diamond Mining Company.

Two years later it was presented as a crown jewel to King Edward VII. Many months after that, it was cleaved, cut into pieces, faceted, and polished. Though 50 percent of its weight was gone, the resulting 105 stones were gorgeous. There were nine major stones, the smallest weighing 4⅓ carats, the third largest 94 carats.

The second largest, the so-called Second Star of Africa, is a square-cut brilliant of 317 carats. It is set in the jeweled band that forms the base of the Imperial State Crown of the British Regalia.

The Star of Africa, the world's largest cut diamond, is a 530-carat pendant-cut brilliant. It is set just below the jeweled cross and orb in the Royal Sceptre, which is held in the British sovereign's right hand at the coronation. Both Stars of Africa were mounted by Messrs. Garrard, the Crown Jewellers, so that they may be removed for the Queen to wear on state occasions.

The Hope

Practically everyone has heard of the Hope Diamond—that deep, rich sapphire-blue gem with a curse. Its owners have known financial disaster; madness; and violent death by gunshot, guillotine, and gurgling waters. It began recorded life in the mid-1600s as a blue diamond of 67 carats, bought in India by wealthy traveler, writer, trader, and gemstone expert Jean Baptiste Tavernier, who sold it in France to Louis XIV. Marie Antoinette wore it; she was beheaded. Then in 1792, in the most sensational gem snatch of the century, the "Tavernier Blue" was stolen from the Garde-Meuble, repository of the French crown jewels. In the form that Tavernier described it, it was lost forever.

In 1830 three sapphire-blue diamonds turned up on the London market. The largest weighed 44 carats and had one oddly cut side. Edwin W. Streeter, a London jeweler of the period, theorized that the three blue stones were the Tavernier, recut. London banker Henry Thomas Hope bought the largest for ninety thousand dollars.

The Hope Diamond was passed to Hope's daughter, the Duchess of Newcastle, then to her second son, Lord Francis Hope, who sold it to pay debts. Selim Habib bought it, and drowned at sea. Fortunately he was not wearing the diamond. Another owner, a Sultan of Turkey, shot his wife while she was wearing it.

In 1911 Edward B. McLean, a Washington, D.C., newspaper publisher, purchased the diamond from Cartier's of Paris. For Mc-

Lean and his wife, Evalyn Walsh, the curse of the blue diamond went on a rampage. Their eldest son died in an auto accident, their daughter under mysterious circumstances. Evalyn divorced McLean; he lost his fortune and died in an institution.

Evalyn Walsh McLean showed no awe of the accursed diamond; she loved headlines and delighted in drawing attention to her famous gem. She wore it as a pendant on a necklace with sixty-two white diamonds in a laid-back hodgepodge of cuts and shapes. Once she pawned it at Simpson's, a famous New York pawnshop, and phoned the news to gossip columnist Ed Sullivan. In a capricious mood, she lent it to her little dog to wear—to the delight of news photographers.

After her death, New York jeweler Harry Winston outbid some forty others to buy Mrs. McLean's seventy-two-piece jewel collection. In 1958, after owning the fabulous blue diamond for nine years, Mr. Winston generously donated it to the Smithsonian Institution. It is one of the most popular attractions of the Smithsonian's Gem Hall.

The Dresden Green

The Dresden Green Diamond was a fine flawless gem, said to be apple green. Its color makes it one of the world's rarest gems. Augustus the Strong, Elector of Saxony and King of Poland who died in 1733, paid forty-five thousand dollars for the 41-carat stone. It was displayed in the famous Green Vaults under the Dresden Palace. The palace was severely bombed during World War II, but the Dresden Green, together with other important jewels, was spirited away to a fortress and thus survived.

At the end of the war, the Saxon Crown Jewels were appropriated by the Soviet Trophies Organization and taken to Russia. It was reported in 1959 that the treasures had been restored to Dresden, but the Dresden Green Diamond was not among them. Supposedly it is in the Kremlin in Moscow.

The Diamond Throne

Under the Tree of Knowledge, where the master Gautama Buddha is said to have received his supreme revelations of truth, there was once a Diamond Throne. This throne consisted of a single diamond a hundred feet around. Its foundations were at the center of all things; the diamond was formed when the earth was formed. When the entire earth quaked, or was covered with water, this splendid throne stood undamaged. Though it was written of in the seventh century A.D., it is now hidden under the drifted bright brown soil of India.

BIRTHSTONE FOR MAY

Emerald

ZODIACAL STONE FOR

TAURUS

(April 21–May 21)

Who first beholds the light of day
In spring's sweet flowery month of May,
And wears an emerald all her life,
Shall be a loved and happy wife.

—OLD SAYING

$\diamond$

Numerologically, emerald is a 4.

Above all, emerald is a woman's stone; or for a man who possesses a marked degree of sensitivity. This gem is perfect for those who cherish graciousness and consideration for others, rather than for themselves first. If emerald is your birthstone, the need for harmony is uppermost in your personality; being nonresistant is intrinsic in your nature.

The emerald appeals to your more refined, gentler side, bringing a soothing, calming effect on you when chaos reigns around your life-style. Indeed, emerald can bestow an energy of cooperation and willingness around you. It is the stone of the peacemakers of the world, those individuals who can gently bring two extremes back into balance without aggression or harsh words, simply through the use of compromise.

Emerald is for people who are still childlike even as adults, people who are creative, original, willing to go out and embrace life fully and wholeheartedly. Nature appeals to them deeply and the green of the stone only enhances that aspect of their personality. And because they are more harmony-oriented, they may wear the emerald as if it were a piece of costume jewelry instead of a very precious and very expensive stone.

Bravo! Emeralds own people, people don't own emeralds. There is an exciting, vibrating energy around this gem that throbs, ebbs, and flows around the wearer or user. It's the color of healing; it's the healer.

. . .

✧

PHYSICAL PROPERTIES

Emerald is a beryl stone, the bold, big-city sister of the delicate aquamarine. Beryl is formed as a thin fluid melt in the seams and fissures of older rocks. Examples of variations in color include not only the blue to sea-green aquamarine and the true green emerald, but also the rose-red beryl, which occurs in a blossom pink, a flame red, and an intense rose pink called morganite. The rare heliodor, a sunny yellow, is said by the natives of South Africa to be a gift of the sun, having fallen to earth in a mighty shower of meteorites.

Within the range of greens found in emerald are "forty shades," like the greens found in Ireland, the Emerald Isle. The finest green of all is called old mine green, and comes from the Muzo mines in Colombia. This was the green of the emeralds discovered by the Spanish conquistadores. Sometimes those gems were called "Chibcha stones" after the Columbian Indians.

The finest quality emerald is a true, true green, transparent, deep and brilliant, with no whisper of yellow or blue in it. The poet Percy Bysshe Shelley wrote aptly of "the emerald heaven of trees." Look upon an emerald—especially if it is your own—and you'll know why this soft-spoken and gentle gemstone is said to soothe away weariness.

The next finest shade of green emerald has a breath of blue in it. These stones came from the original mine at Chivor in Colombia and were being mined and shipped throughout the world before the seventeenth century.

Emeralds in nature do not often grow large, or without pleasant inner quirks. The stones are typically distinguished by a cloudiness called the *jardin*—the garden. Sometimes under the microscope an emerald will reveal a perfectly formed cloud suspended in the green atmosphere. Or there may be designs like moss. Other inclusions may be fine channels, a golden-faceted ball of pyrite crystal, or a little cave in which there floats a gas bubble and a tiny salt crystal.

For all their hardness of 7.5–8 on the Mohs' scale, emeralds aren't a tough stone. They are sensitive to knocks or blows. When wearing them, especially in a ring, one must take care not to whack them on hard objects.

The major sources of emeralds today are at Muzo and Chivor in Colombia, South America. The finest emeralds in the world (by gemologists' criteria) occur at Muzo in cavities in the ground which are known to be 130 million years old. Emeralds are also found in veins near the surface. From the latter some well-developed, relatively clear emeralds have been taken.

In 1956 in Sandawana, Rhodesia, emeralds were discovered. These stones are usually under one carat; and their green color, though lively, is less intense than those from Colombia. Their unusual brilliance and reasonable price have made them sought after for jewelry.

The mines at Sandawana produced in quantity for only twenty years, but some stones still come from that locality.

Emeralds are mined by a rather odd process. Since the emerald-bearing cavities are within rocks, and not visible from the outside, the entire rock must be broken up so as not to miss any treasure. Steps or terraces are cut around an entire hill, or over an entire mountainside. The miners stand on one level and plunge nine-foot-long crowbars into the next level below them, penetrating and breaking up the rock. In other types of deposits, in which the emerald-bearing mineral has formed great cones, modern mining methods can be used. Where the mineral forms walls, workers use strong jets of water to wash out the unwanted minerals. The emeralds are then raked and shoveled into baskets and sent to the surface to be sorted later.

There is an unusual fact that seems to apply to all gemstones. Some stones are called old mine, meaning that they were among the first to be discovered in a particular location, which may by now have been mined for several hundred or even several thousand years. The peculiar fact is that the "old mine" stones are the largest and finest by all the customary standards of the gem trade. Something in nature seems to heave these big gems up toward the surface, whereas the somewhat smaller but still quite fine stones may stay buried a bit deeper. For this reason, gems that were mined twenty, fifty, or five hundred years ago are likely to be bigger and better than the ones found today.

◇
SHOPPING FOR EMERALDS

Perhaps the most important thing to know, in comparison-shopping for emeralds, is what a genuine emerald looks like. Learn what its color range includes, the general look of the stone, the feel of it in your fingers, the feelings you get about the genuine article. Ask to see it under magnification. These instructions make the assumption that you'll see at least a few stones that you'll get some vibrations from. Pay a lot of attention to your instincts with this stone, so that if one comes along that isn't any of the things you've learned about emerald but the stone claims you, you'll have some basis for a decision.

A flawless emerald is almost unknown; indeed, those of the most appealing colors may have many cracks and imperfections. Only about 1 percent of the emerald found is of fine gem quality.

For more than forty years emeralds have been man-made by various processes that duplicate the chemical composition and other characteristics of the genuine. These are called synthetics. Chatham emeralds and Gilson emeralds are synthetic, though hardly less expensive than natural ones. These synthetics have fewer inclusions than natural ones; those which do occur may be like bubbles or wisps of steam.

A type of glass is manufactured that is very similar to genuine emerald. Green garnets, peridot, and even jade may be passed off as emerald by an unscrupulous or ignorant dealer. Be wary of any emerald that has a first name, such as Evening Emerald, or Crystalline Emerald, for they are some other stone.

As for cut, the step cut called emerald cut is beautiful if the stone is large enough; but any of the step or brilliant cuts will bring out the dazzle in this magnificent gem. Also consider whether you prefer yellow gold or white gold or platinum around your emerald. Educate your eyes until you meet the combination of cut, stone, precious metal, and mounting that appeals to you the most.

· · ·

✧
CHARACTERISTICS AND ATTRIBUTES

Emerald is guarded by the fabled Arimaspi, a one-eyed race whose home is near the Mountains of the Moon in Africa; the Arimaspi are known to battle with the half-eagle, half-lion creatures called gryphons.

Worn by men, emerald represents joyousness, but also inconstancy. On the hand of a woman, the gem stands for ambition, change, and childish delight. Emerald is one of the stones of Mercury, of Venus, and the moon. According to eighteenth-century author Giacinto Gimma, youth is the age of man, and 5 is the magic number of this green gemstone. The animal that corresponds to emerald is the clever fox.

Engraved with a frog, emerald has the power to reconcile enemies and restore friendship where there has been discord. It is a gem for springtime and for the first half of the week. It's the lucky talisman for Monday and the gemstone for Tuesday and Wednesday. Its favorite hour is two in the afternoon. For a fifty-fifth anniversary, the significant gemstone is emerald.

Emerald is recommended as an amulet above all other stones. Worn in a necklace or ring, it is said to prevent epileptic attacks, stop bleeding, and cure panic or fever.

Emerald in other languages has some interesting variations. In French it is *emeraude*. In Spanish it is *esmerelda*; in Italian, *smeraldo*. The German word is *smaragd*. The Latin work is *smaragdus*.

Emerald is the fourth foundation stone of the Holy City and the fourth stone of the High Priest's breastplate. It is the gemstone of the apostles John the Baptist and James, son of Zebedee, as well as of the Israelite tribe of Judah.

According to a fourth-century Christian book on gemstones, emerald is capable of foreshadowing things to come. It has the power of transfusing the air surrounding it with green, thus calming small irritations. In that same regard it is said to refresh the memory and to restore clear sight to weary eyes. It helps in divination, particulary in recovering lost items. Its basic nature attracts to it kindness and goodness; it strengthens faith when its owner is undergoing adversity.

Emerald is a living energy field that represents universal intelligence. It is associated with the emerald tablets of Hermes, the messenger of the gods. The gem contains a perfect balance of the creative force, which is intelligent thought combined with correct action.

Spiritually, emerald works a transformation, nurturing, stabilizing, harmonizing wisdom with free will, bringing ever to mind the Golden Rule. It educates to bring understanding. It promotes openness and inspiration, and divine order in one's life.

Emerald signifies a clear conscience, and people who gladly give of their wisdom and love to others. The wearing of emerald enhances perception and evaluation of that which is perceived. The vibration of this stone is love, projected from itself and through itself.

Andreas, Bishop of Caesarea in the latter tenth century, was one of the earliest writers to make the association between the Foundation Stones of the New Jerusalem and the apostles. He stated that emerald is nourished with oil to preserve its beauty and transparency. Andreas connected the stone with John the Evangelist, who soothed the souls dejected by sin with a divine oil.

Around A.D. 600, Pope Gregory the Great (who was the first monk elected Pope) listed the nine ascending orders of angels, and to each he assigned a gemstone. Bear in mind that even the youngest angels of least rank are highly evolved spiritual beings who are unceasingly ardent in their adoration of the Creator and the manifestation of His will in the universe. Pope Gregory assigned emerald to the highest rank of angels, the Angel Princes. It is said that by wearing the corresponding stone, one may attract angels of that rank.

For the guardian angel Muriel, emerald is the talismanic gem. Muriel is the angel of the month of June and ruler of the zodiacal sign Cancer. He is one of the rulers of the order of Dominations. He serves as one of the chief angelic officers of the third hour of the day.

Among the Chaldeans, emerald was associated with the planet Venus. A manuscript of 1604 attributed it to Venus and Mercury and to the fixed star Spica Virginis, at 17 degrees Libra.

As the birthstone for May, it was used by the Arabs, the Poles, and the Russians. It has been used since the fifteenth century with agate as the alternate birth gem for May. Emerald was reportedly efficacious against venom and possession by evil spirits.

✧

HEALING MAGIC

Well into the mid-eighteenth century, chemists' shops sold powdered emerald as a medication. Doses of the "elixir of precious stones" were given to Charles VI of France and Lorenzo de Medici on their death beds. Francis Bacon wrote that "precious stones may work by consent upon the spirits of men to comfort and exhilarate them." (In other words Bacon felt that, mostly, people cured themselves.) Liquids in which emerald had rested were considered effective healing potions against weakness and pains of the internal organs; these were much used during the Great Plague of 1548. Present-day emerald gem elixir has much the same application.

An overwhelming mixture of gems called an electuary was popular in France in the early 1700s. It was considered an efficacious remedy for most of the ills the flesh fell heir to. Its ingredients included emerald, sapphire, topaz, pearls, coral, jacinth, silver leaf, gold, and several powerful herbs. In Florence and Languedoc, practically every house had a vial of it sitting around waiting for some ailment to cure.

In modern-day Gem Therapy, which uses the stone's vibrations, emerald is the single gem recommended for treatment of biliousness, heartburn, colitis, and digestive glitches in general. Emerald is used in about 60 percent of the gem mixtures.

As with all gemstones, emerald's vibrations may be passed on to a person either through wearing the stone; through Ayurvedic methods, Teletherapy, or Radionics, or by taking the elixir.

Here follows a partial list of the body organs or areas, physical and emotional maladies, and psychological ailments for which emerald elixir may be used.

It treats digestive conditions, the immune system, the intestinal tract, and the kidneys. It is helpful in childhood diseases. It is used in eye and heart problems and treats the nervous system and the skin. Working with the heart chakra and the etheric, astral, and emotional bodies, it is good for bringing mind, emotions, and spirit into balance, and for handling family affairs or father-image problems. The major organs—liver, heart, kidneys, pancreas—benefit from emerald elixir. It helps with meditation, elevating one's consciousness and psychic abilities.

Wear emerald or its elixir over your heart or thymus gland, or close to the nasal passages. Use seven drops in your bath water. Just as with the other elixirs, use the cycle of two weeks on, a week off, two weeks on.

✧
EMERALD DREAMS

If you dream of emerald, you will know a life of affluence. You'll marry into a wealthy and respected old family, and their luster will complement yours. But you'll overcome obstacles and triumph over trials before you know happy success.

If you dream of emerald with other jewels, you'll have riches and social prestige. If your dream is of an old emerald, you'll inherit money and real estate from a surprising source. Be very cautious and get good counsel, as there may be some trouble with others over your inheritance.

Should you buy an emerald in a dream, you may have some unfortunate dealings with someone you have trusted. If your lover wears emeralds in your dream, you may be jilted for someone of greater wealth; and one you are fond of may move to a distant place.

✧
EMERALDS THROUGH HISTORY

The vivid green of emerald signifies the youth of one's life, and eternal life. It is the gemstone of Ceres, Roman goddess of agriculture. In Roman and Greek times, green was used in the final services for those who died young. The graves of young virgins and of children were covered with green branches. The lower part of the torches used in the ceremony was colored green. An emerald ring was sometimes placed on the index finger of the deceased, as a sign of hope in resurrection. In the tomb of Tullia, dearly loved daughter of Cicero, there was found the most beautiful emerald ever seen at that time.

Emerald beads and scarabs have been found in Egyptian tombs. The Egyptians used emeralds for the eyes of their sacred images. In the mummies of their dead, engraved scarabs of precious emeralds, rubies, or turquoises were used to replace the heart. (Since emerald was not always available, the Egyptians invented faience, an exquisite glazed pottery which skillfully substituted for the genuine gemstone.)

The Aztecs carved emerald into brilliant forms of fishes and flowers. The treasured gold of the Incas, plundered by fifteenth-century Spaniards, was set with quantities of emeralds and pearls.

Emerald was among the most expensive treasures of the gem markets of Babylon. Today, nearly six thousand years after the heyday of this ancient civilization, emerald remains one of the most valuable gemstones available.

Leaders of all eras wore and used emerald. Cleopatra, Queen of Egypt, wore magnificent emeralds that came from her own mines in Upper Egypt. The Roman emperor Nero used to watch the gladiators through an emerald, because he believed it sharpened his eyesight. In the days of the czars of Russia, emeralds were the most prized of the Russian Crown Jewels; they were a personal favorite of Empress Catherine the Great.

At the time of the Spanish conquest of New Granada, the Indians of that locality burned gold and emeralds as love offerings before the images of the sun and the moon.

The ancient Peruvians worshiped emerald. A chronicler of the time reported that they had a "mother stone" the size of an ostrich egg. On important feast days the emerald was on display for the people. Priests urged the peasants to bring in emeralds as gifts, because the mother was lonely for her children. The peasants traveled long distances to worship the stone and offer it daughter stones of smaller emeralds.

Emeralds do occur in large masses occasionally. However, these are not gem-quality stone but rather used in building. The writers Herodotus and Pliny spoke of gigantic masses of stone which they believed to be emerald. The Greek philosopher Theophrastus, who lived about 372–287 B.C., also wrote of an emerald 72 inches long and 54 inches thick, which the King of Babylon sent to the Egyptian Pharoah. An obelisk in the Temple of Ammon was made of four emeralds, 160 inches long and in places 16 inches thick. In the time of Theophrastus there was still in existence an upright column formed from a single emerald, in the temple of Hercules of Tyre.

Some large emeralds still exist in museums and private collections. A wealthy American owns a 225-carat emerald with a portrait of Caesar engraved on it. Charlemagne's crown was set with emeralds and other precious stones. In the 1600s the Hapsburg Empire acquired a jar carved from one massive emerald crystal. The jar, four inches high, weighing 2,680 carats, is in Vienna.

In the Bank Melli in Tehran are the former crown jewels of Iran, lavishly adorned with emeralds, some of which are hundreds of years old. In this collection are many boxes of emeralds; there are emerald-studded crowns and belt buckles. The high quality of these old gemstones is hardly ever matched by emeralds found today.

BIRTHSTONE FOR JUNE

◇

Pearl

ZODIACAL STONE FOR

GEMINI

(May 22–June 21)

The hours I spend with thee, dear heart!
Are as a string of pearls to me;
I count them over every one apart—
My rosary, my rosary.

—ROBERT CAMERON ROGERS
"THE ROSARY"

Pearl is a numeral 6.

There are always many people of all nations who demand to have pearl; it is a world-class gem with a worldwide market value. People who are generous, artistically gifted, and enjoy a sense of peace and harmony will be drawn initially to this gem. A serenity emanates from it that appeals to their quiet inner space.

Pearl inspires cooperation, loyalty, fairness, and emotional attunement with self and others. It seeks to soothe and calm rather than agitate or energize like some other gems.

Pearls are for those with a discerning eye and a strong, intuitive sense about themselves and their personal world. Pearls are for people who listen to their own special drummer in life and who never march where the crowd is going. Those who feel this special affinity for pearl are often alone but seldom lonely.

Once in your possession, pearls will become part of the family heirlooms handed down from one generation to the next. Pearls invite you to wear them often, even daily. The aura around them is one of brotherhood and humanitarian harmony; it will give sustenance and peace even in a chaotic environment.

Pearls are for the masses of any social stratum and any class. This widespread popularity cannot demean or devalue the glowing beauty of this priceless gem from the womb of the ocean. It can only add a new luster, warmth, and tranquillity to your flagged spirit, picking you up and making you whole again.

. . .

✧

PHYSICAL PROPERTIES

Pearl is the only birthstone that is not of mineral origin. In other words, it is not a stone. Pearl is an organic substance. It is formed inside the shell of live oysters and mussels as a result of foreign matter—a grain of sand, for example—which has entered the shell. Unable to expel its irritating guest, the oyster covers the intruder with thin alternating layers of conchiolin and aragonite. Conchiolin is organic matter. Aragonite (also called nacre or mother of pearl) is the mineral that lines the oyster's shell. The layers that make up a pearl are like those of an onion.

The result, after several years' oyster labor, is an object that may or may not be a "true," or gem quality, pearl. The true pearl can be any shape or size, but its value and beauty are determined by the shimmering luster from the various layers. Pearls of gem quality are formed by a particular species of pearl-bearing oyster. Those which occur in the edible variety are rarely gems. Though if you like oysters, you may go on eating them in hope.

Around 1904, the Japanese perfected the method of producing what are called cultured pearls. An irritant (a mother-of-pearl bead) is inserted into a living oyster. The oysters are returned to beds in the sea. Thereafter the cultured pearl is formed by exactly the same method as a natural pearl. After several years, the oysters are harvested and the cultured pearl removed.

The primary difference between true and cultured pearls is in their number of layers. The bead nucleus of a cultured pearl is several times the size of the grain of sand that forms a natural nucleus, so for pearls of similar size, there would be fewer layers formed to cover the nucleus in a cultured pearl. The cultured pearl may fracture or the layers separate more readily, or be less lustrous. (These are worst-case occurrences, and do not usually happen.)

Even gemological experts must use instruments to distinguish true pearls from cultured pearls. In an X ray film, the large nucleus shows clearly.

Pearls may also be simulated. These are the costume-jewelry pearls, made of beads dipped in a solution made from fish scales, which gives the pearly look. The dipping is usually one or two layers, so this type of pearl lacks the deep luster and translucency of one that comes from the sea. They are subject to chipping and peeling. However, they wear well enough for the price; and when after a while they molt sadly and their color goes ashen, they can be inexpensively replaced.

The size and shape of pearls vary. They may be tiny, called seed pearls. They may be as big as a child's marble. The perfect ones are perfectly spherical. They can also be oval in outline, or pear-shaped, or wing-shaped, or baroque, which describes a basically round pearl of irregular shape or texture. The baroque pearls are stunning when imaginatively mounted. During the Renaissance, the baroque pearl became fashionable. Its strange or distorted shape formed the core of imaginative designs of animals or gods.

Pearls come in several colors: white, creamy white, rosy, yellow, green, black, and rarely, grey. Freshwater pearls do not have the fine colors possessed by those grown in salt water. The matching of pearls is difficult, for all these factors must be considered: size, freedom of the "skin" from imperfections, the closeness to perfect roundness, luster, and tint. A necklace of perfectly matched pearls represents time, study, care, and attention. An old saying held that every time a pearl was matched, it doubled in value.

To grow cultured pearls, growers first locate a large, shallow, calm body of water. There divers place a particular species of pearl oyster onto rafts inside enclosures. After one year the oysters are removed, cleaned, and put into new cages. Two years later the shells are opened, and bits of nacre and segments of mantle tissue from live oysters are surgically inserted between the muscle and the internal organs of the recipient oyster. They are returned to the water. For the next three and one-half years they are inspected regularly.

All the diving is done by Japanese women, called *amas*. They wear white outfits and glass masks. In the shallow waters, they stay down only about one minute per operation.

After the oysters are opened and the pearls harvested, the process of cleaning and bleaching begins. The pearls are expertly sorted by shape, size, and color. Here the critical criterion of luster is evaluated; poor-quality pearls must be destroyed.

One copyrighted and trademarked grading system of pearls describes them first in terms of color. Next a 1-to-5 scale (1 being lightest, 5 darkest) describes the intensity of color. Cultivation is on a 1-to-5 scale, with 5 being a thick cultivation with many layers of pearl. The same scales are used to grade luster and cleanness. Physical measurements are also exact. Dealers using this system can exactly match two pearls that are half a world apart.

Late in the 1920s cultured pearls glutted the market. The Wall Street Crash of 1929 was followed by the Pearl Crash of 1930, when bankers refused credit to pearl dealers on their stocks of cultured pearls. In a single day, pearl prices dropped by 85 percent. Today cultured pearls represent 95 percent of the market. Sad to say, worldwide water pollution threatens the pearl industry.

✧

SHOPPING FOR PEARLS

When you're comparing pearls, you'll want to consider not only color, shape, and size, but also luster and orient.

Color is the body tint of the pearl. Over this may be another color, called the orient. A slightly pinkish orient is much desired.

The luster of a pearl depends on the relative smoothness of the surface, the thickness of the nacre coatings, and its ability to reflect light. Pearls with a high, silky sheen are the finest quality. The more translucent the pearl, the more beautiful it is.

To take proper care of your pearls, have them restrung at intervals, as the rubbing together of pearl and stringing material causes wear. They should be strung with knots between them to prevent the edges of drill holes from coming in contact. Pearls may be injured by hair spray or perfume, scratched by harder gems, or shattered by a single sharp blow. After you wear them, wipe them with a soft cloth to remove any slight film of body acids or cosmetics. Don't wet the string if you can avoid it. Wearers of pearls should not drop them or throw them down carelessly when taking them off.

In time pearls "die," losing their natural beauty or actually disintegrating. Lustrous life expectancy of the average pearl necklace is a century and a half. A few pearls known to be 1,300 years old are still faintly gleaming.

✧
CHARACTERISTICS AND ATTRIBUTES

A fifteenth-century book on gemstones said that pearls are formed from the dew of heaven. Some say that pearls are the tears of angels. In the Orient, where pearls were first widely used, it is believed that wearing a pearl brings enlightenment and instills courage. Because pearl stands for modesty, purity, and innocence as well, it is the ideal gem for a young girl. It also strengthens the heart. The perfect pearl—one that is perfectly round—signifies beauty and great love.

The peaceful energy pattern of pearl is not one that is transmitted to others, but is more for the wearer, soothing one's pituitary and promoting wholeness; it rejects negativity and holds only positive energy.

In Madagascar as late as the 1920s, it was a custom for one who had been born to bad luck to change his luck into good. This was readily accomplished by buying one or two cheap pearls (price about one cent each) and burying them. Once the person had symbolically "thrown away wealth," then capricious fate, seeing that he did not crave it, would provide him with it.

Pearl is a soothing, peaceful gem, helping to promote trust and balancing relationships. It enlarges the spirit with compassion and willingness. Gazing upon a pearl helps one comprehend divine grace.

Pearl is associated with Venus and Mercury, and the fixed star Umbilicus Andromedae at 20 degrees Aries. Wearing pearls counteracts the negative effects of Jupiter retrograde.

Pearl is symbolic of the angel Nelle, a household angel of exceptional loveliness.

✧
HEALING MAGIC

By the seventeenth century, the medicinal use of gemstones was generally accepted. Pearls, crushed and administered as a potion, were recommended as an antidote for many ills. Sir Francis Bacon, the English philosopher, essayist, and statesman, was recorded as having ingested a paste of powdered pearls made with lemon juice. We don't know what his ailment was; but he did live for at least three years afterward. On the other hand, there is Kokichi Mikimoto, the pioneer of pearl culturing and merchandising, who swallowed two pearls each day for at least seventy-four years, and enjoyed excellent health well into his nineties.

As a remedy for ailments, Gascoign Powder enjoyed a vogue until 1715. This mystical feelgood powder consisted of pearl, white amber, powdered hartshorn, red coral, crab's eyes and the black tips of their claws. Then a Dr. Slare proved that the medicinal action of all its ingredients was negative. However, the doctor's scholarly approach to a rival medication could have been somewhat tinged by the fact that he was advancing his own remedy of chalk and "salt of wormwood" as more efficacious.

About the same time, an electuary of gems was a renowned antidote for practically everything that ailed men. The electuary was made of pearls and several other gemstones, either crushed to powder together, or the water in which the gems had rested was used, or both gem powder and water in a slurry.

This electuary was distantly related to the Gem Rasayana, the nine-gem remedy used today in Gem Therapy. As a single gem in this therapy, the vibrations of pearl help to restore the cosmic color orange to the human spectrum.

Because creatures that live in the sea have an attunement to the moon, pearl allows the individual to understand the influence of phases of the moon on his own emotions. The properties of pearl concentrate and balance these forces to bring them to their highest potential.

As with all gemstones, pearl's vibrations may be passed on to a person either through wearing the stone; through Ayurvedic methods, Teletherapy, or Radionics; or by taking the elixir.

Here follows a partial list of the body organs or areas, physical and emotional maladies, and psychological ailments for which pearl elixir may be used.

It treats white blood cells, cancer, and precancerous conditions; stomach and abdomen, ulcers, and the intestinal tract. It helps with mother-image problems, emotional balance, anxiety, and initiative. It acts as an aphrodisiac, enhancing vitality and the life force.

Spiritually it helps one attune to devas, raising consciousness and spiritual understanding. It works with the base, heart, sexual and emotional chakras, and the astral and emotional bodies. By improving the working of pancreatic enzymes, it also stimulates the absorption of all nutrients and changes excessive appetite into a more intuitive approach to eating.

Apply pearl elixir, mixed seven drops with coconut and jojoba oils, to the solar plexus, abdomen and lower back to ease emotional imbalances. Add seven drops of elixir to bathwater. Powdered pearl, placed on the tip of the tongue or underneath the tongue, can ease a stomach ulcer and strengthen the adrenal glands.

✧

PEARL DREAMS

If you dream of pearl, especially if your birthday comes in June, you will know success through hard work and patience. If a string of pearls is given to you in a dream, you will have a happy and successful marriage; but if you dream that the string breaks, you'll know misunderstanding and sorrow. Should you dream that you have gathered up a broken string, or that you restring them, you'll have minor reverses and inconsequential delays before fulfillment of some desire of yours.

Dream that someone admires your pearls, and this means you will strive for love or material things with a commendable purity of purpose. A display of pearls in a dream portends good business, brisk trade, and pleasant social affairs.

For some, a dream of pearls forecasts a torrent of tears—but never fear, the tears will completely wash away some old sadness. A maiden who dreams of receiving a pearl necklace will enjoy a calm and peaceful life with a man who will grant her every wish. A man who gives pearls should consider his dream a warning about female vanity. Dream of losing your pearls, and you'll face financial reverses and loss of love.

Those who dream that they are collectors of pearls are prophesying that their business genius will win large rewards for themselves; they will experience a dramatic increase in wealth or social position.

✧

PEARLS THROUGH HISTORY

Pearls are the immortelles of fashion. They always seem to be in. Pearls on the wedding tiara, seed pearls forming a design, pearls in strings and earbobs, on wrists or fingers, on an evening bag or a jeweled wrap—pearls are there. And as a statement of elegance, basic black (or basic colors) and pearls have endured for decades. Perhaps it is their perfect roundness, but pearls have a "forever" feeling about them. They were, they are, they will always be.

In the time of Jesus, pearls were highly prized as gems. Evidently they were reserved for holy purposes and for men, because women who adorned themselves with pearls didn't get very good press. In Biblical accounts, Jesus referred to pearls several times. He is quoted as discouraging the wearing of pearls by women. He defined wasted efforts as "casting pearls before swine." Jesus spoke also of the merchant who, on finding one pearl of great value, went and sold all that he had and bought it.

Hindu mythology describes a beautiful tank formed of crystal, the work of the god Maya. Its bottom and sides were set with perfect pearls. In the center was a platform gleaming with precious gems. The tank was otherwise empty, yet it was so skillfully fashioned that it appeared to be filled with clear refreshing water, and anyone nearing the tank felt a great urge to cleanse himself in it.

During the height of the power of Rome, pearls were the most desired possessions of her princes and women of fashion. In every royal treasury are quantities of pearls in necklaces and every other jewel form. His Highness the Gaekwar of Baroda owned a sash of one hundred rows of pearls, seven rows of pearls whose value is over a million dollars, as well as a litter set with seed pearls. The most remarkable treasure in his collection is a carpet of pearls ten and one-half feet long by six feet wide. The story was told that there were too many pearls in the treasury to keep track of, so they were sewn into that marvelous carpet. It is worth many millions of dollars.

Warriors of ancient India set pearls in the handles of their swords as symbols of the tears and sorrow the sword might bring. Today we have the pearl-handled revolver, which speaks the same language as the sword.

Perhaps the most fabled pearls of all time are the pearl ropes of Catherine de Médici, great-granddaughter of Lorenzo the Magnificent. Upon her marriage in 1533 to the future King Henri II of France, Catherine's kinsman, Pope Clement VII, made her a gift of six ropes of pearls and twenty-five teardrops, called "the biggest and finest ever seen." Catherine wore the pearls constantly like talismans, the teardrops sewn to her clothing, the heavy ropes strung on their gold wire weighting down her neck.

Catherine, a skillful manipulator, had always entertained ambitions. When in 1559 Henri was mortally wounded in a tournament, she hoped to become ruler of France. But instead their fifteen-year-old son Francis took the throne as dauphin. He promptly married Mary, Queen of Scots, who was seventeen. Tired perhaps of having the things hanging on her all the time, Catherine gave her pearls to Mary as a wedding gift. Within about a year Francis was dead.

The following year the eighteen-year-old Dowager Queen Mary was called home to her rulership over Scotland. The pearls went with her, in a velvet-lined sandalwood casket. As granddaughter of James IV of Scotland and Margaret, sister of Henry VIII of England, Mary was high also in the succession of the English throne. She married her cousin Henry Stuart, Lord Darnley. Their son became James "Sixth and First," as the Scots put it; James VI of Scotland in 1567, James I of England in 1603. Darnley was murdered, perhaps by the Earl of Bothwell, who became Mary's third husband. Mary was compelled to abdicate in 1567. She escaped to England, where she was accused of conspiracy to overthrow Queen Elizabeth I and assume the crown. After eighteen years' imprisonment Mary, age forty-five, was beheaded.

Queen Elizabeth bought Mary's pearls from Murray, the Regent of Scotland, at her own price of three thousand pounds. Elizabeth loved pearls. She had pearls by the thousands (real and imitation) sewn into all her sumptuous gowns. She wore the great ropes as

Catherine had, constantly, with delight; the drops gleamed wickedly from her ruff and dangled saucily from her earlobes.

Just before she died, she named King James VI of Scotland her successor. He allowed the beautiful pearls to languish in his jewelbox for ten years. When his daughter Elizabeth married Frederick of Bohemia in 1613, the pearls became her wedding present. Frederick reigned for one winter; in 1620 Frederick and Elizabeth slipped away to Holland, taking the pearls with them. Of their thirteen children, their daughter Sophia married the Elector of Hanover. Sophia's son became George I of England.

When his son George II came to the throne, the pearls went to his wife Caroline. By now the large single pearls were strung into a necklace. There followed George III (his wife Charlotte Sophia had the pearls) and George IV, who ruled both England and Hanover. In 1830 William IV became ruler of England and Hanover. His wife Adelaide wore what were by then called the Hanoverian Pearls.

In 1837 Victoria succeeded her uncle William. By Hanoverian law, no woman could rule that country, so at age eighteen Victoria became Queen of England—and possessor of the pearls. Ernest Augustus, who became King of Hanover, immediately began demanding the return of the Hanoverian jewels, especially the necklace of thirty-seven large pearls. When in 1843 he still hadn't gotten satisfaction, he went to England to beard Victoria in her own court. She was diplomatic and regal, but not amused; she simply turned the nettlesome matter over to the law. After more years of delay, when Ernest Augustus was finally permitted to identify the pearls, he couldn't.

In 1858, after Earnest Augustus had been dead for six years, England gave a magnificent pearl necklace to Hanover. Were they the pearls of Catherine, of Mary Queen of Scots, of Elizabeth I, of Caroline, of Charlotte Sophia, of Adelaide? Indeed, of Victoria? The pearls of a Pope, gifts to queens for three and a quarter centuries? Perhaps.

Moonstone

ZODIACAL STONE FOR

GEMINI

(May 22–June 21)

> . . . *Sweet the coming on*
> *Of grateful evening mild, then silent night;*
> *With this her solemn bird, and this fair moon*
> *And these the gems of heaven, her starry train.*

—JOHN MILTON
PARADISE LOST

$\diamondsuit$

Numerologically, moonstone is a 4.

You who are in positions of authority and power, or in business, are initially drawn to this stone. Although this gem appears quiet and unassuming, the energy it possesses is not for everyone. But people who are ambitious, self-assured, seek financial and material success, and are able to relate to others, will want this stone.

Beneath the obvious, you will want it because it is fascinatingly unusual. Moonstone appeals to your sense of individuality, which you prize greatly. If it is your birthstone, you are different from what you appear to be; you are more than that—and so is moonstone.

Moonstone is an anchoring, foundation, earthy type of energy. It is worn best by those who are hard workers, organized, patient, economical, and have great personal integrity. Those who would choose to manipulate instead of earning their rightful way in the world will feel uncomfortable wearing moonstone; for there is a solid gold force of incorruptibility like a beacon around this gem. On those honest and enduring individuals who deserve it, moonstone will bestow a steadiness that will iron out inner tension and get them to relax.

$\diamondsuit$

PHYSICAL PROPERTIES

One of the two alternate birthstones for June is moonstone. It is also called selenite, from the Greek *selene*, meaning moon. Its mineralogical name is adularia, from its place of origin, the Adula, a peak in the Saint Gotthard Mountain range in the Swiss Alps. Moonstone, a gem from the common mineral feldspar, is an aluminum silicate containing potassium. The gem is made up of thin, microscopically fine plates or scales of two alternating types of feldspar. The structure of the scales, when the stone is turned in the light, causes the romantic and harmonious blue or silvery white shimmer to chase across the surface of the stone. This captivating manifestation is called adularescence.

Moonstone, generally thought of as milky bluish, occurs in several subtle colors: beige, pink, green, yellow, white, grey, or brown. The island of Sri Lanka, home of most of the major gemstones used today, produces moonstone in shades of soft gray melting to a silvery white. Recent mining activities in Kangyam, India, have uncovered moonstones of brown to reddish brown, black to lead grey, yellowish or pinkish hues, and green or nearly orange. In these the glimmer of light will be an evanescent hue the same color as the stone. Some of these gems have the cat's-eye effect; occasionally a stone will show a cross-shaped bright spot caused by two rays at right angles to each other. These stones, cut into cameos and cleverly using the stone's natural phenomena to greatest advantage, are popular in the United States.

Moonstone, with a Mohs Scale value of 6, is a relatively soft stone. It is never faceted, but is cut cabochon for the greatest play of light.

A peculiar flaw occurs in this extraordinary gemstone. Occasionally under magnification there can be seen a long inclusion resembling a centipede.

Small deposits of moonstone are found in Brazil, several places in North America, and Australia.

✧
SHOPPING FOR MOONSTONES

In shopping for moonstone, you will want to consider color and shape of the stone, as well as its adularescence. You may buy it unmounted for later mounting. Perhaps you'll find the perfect combination of precious metal, stone, and mounting already made up. It may be set in a ring, pin, amulet, lapel jewelry, or whatever you like.

Protect your moonstone jewelry from knocks, strong chemicals, soap scum, and grease. Clean it with a soft brush using a solution of mild detergent and water, rinse well, and pat dry on a towel. Store it so that it will not touch other gemstones which could scratch it.

✧
CHARACTERISTICS AND ATTRIBUTES

Moonstone signifies winter. It is the phenomenal gem for Monday (*phenomenal* here meaning that the stone itself contains a visible, extraordinary something); and is especially powerful when worn on its day with white or white and silver fabrics.

It is the talismanic gem for Ofaniel, angel who exercises dominion over the moon. Ofaniel is chief of the order of Ofanim, or Thrones. He is sometimes referred to as "the angel of the wheel of the moon."

Moonstone is the proper gift for the thirteenth wedding anniversary. It is said to counteract the negative influence of 13 also for the twenty-sixth, thirty-ninth, fifty-second, and sixty-fifth anniversaries.

Amulets of this gentle gemstone, hung upon fruit trees, help in producing abundant crops of fruit. It assists all vegetation in orchards and gardens. It protects against wandering of the mind, insanity, and epilepsy.

It is said to strengthen one physically. It also acts to reconcile lovers and gives good fortune in love relationships. Though it is thought to increase care and drive away sleep, these odd characteristics of this lovely gemstone might prove beneficial for people who are indifferent and sleep too much.

For travelers, a moonstone amulet will protect from harm or danger. If the gem is engraved with a swallow, the amulet establishes and preserves peace and concord among men.

It brings inspiration and success to those who use it well. Held in the mouth, a moonstone will help one decide on matters, whether they should be pursued or dropped. If the goal is to be pursued, it is fixed in the memory; if not, it is wiped out.

Moonstone, turned slightly while the subject watches, can be used to hypnotize people. In the Orient it is believed that the stone is the solidified rays of the moon; and that the glimmering light is the light of the good spirit who lives in the stone.

A manuscript of the 1660s called selenite "snayle stone or the moone stone," of purple color, found in the body of a large snail in the Indies. This snail's shell shines like mother of pearl; two such lavender-colored shells from Siberia, with many diamonds, were used by Carl Fabergé in 1890 to make a unique brooch.

Moonstone helps develop psychic gifts, such as psychometry (holding an object and through the higher consciousness drawing information from it) and clairvoyance. It attunes one to the energies of nature and the earth.

It is said that the wearer's character permeates the moonstone. One wishing to read the aura of the person will find that the stone shows the true and total nature. To be most effective the moonstone should belong not to the reader but to the one being read.

In India moonstone is believed to bring good fortune, for there it is sacred. When moonstone is displayed for sale it is always placed on a yellow cloth—the most sacred color for the sacred stone. It is revered as a gift for lovers, arousing tender passions when the stone is placed in the mouth at the time of the full moon. It also gives lovers the power to read their future together. Not so long ago, psychics used a crystal ball made of moonstone as a focus for clairvoyant energies.

Moonstone is the feminine quality of our subconscious minds, imparting to us the self-confidence to recognize proper timing in the fulfillment of each step in our individual pattern of destiny.

In 1571 a writer told of a moonstone owned by a friend. The stone was the size and thickness of a small coin; and on it there was a white point about as big as a seed of millet. This point grew or shrank as the moon waxed or waned. The writer borrowed the moonstone and observed it for an entire month. The point was first visible at the top of the stone, then it moved gradually down toward the center, increasing in size and yet maintaining the form that the moon was in at the time. When the moon was full, the white point was round and occupied the center of the moonstone. As the moon waned, the mark grew smaller and moved upward to its original position.

· · ·

✧

HEALING MAGIC

By the application of moonstone, sores are said to dry out without stinging. It is therefore good against stubborn ulcers on the inside or outside of the body, bedsores, and burns or cuts that are slow in healing.

This subtle gemstone calms the mind. Its cooling energy relieves excessive body heat and emotions. At the full moon, the water element in the external environment is stimulated; the high tides cause excess water in all life forms. Asthma, epilepsy, and menstrual difficulties can be exaggerated during the full moon. If one is under physical or emotional stress, which grows worse under the new or the full moon, wear a moonstone set in a silver ring on the right ring finger.

As with all gemstones, moonstone's vibrations may be passed on to the person either through wearing the stone; through Ayurvedic methods, Teletherapy, or Radionics; or by taking the elixir.

Here follows a partial list of the body organs or areas, physical and emotional maladies, and psychological conditions for which moonstone elixir may be used.

Moonstone is good for treating conditions of the stomach and abdomen: ulcers, cancer and precancerous state, the spleen, pancreas, and intestinal tract. It is especially effective in female problems, pregnancy and childbirth.

A specific in treating edema, moonstone elixir is beneficial in detoxification and restoring mental balance.

This elixir is also quite effective in treating emotional conditions, in relieving anxiety and sensitivity, and in restoring mental balance. It helps in the absorption of all nutrients.

Moonstone elixir works with the brow, crown, and solar plexus chakras, as well as with the astral and emotional bodies.

Wear the gemstone on the finger, the solar plexus, or at the base of the skull. The elixir can be sprayed in these places with an atomizer.

. . .

✧
MOONSTONE DREAMS

A dream of moonstone speaks to the dreamer of danger ahead. If the dreamed-of stone has lost its flickering light, the dreamer will suffer keen disappointment in attaining her or his highest goals. But if the light can be seen, it is a promise of renewed hope and the rapid solution of a long-standing problem. To dream of giving or receiving a moonstone presages good luck for the dreamer.

Whoever wears moonstone near the heart in a dream will know honesty and fairness in business dealings. Dreaming of a moonstone whose light moves of itself is a sign of humor and adventure with someone you are fond of. Moonstone seen against a background of color is a sign of healing and transformation. Dreams of a moonstone with a cross-shaped light predict that one will show gratitude for actions.

✧
MOONSTONES THROUGH HISTORY

The moonstone's period of most popular use in jewelry was in the nineteenth century and up through the 1920s. Men wore moonstones in tie stickpins, in watch fob ornaments, rings, and cuff links. Jewelry for women used moonstones in rings, earrings, brooches, bracelets, and necklaces. For some years this unusual gemstone was hardly found at all. Even now with the new discoveries, it is available only in limited quantities.

About 1100 B.C. in Ceylon, the Moonstone Temple was built. It is a legend of the temple that the altar steps were faced with mosaics of shimmering moonstones. The ruins of this edifice can still be seen at Anuradhapura.

The French author François Rabelais, in *Pantagruel*, his masterpiece of comedy and satire, described the Temple of the Oracle of the Bottle. The Oracle resides on an island in an extensive underground temple. Those wishing to consult the Oracle pass through an extensive vineyard planted by Bacchus himself, which bears leaves, fruits and flowers at all seasons. The traveler must eat three grapes and put vine leaves in his shoes to signify that he despises wine, has conquered it, and tramples it underfoot.

He passes through a vault decorated with paintings of women and satyrs dancing, down many flights of marble stairs to the temple entrance. On the jasper portal is inscribed in gold, "In wine lies truth." Through bronze doors carved with vine tendrils he enters the temple, walking carefully over the mosaic floors realistically portraying vine leaves and grapes. Everywhere are reminders of wine and revelry.

Centered in the temple there stands a seven-sided fountain. Its base is of purest transparent alabaster. Around it are seven columns. The first is of heavenly blue sapphire; the second, of hyacinth; the third, of diamond, as dazzling as lightning; the fourth, of the "male" ruby or amethyst. The fifth column is of emerald; the sixth, of agate. The seventh column is of transparent moonstone, "with a splendor like that of Hymettian honey, and within appeared the moon in form and motion such as she is in the heavens, full and new, waxing and waning."

Above it a crystal cupola is carved with the signs of the zodiac, the solstices, equinoxes, and fixed stars. The water of the sacred fountain tastes like the drinker's choice of wine; as the fountain empties, it produces faraway music.

The Oracle of the Bottle is housed in a perfectly symmetrical circular building of transparent stone which admits the sun's light. The Bottle is half-immersed in a second alabaster fountain holding limpid water. Bacbuc, priestess of the Oracle, leads the visitor in, and after he has performed certain rites, he may ask his question. If the answer needs interpretation, the priestess gives him wine disguised as a book.

The traveler returns the way he came, dazed not only by the answer to his question, but also by the wine-rich atmosphere and the lavish display of precious metals and gems of every kind.

ALTERNATE BIRTHSTONE FOR JUNE

Alexandrite

ZODIACAL STONE FOR

GEMINI

(May 22-June 21)

Youth's for an hour
Beauty's a flower
But love is the jewel that wins the world.

—MOIRA O'NEILL

Alexandrite is a numeral 5, quite appropriate for a gemstone full of surprises.

Initially, women or men who share their sensitivity and emotions with others are drawn to this changeable gem. Alexandrite has a soothing, tranquil emanation that invites the viewer to hold or touch it. Because the gem is unique in its potential color changes, it appeals on a deeper level to those who cherish creativity and change or flexibility.

If alexandrite is your birthstone, then be aware that it is for the daring, the different, those who crave freedom, adventure, the liberal rather than the conservative life-style. Interesting and unusual people wear alexandrite; it is not a gem for those who are passive or shy. The gem reflects the gamut of moods of the wearer, which will be many and diverse in expression. It can be dressed up or dressed down, worn to a pizza palace or to an opening night.

Alexandrite's aura is one of restlessness, quick boredom, quicker change. It asks the wearer to be constantly adaptable as are the gem's complementary colors. This is a stone that likes to be flaunted, flashed, and set in highly imaginative mountings, mirroring the personality of its owner.

✧

PHYSICAL PROPERTIES

Alexandrite, June's second alternate birthstone, is a strange gem. It has the rare ability to change color completely from day to night. Many gemstones either deepen in color or wash out under artificial light, but the transparent alexandrite, bluish green by daylight, becomes deep raspberry red under artificial light.

This bewitched gem of the Ural Mountains is a variety of chrysoberyl, a mineral that produces stones in shades of yellow and green. Sister stones of alexandrite are cat's-eye, golden chrysoberyl, and the pale yellow to pale green chrysoberyl. None of these gemstones is plentiful anywhere on earth.

The color of alexandrite is due to chromic acid. The striking change from green to red is the stone's reaction to the differing composition of the light shining into it. The finest alexandrite appears almost emerald green when viewed in most directions, and shows red in others. These gemstones have a pronounced toughness, accompanied by a high hardness rating of 8.5, just below ruby and sapphire.

Alexandrite is not much inclined to develop flaws. And because of its hardness, it takes and keeps a lively, brilliant polish.

Alexandrite is known as a phenomenal gem. In general, transparent gems which have been cut either in facets or in cabochon simply reflect and refract the light that comes into them. Phenomenal stones will change color, or do whimsical things with light, like magicians performing for an audience. Other phenomenal stones are moonstone, cat's-eye (another chrysoberyl gem), opal, star rubies, and star sapphires.

Rarely, an alexandrite cat's-eye is found. In addition to its unique habit of alternating between red and green, a moving line in the stone imitates the effect of light on the eye of a cat. In the usual cat's-eye, a silvery band of light hovers above the surface, apparently related but detached by some mystical means.

This phenomenal gemstone is always cut to let the light play and refract to the greatest degree possible.

Alexandrite is found in the gem gravels of Sri Lanka along with several of the other precious gemstones.

Mining operations in that country have not undergone appreciable improvement in twenty-five hundred years. Attempts at modernization have hit the hard wall of opposition from the workers, who prefer modes of operation hallowed by tradition. The methods of mining in Sri Lanka are fairly primitive but adequate, as in this magical land the gem deposits are not far underground. Workers may rake them out of riverbeds with long-handled rakes and dump them into baskets for washing and sorting.

In the alluvial valley bottoms, pit mining is used. Bamboo scaffolds and small huts—the telltale signs of a gemstone mine—are erected over the pit. Shafts are excavated down forty to fifty feet to the gem-bearing gravel, called *illam*. Down in the pit, a miner scrapes away the soil, gradually widening the excavation until all the several layers and the little side roads of the gravel strata have been cleaned of gems.

The miner then puts the gem-bearing gravel into baskets, which are pulled up out of the shaft by means of a windlass. At the surface the possible gems are sorted out of the mere rocks and the illam set aside in piles. The piles are kept under constant guard, for the gems may not be washed and sorted until the "first washing day," which is decreed by astrologers.

All stages of gem mining in Sri Lanka are accompanied by advice from astrologers on the correct day and time and place to begin, and by prayers and sacrifices to the gods.

When washing day comes, the washers rotate their woven conical baskets, filled with illam, in water so that the lightweight unusable material is swished out and the heavier gemstones are caught in the conical bottom. In a given location the gem gravels may bear topaz, zircon, tourmaline, spinel, ruby, sapphire, garnet, the chrysoberyl gems, and more. Once there are sufficient stones in the basket, and after a prayer to the god of minerals, the overseer begins his search. Quickly he locates the valuable gems and removes them; he checks a second time, then gives the basket which still contains some stones of low value, to the washer for his own disposal.

When, much later, the alexandrite found in a river bottom has been cut, polished, and mounted for you, it will give you much satisfaction—and a lifting of the heart.

· · ·

✧

SHOPPING FOR ALEXANDRITES

It pays to phone ahead when you're checking out alexandrite, to find out if the jeweler has them in stock. When you're looking at them, ask yourself the usual questions: Do I like the cut? Do I want a larger stone? Is this the type mounting I really want? Is the color change from daylight to artificial light what I expected? How do I feel, down deep, about this very stone? Listen to your intuition, and you'll find the alexandrite that is yours alone.

✧

CHARACTERISTICS AND ATTRIBUTES

Because of its comparatively recent discovery and its relative scarcity, alexandrite doesn't have many romantic traditions such as those associated with longer-known gems. In Russia, it was used as the birthstone for August. In the Orient, alexandrite is the phenomenal gem for Friday.

However, newly channeled information reveals the exciting potential of this remarkable changing stone. Its changeability is only for the eyes, for at its serene heart is a consistent spirituality and fixity of high purpose.

Alexandrite is identified with the angel Geburathiel. Geburathiel is one of the great angel princes, an upholder of the left hand of God. He is the chief steward of the fourth hall in the seventh heaven; he represents the divine strength, might, and power.

Alexandrite is a teaching stone on the spiritual level. Holding it in the palm or wearing it on the forefinger or at the throat, you will feel an openness of mind and heart that will enable you to receive new information, to evaluate and clarify it for your own understanding. The presence of the stone will help you to raise your level of integrity in interactions with others.

The wearer of alexandrite will soon place more trust in the positive nature of events, and readily form the habit of synthesizing her/his new knowledge, new integrity, and new outlook into a more spiritually aware pathway of life.

In a marquise cut, alexandrite provides the ideal amulet for pregnancy and childbirth. Its green aspect represents the process of growth; the red, the wonder and vitality of new life. The stone provides balance, smoothing out the jagged hormones and bringing to the fore the joyous side of this amazing, bewildering experience.

Used in healing, alexandrite is associated with Suriel, one of the angels who preside over the fixed stars. In the female aspect, Suriel heals the mind and emotions. It was Suriel who instructed humankind in the laws of hygiene.

✧

HEALING MAGIC

The influence of alexandrite is more feminine than masculine. Its vibrations are very helpful in enhancing color therapy.

As with all gemstones, alexandrite's vibrations may be passed on to a person either through wearing the stone; through Ayurvedic methods, Teletherapy, or Radionics; or by taking the elixir.

Here follows a partial list of the body organs or areas, physical and emotional maladies, and psychological ailments for which alexandrite elixir may be used.

This elixir is effective in treating leukemia, the lymph glands, the spleen, and the nervous system. It increases self-esteem, restoring emotional balance.

Working through the spleen chakra, and the emotional, etheric and mental bodies, it balances and helps one attune to the energies of the earth.

The elixir may be used in a bath; or taken in doses of seven drops each, four times daily for two weeks, then off one week, then resume cyclically.

✧

ALEXANDRITE DREAMS

Should you dream of a square-cut alexandrite, it means you may be limiting your own expectations. But if the stone you dream of is oval, you will get more flexibility and spontaneity into your daily life. If while looking at an alexandrite you hear music, it signifies that you are a free spirit, able to roam wherever you wish—even if mainly in dreams.

You might see alexandrite shining up at you from a dark hole; this indicates that you have unsuspected courage. A sparkling, dancing gemstone of any kind signifies the social whirl, parties, and good clean fun. A single alexandrite in a collection of gemstones means that you need to simplify your thinking and your life-style.

Peace and mercy are indicated when you dream of alexandrite on the forehead of a friend. Worn on your own hand in a dream, this beautiful gem brings you the warm light of a lifelong love.

✧

ALEXANDRITES THROUGH HISTORY

Alexandrite may have been known in early times, but there are no records that refer to a stone of its description. Three different gem authorities date its discovery as three different years: 1818, 1830, and 1831. Whatever the year, all agree that the gem was discovered in the Ural Mountains near Ekaterinburg, (now Sverdlovsk) Russia, on the birthday of the future Czar Alexander II. In that mining location there were known to be emeralds; it was emeralds the miners were looking for. Thinking that the green stones they found were emeralds, they took some back to camp. Oddly enough, by campfire light the stones looked red. In the morning they seemed to be green again. Either the stones were magical, or they were something brand new.

In 1839 they were identified as a new gemstone species. The mineralogist Baron Nils Adolf Erik Nordenskjöld named the fantastic gem Alexandrite. Since it bore Russia's imperial colors, it became and remained for nearly a century the Russian national gem.

Stones of the gem quality found in the Urals have never been plentiful. Weight up to a carat is most common; alexandrites seldom weigh more than three carats. However, in Ceylon at the turn of the century, a few were found that weighed as much as sixty carats each. These were the exception even in that fantastic island of gemstones; here too, their usual weight is less than one carat.

For almost a hundred years, alexandrite came only from the Ural Mountains. Among them all, it is the Russian stones which show the most beautiful colors with the most intense color changes. The deposits there may have been worked out; now they are neglected, and no more stones come from the Urals. The gemstones today found in Sri Lanka, Rhodesia, and Tasmania are often clearer, but the perfect bluish-emerald green has more of yellow in it, and the change to red is less remarkable than in those from Russia.

BIRTHSTONE FOR JULY

◆

ZODIACAL STONE FOR

CANCER

(June 22–July 22)

"*. . . Give crowns and pounds and guineas
But not your heart away.
Give pearls away, and rubies,
But keep your fancy free. . . .*"

—A. E. HOUSMAN
"A SHROPSHIRE LAD"

$\diamond$

Ruby, July's birthstone, is a numeral 3.

Those who have great perceptivity, compassion, gentleness, and inner resources are drawn to this vivid gem. Many women will be attracted to it; also men who permit their responsiveness and their emotions to surface. There is a fusing rhythm about ruby that makes nearly everyone want to own it.

On a deeper level, those men and women who are rugged individualists, self-starters, and strong-willed original thinkers will call this gem their own. Ruby likes a challenge. It wants to swagger in glittering settings, preferring a childlike owner who, while having the world by the tail, is still in awe of it, and never loses his or her raptness for life.

This deep, brilliant gem vibrates to the sound of its owner's inspiration, positively craving parties, joy, festive occasions, and enthusiasm. Ruby likes being set alone, wanting center stage, enjoying the flair of the dramatic from its owner. It is happiest when worn constantly, lending an assertive, take-charge energy that literally throbs around the stone.

Without question, ruby is for the strong!

$\diamond$

PHYSICAL PROPERTIES

Ruby is a gem of the corundum family. The word for this mineral comes from the Hindi *kurund* and the Sanskrit word *kuruwinda*. Corundum is formed of crystallized aluminum and oxygen (a light metal and a very light gas), which combine to produce a hard, heavy, tough mineral. In industry, the abrasive known as emery is corundum. Corundum yields splendid gemstones in opulent hues of yellow, orange, pink, blue, green, violet, and brown. Whether the color is muted or flamboyant, it is pure, the gem itself clear and deeply transparent.

Only the red corundum is called ruby; all the other colors are called sapphire, with its color mentioned before it, such as pink sapphire, yellow sapphire, and so on.

It is typical of ruby to have inclusions of foreign microcrystals. It is these inclusions which prove conclusively that the ruby under inspection is natural and not man-made. Some inclusions are lacy winglike arrangements of tiny drops of fluid. If the inclusions are rutile needles, they may show as "silk," a delicate shimmer of silvery light, or they may form a six-pointed star.

These star stones, or asterias, are never perfectly transparent, and their colors tend toward pale tones. Sharply delineated stars appearing in rubies and sapphires with deep color are so singularly rare that they are very expensive. Asterias are cut cabochon in order to display the effect of a white star fleeing across the stone when the stone is turned.

Asterism results from the light reflection of three sets of needle-like inclusions arrayed at 60-degree angles from each other.

For a fuller explanation of star rubies, see Star Garnets (page 43).

Very seldom will rubies grow in large crystals. A 138-carat star ruby, of perfect shape and the size of a Ping-Pong ball, is in the Smithsonian Institution in Washington, D.C. The Delong star ruby, weighing 100 carats, was kidnapped from the Natural History Museum in New York City and, after a handsome ransom was paid, was recovered from a phone booth.

Possibly the world's last large ruby discovery was made seventy years ago. It weighed forty-one carats. Found on Armistice Day in 1918, it was named the Peace ruby.

Rubies and sapphires are the hardest of the so-called colored gemstones. (Diamond, which occurs in colors other than white, is not considered a colored gem.) They are tough, meaning that they do not break or chip readily. Their brilliance and their color purity make them easy to distinguish in the rough from other gemstone minerals.

That seventeenth-century traveler and chronicler of fabulous gemstones, Jean Baptiste Tavernier, noted that in his time both rubies and sapphires were being heat-treated to intensify their color. Heating somewhat dulls the "life" of the stones; however, the intensified color is permanent. Gemstones were heat-treated by baking them in small ovens, sometimes with just the bare stones cooking in the heat, sometimes with the stones encased in mud. This seems a chancy proposition, especially considering that the fuel was wood or dung, and that a specific temperature and a specific time is needed to do the optimum job. But considering the empathic relationship of the Indians and the Ceylonese with gemstones, perhaps they performed the entire process psychically. Somewhat more scientifically today, gemstones are still heat-treated to increase or even change their colors.

Deposits of precious corundums occur in all the continents. They are even found in Switzerland in the Ticino River, and around Rock Creek and the Missouri River in Montana. The most prolific producer of corundum—indeed, of most gemstones—is Sri Lanka. There, original deposits were formed inside mountains. The annual monsoon rains, falling over all the years of earth's existence, weathered away the rocks and their pockets of gemstones and washed them all downstream. There the heavier gemstone gravels sank to river bottoms and formed rubble banks and terraces on the slopes of hills. These alluvial, secondary gem deposits, which were completed about one million years ago, rest upon much older bedrock.

The most beautiful rubies now come from an area near Mogok, Burma. The white mother rock there has been dated at over 500 million years old. Rubies occur in splendid, well-developed crystals, and are a glorious sight against their white matrix.

There is a legend about the Burmese ruby fields. Sometime in the fifteenth-century a band of robbers was banished to the wild Mogok Valley. They saw the luxurious red stones and reported them to the king, who ordered that the secret be maintained. Then, beaming in the friendliest way, he arranged with the Shan prince-owners to trade his worthless land for their valley of treasures. The ruby fields became the property of the Burmese throne. The first known reference to them is a royal edict of 1597.

The story is often told that sovereigns of Burma and India commanded that any ruby over six carats become the property of the royal household. One Burmese king, hearing of the unearthing of a large ruby, sent a regiment of soldiers to fetch it to him with pomp and ceremony befitting such a fine stone.

After the British conquered Burma, they attempted to put ruby mining on a commercial basis, with modern equipment. This attempt, financially unsuccessful, was abandoned. Today rubies are mined by ancient methods involving manual labor, mainly because that way seems to work best.

Currently, the second most important ruby fields lie in Thailand, at the frontier with Kampuchea. Rubies from Sri Lanka are primarily light to raspberry red, and have a brilliant luster. Rubies have also been found in Tanzania.

✦

SHOPPING FOR RUBIES

The color of the stone is more important than the relative degree of perfection. Rubies are graded according to color and quality. The most desired color is blood red, called pigeon's blood. The next desired color is dark garnet red to red-brown. Last of all—but still very desirable—are those of paler color with good brilliance. A clear, transparent, flawless ruby of any size is the rarest of all gems.

As with other dark stones, try them against your skin or your clothing to see if you are at ease with the lush color of this dazzling gemstone. And if you're looking for *real* temptation, try them with diamonds.

Ruby, being tough as well as hard, does not scratch easily. But give it the respect it deserves, and cushion it in storage. Keep your rings gleaming, free of soap scum or hand lotion. First close the sink drain, then clean them with a soft brush and mild detergent, rinsing with clear water. As a precaution, when you take off your rings, never lay them on the lavatory or sink counter. Have a safe, particular place where you always put them.

• • •

✧
CHARACTERISTICS AND ATTRIBUTES

In India, ruby is called in Sanskrit, *ratnanavaka*, "Lord of the Precious Stones," for there it is prized above all other gems. He who possesses a flawless ruby may walk without fear in the presence of his enemies. Ruby brings to its wearer health, wisdom, and contentment. The fortunate owner of a ruby will live in peace with all men; he will be protected from all perils, and his social position, land, house, and crops cannot be taken away from him.

Other powers attributed to ruby include removing unclean thoughts, controlling the passions, and evaporating the vapors of pestilence. Ruby was also a specific cure for digestive gas or liver complaints. Ruby is the eighth stone on the Breastplate of the High Priest. It is a gem of summer, the Hindu gemstone for August. It is the talismanic gem of the guardian angel Malchadiel. Malchadiel is the governing angel of March; also ruler of the zodiacal sign Aries. He "rises and rules in the beginning of the year," for ninety-one days, from spring to summer.

In Arab tradition ruby represented the zodiacal sign of Taurus. Its favorite hour is five in the afternoon. Ruby commemorates a fortieth wedding anniversary.

A ruby, engraved with the "beautiful and terrible figure of a dragon," has the power to increase material possessions and bring the wearer joy and excellent health. In the Orient, it is called a "drop of Mother Earth's heart's blood."

Ruby amplifies our values. It can be either a gem of universal desires or earthly idolatry, depending on the individual's development. The ruby refines and purifies the heart.

Since ancient times the warm glow of ruby has been associated with fire. Rubies were thought capable of boiling water or melting wax. A legend of India says that the home of the gods is lighted by massive gleaming rubies. The Chaldeans attributed ruby to the planet Mars. Ruby and Tuesday go together. A star ruby is the phenomenal gem* for Wednesday, but the transparent ruby is

---

* A phenomenal gem is one having unusual qualities or characteristics within the stone.

the talismanic gem for Friday. (Viewing this abundance of associations, one might assume that if all the lists of all time were available, some variant of ruby would be found hard at work for every
day of the week.)

✧

HEALING MAGIC

Ruby is an amazing feel-good gem, for both physical and spiritual ailments. Its vibrations are a concentration of the cosmic color
red. In Dr. Bhattacharyya's Gem Therapy, which differs only
slightly from Gurudas's Gem Elixir treatments, the single gem is
used to treat diseases of the blood, arthritis, constipation, debility,
endocarditis, palpitations and intermittent heartbeat, poliomyeli-
tis, and fainting. It is also used in about 20 percent of the multi-
ple-gem mixtures and is one of the Nine Gems used as a formula
in Gem Therapy.

As with all gemstones, ruby's vibrations may be passed on to a
person either through wearing the stone; through Ayurvedic
methods, Teletherapy, or Radionics; or by taking the elixir.

Here follows a partial list of the body organs or areas, physical
and emotional maladies and psychological ailments for which ruby
elixir may be used.

In either gem form or elixir, it is probably the master gem in
treating the circulatory system and the heart, not only the physical
heart but also its cells and their action, as well as the heart chakra,
the heart meridian, and the neurological tissues associated with
the heart. It replenishes vitality that has become depleted.

Ruby is effective in infectious diseases and fevers, including
childhood diseases; and treats leukemia, sickle-cell anemia, immune system problems, and bubonic plague. It treats problems of
the digestive tract.

On the emotional level, this gemstone removes obstacles, especially the big dog of negativity. It promotes tranquillity in oneself and one's relationships. Where the passions are divided, ruby
enhances intuitiveness and brings matters into perspective. It amplifies skills of negotiation, decision making, self-confidence, and
self-esteem.

Spiritually ruby is influential in attuning one to devas (nature spirits) and divine love, raising consciousness, and bringing spiritual balance and inspiration. It amplifies the kundalini energy and permits one better control of this powerful creative force. It works through the heart chakra and the mental and spiritual bodies. It cleanses the aura.

It helps in the assimilation of calcium, iron, magnesium, and vitamin E.

Wear the gem or the elixir on your tailbone, heart, base of the skull, or thymus gland. Use seven drops in your bathwater.

✧

RUBY DREAMS

The deep radiant red of a ruby, seen in a dream, is a symbol of passionate love. (Not incidentally, scientific analysis has demonstrated that the red rays of the spectrum give heat and make one more lively.) If you dream of wearing one or more rubies, you will have many ardent sweethearts. Dreams of being given a ruby are dreams of success in business or triumph in winning the one you love. Should you dream of losing a ruby, it foretells that your lover will become indifferent.

If you buy a ruby in a dream, the size of the ruby will indicate how powerful you perceive yourself to be. Seen on anyone in a dream, a large ruby, centered in diamonds and gold in a heavy framelike mounting, reveals that person's honesty and strength of character. A small stone, seen as if from a distance or in a fragile setting, is an indicator that you are able to let even important matters rule themselves. A battlefield scene, with some of the combatants wearing ruby red, predicts that you will eventually surrender to your own good.

✧

RUBIES THROUGH HISTORY

An ancient gemstone book labeled ruby the most precious of the twelve stones God created when He created all creatures. "The ruby, called the lord of gems, the highly prized, the dearly loved ruby, so fair with its gay color." It was the ruby which, by God's command, was placed on the neck of Aaron, the High Priest of the Jews. Ruby is the eighth stone on the breastplate of the High Priest.

In the Bible, in Proverbs, are references to rubies. One asks, "Who can find a virtuous woman? For her price is far above rubies." Another states that "wisdom is better than rubies."

Episcopal rings found in the tombs of three bishops, two of the thirteenth century, one of the fourteenth, were each set with a ruby. Episcopal or bishops' rings were like betrothal rings, wedding the bishop to his diocese. At one time such rings, in accordance with liturgical requirements, were made large enough to be worn over a glove.

There was a symbolical significance to the color of the stones set in these rings. Ruby's glowing red designated glory; the blue of sapphire symbolized chastity and happiness; amethyst, the wine used in communion; emerald was the constant promise of the Resurrection; while the clear white of rock crystal denoted guilelessness.

The famous ring of Edward the Confessor, which was used as the Coronation Ring of the kings of England, had "a precious ruby inserted therein." In 1389 King Richard II granted this ring to Westminster Abbey for the shrine of the Confessor there. The King reserved the privilege of wearing the ring while in England, but agreed to return it to the shrine when he traveled out of the country. Once the Abbot was dilatory in sending the King the ring, and in his apology to his monarch prayed that his tardiness should not invalidate the rights of the church to possess the relic. Evidence indicates that it did not, for later records show the ring still among Edward's belongings kept at his shrine.

The Imperial Crown of India, worn by its emperor or empress the King or Queen of England, is set with four stunning Burmese rubies set in four Maltese crosses glittering solidly with diamonds.

The Romans, Jews, Italians, and Arabs considered ruby the natal stone to warm cold December. From the fifteenth to the twentieth-century it was in general use as December's birthstone; the exceptions to this rule were the Russians and the Polish, who preferred that ruby go with July, as it does today.

138 · GEM MAGIC

FABLED RUBIES OF HISTORY

The Ruby of the Black Prince of England

In Biblical times and later on, a red stone was called a carbuncle, because of some slight resemblance to the medical condition of the same name. Sometimes the stone was called balas, or balas ruby. Both carbuncle and balas were later interpreted as meaning ruby. More likely, depending on size and other considerations, the stones anciently called ruby were either spinels or garnets. Some of the famous old "rubies" have proved to be spinel.

The Imperial State Crown of England has, prominently displayed in the front above the large diamond Second Star of Africa, the Ruby of the Black Prince. Some whisper that this cabochon-cut red stone is congealed blood. More or less a diamond shape, the beautiful gem measures about two inches by one and one-half inches. It originated in India and was centuries old when it first came to the attention of the English.

Sometime before 1367, the gem belonged to Abu Said, the Moorish ruler of Granada. Don Pedro el Cruel, King of Castile, heard of this unusually large and beautiful ruby, and invited Abu Said to his court. There Don Pedro had Said's entire entourage murdered and took possession of the stone.

But soon afterward, Don Pedro lost a war and his kingdom, so he fled to the protection of Edward the Black Prince, eldest son of Edward III of England and father of Richard II. Don Pedro won Edward's assistance in battle, and after triumph near Nájera in 1367, he gave the precious gemstone to the Black Prince.

Upon Edward's death, Richard II inherited the stone. King Henry V wore it in his golden coronet at the battle of Agincourt. In Shakespeare's play *Henry V*, the king cries, "Once more unto the breach, dear friends, once more—or close up the wall with our English dead!"

Seventy years afterward, in 1485, Richard III wore it into battle at Bosworth Field. Richard fell in battle. The coronet, which is said to have been hidden in a hawthorn bush, was snatched up and used on the spot to crown Henry VII, first of the Tudor kings. Some time later, when the ruby was stored in the Tower of London, the notorious Captain Blood attempted to steal it. Then in Cromwell's time, when all reminders of the monarchy were destroyed, the ruby was sold for four pounds.

The fabled gem was recovered after many years and was set into the British State Crown, where it remains today. Despite its numerous adventures, the Ruby of the Black Prince is not a ruby, but a 170-carat spinel.

The Timur Ruby

Timur Lenk, or Tamerlane, the fourteenth-century Islamic conqueror of much of central Asia and eastern Europe, named the great gemstone for himself. Weighing 315 carats, it was originally named Kiraj-i-Alam, "Tribute of the World." Its history began sometime before the end of the twelfth century and the beginning of the Muslim dynasties in India.

In 1398 Timur captured Delhi, killing thousands of its inhabitants and sacking the city. In his loot was the huge red ruby which he felt was worthy to carry his own name. And so it did, down through generations of gradually waning power into the seventeenth century. The ruby became the property of Abbas I, the new ruler of Persia who, to save his own skin, presented it to the mighty Mogul Emperor Jehangir.

Jehangir was an unusual man, with far-flung interests and a critical awareness of history. Timur had merely named the ruby for himself, but Jehangir had the names of several Persian kings (including his own) engraved on it, knowing that so long as the stone existed, so would those names. In 1627 the Timur came to Jehangir's son, the well-memorialized Shah Jehan, who built the Pearl Mosque at Agra, the Diwan-i-Am, and the Taj Mahal. The Timur hung on Shah Jehan's Peacock Throne, suspended from a golden chain.

Mogul emperors reigned and were replaced; and their deaths—usually violent—often had a lot to do with the great wealth of which the Timur was a part. In 1739 Nadir Shah breezed in from Persia, overthrew the incumbents, sacked the city, and rode back to Persia with all the jewels and the Peacock Throne to boot.

Nadir Shah went mad, and was assassinated; his pale and shadowlike son, Shah Shuja, ascended the throne. Shah Shuja was seized, blinded, and tortured to make him reveal the hiding place of the Timur ruby, the Koh-i-noor diamond, and other jewels. Shuja was rescued from death by Ahmad Shah, who had ridden up from Afghanistan. As a reward Shah Shuja gave Ahmad Shah the Timur.

Ahmad Shah was a short-time owner. From him Ranjit Singh snatched the Timur and the Koh-i-noor and had them for a while. In 1849 Ranjit Singh's number came up, and the British took possession of the noble Treasury of Lahore in the name of Queen Victoria.

The blood-covered ruby—which too proved to be a spinel—no longer was witness to stabbings, intrigues, blindings or sackings. Surrounded by guardian diamonds, exiled forever to the quiet life, the mighty Timur—"Tribute of the World"—was set into a necklace. But—lest we forget—on its back, still readable after centuries, are carved the names of Persian kings.

BIRTHSTONE FOR AUGUST

◇

ZODIACAL STONE FOR

LEO

(July 23–August 23)

Rich and rare were the gems she wore,
And a bright gold ring on her wand she bore.

—THOMAS MOORE
  "RICH AND RARE WERE THE GEMS SHE WORE,"
  STANZA I

Sardonyx is a numeral 3.

Although it is the same numerologically as ruby, this gentle brown gemstone shows another aspect of the 3 personality. Sardonyx is opaque, preferring to gleam instead of sparkle. Its sturdy nature draws mainly those women and men who are connoisseurs. It is the birthstone of those who are logical, analytical, or love numbers; you who have a field of specialty appreciate the finer aspects of this honored gem of ancient days.

There can be a mystical invitation from the gem to the potential buyer; if that occurs, the gem is for you. On a deeper level, sardonyx reflects the inner person's many facets, qualities such as talent, diversity, imagination and energy. The gem mirrors your calm statement of individuality and originality with tasteful reserve.

Like ruby, sardonyx enjoys change, travel, and festivities. It is quite at home wherever it may wander with you.

Because that magical reaching out has to take place, sardonyx is not popular with everyone. The adage "many are called but few are chosen" applied to the aura of sardonyx. Those attracted to this rose-orange-red-brown gemstone will feel a harmonious kinship with it that will rival their innate creative urges and enjoyment of life.

PHYSICAL PROPERTIES

Sardonyx, the birthstone for August, is an opaque gem. The word comes from the Roman writer Juvenal, who first called it a precious stone.

Like amethyst and bloodstone, sardonyx is a quartz gem. It is one of the varieties of chalcedony. The chalcedonies are distinguished by the lack of a visible crystalline structure. Their composition is more fibrous. Under magnification one can see a mass of tiny individual crystals. The stone is porous, meaning that it can be stained by chemical processes. (The ancient Greeks boiled it in honey to change or amplify its color.) Most gemstones of sardonyx have had their color enhanced by this method.

Sardonyx has parallel flat bands, the layers having sharply delineated colors of rose-orange-red ("sard"), white, and brown. It is often used for cameos, with the white layer cut to stand in relief against the darker backgrounds. It is also used for cutting intaglios, in which the design is cut down into the stone.

The contrasting layers give particularly effective results. Such cameos are finer and more durable than shell, which is also cut into cameos. Many old fine sardonyx cameos were made into brooches and seals. Archaeological investigations in a predynastic tomb in Egypt revealed a necklace of sardonyx and carnelians.

Today sardonyx is found in Germany, India, Brazil, Asia Minor, and Madagascar. Its period of greatest popularity was in biblical times, ancient Roman and Greek times, and the 1800s.

✧

SHOPPING FOR SARDONYX

When you're shopping for sardonyx jewelry, first take a look at what's available already mounted. This will give you a basis for deciding whether you want your sardonyx (or sardonyxes) in a ring, lavaliere, bracelet, or some other piece of jewelry. Color is important in this stone. You may find one that's too pinky or orangey to blend nicely with your wardrobe; so keep looking. Somewhere out there may be a stone with beiges or red-browns, or greens, or greys and whites and blacks, something that is right for you.

Or you just might decide not to have your sardonyx mounted at all, but to get a tumbled stone for your lucky piece. The glassy smoothness of this rather unusual gem makes a wonderful "worry stone" that you can hold in your hand.

✧

CHARACTERISTICS AND ATTRIBUTES

Sardonyx was thought to be generated by the sun. If it is frequently worn against the skin or placed in the mouth, it vanquishes stupidity, strengthening intellect and understanding and sharpening all the bodily senses. It cools anger and overheated passions.

Pliny wrote that the stone was good for treating wounds inflicted by scorpions or spiders. It also inspires courage and strengthens marital love. Its wearer will gain new self-control and good luck and be protected against all evil.

Emanuel Swedenborg, Swedish mystic, theologian, and scientist, called the sardonyx a symbol of "love of Good and Light."

The fifth Foundation Stone of the Holy City is sardonyx. It is one of the gems given as sixth on the Breastplate of the High Priest. Its hour is seven in the evening. It is a gemstone of the apostle James, who was the son of Alpheus. It is also the gem of the apostle Philip. Further, the archbishop of Mainz, about A.D. 800, said that the sardonyx represented the apostle Paul, and signified the strength of the spiritual life and the humility of saints despite their virtues.

Because of the variety and depth of its colors, it represents divine power and purification, and the turning over of worldly concerns to a higher intelligence.

Sardonyx is associated with the angel Derdekea, a heavenly female power who descends to earth for the salvation of humankind. The stone has been attributed to the planets Saturn and Mars, and to the right and left wings of the fixed star Raven at 8 degrees Libra.

✧

HEALING MAGIC

When used in healing, sardonyx has an effect upon the bone marrow and can give relief to cell disturbances therein. Lenora Huett, a spiritual channel, predicted that in the future sardonyx could be used with laser beams in treating cancer.

As with all gemstones, the vibrations of sardonyx may be passed on to a person either through wearing the stone; through Ayurvedic methods, Teletherapy, or Radionics; or by taking the elixir.

Here follows a partial list of the body organs or areas, physical and emotional maladies, and psychological ailments for which sardonyx elixir may be used.

Several sources recommend the use of sardonyx in alleviating grief, depression, and general woe. It relieves anxiety and stress, gives inner strength and self-confidence, and promotes understanding in relationships.

It increases intuition and provides one with stronger mental discipline and self-expression.

Sardonyx works well with the vertebrae, the thyroid, and the larynx. It balances the metabolism.

This opaque gemstone works with the throat chakra and the emotional body.

✧

SARDONYX DREAMS

If you dream that someone hands you a sardonyx, it means that you'll soon be given greater responsibility. Rolling it between your thumb and fingers in a dream, as you would a worry stone, indicates that someone you love will receive healing. Seeing a selection of sardonyxes represents a flow of abundance; but you must be willing to share sensibly to keep the flow going.

Seen in a dream, a sardonyx lying half-hidden in the earth indicates that you will receive some new truth in a spontaneous way. Buying a sardonyx predicts that you'll soon become involved in a new creative venture. Dreaming of a sardonyx that is "in your way" means you will take definite steps to start that exercise program and/or go on a diet. An extremely large sardonyx, in a dream, reminds you to maintain balance among the varying elements in your life.

Sardonyxes seen as rectangles, squares or cubes point out that you are wasting a lot of time and that you should become more efficient in everyday things. In a dream, a floor tiled with sardonyx is a reminder that you have something yet to learn.

✧

SARDONYX THROUGH HISTORY

One of the earliest mentions of rings is in Genesis 41:42. Joseph (son of Jacob and Rachel; Joseph of the coat of many colors) had interpreted Pharoah's dream for him and given him sound advice, and Pharoah was immensely pleased with his servant. Not only did he make Joseph a ruler in Egypt second only to himself, but "Then Pharoah took his signet ring from his hand and put it on Joseph's hand, and arrayed him in fine linen, and put a gold chain about his neck . . ." This occurred about 1700 B.C. It is not known if the ring was set with a gem, or if the gem was a sardonyx—but the sardonyx was the gemstone of the Israelite tribe of Joseph.

When the biblical Daniel was shut up in the lions' den, "a stone was brought and laid upon the mouth of the den, and the king sealed it with his own signet and with the signet of his lords, that nothing might be changed concerning Daniel."

In Persian poetry, great power and authority are attributed to the sovereign's ring, for the impression of the royal signet placed upon letters or documents confirms that they are royal ordinances. The same has applied throughout history in other lands as well. And in Victorian novels, the villain or villainess—with self-serving intent—sometimes used the hero's signet ring on letters or documents. The Louvre in Paris contains the gold signet ring of Aahhotep I, an Egyptian queen of the period around 1600 B.C. She might have used her signet to seal doors or parchments, or to verify inventories.

Rings from ancient Minos and Mycenaea (from about 1700 to 1000 B.C.) have a great many different designs, either in relief or in intaglio. They appear at first to be signet rings. However, some of the designs are so shallowly engraved that they could not have been used for seals. Also the circlet is too small for a man's finger. Therefore, the rings must have been adornments for women.

There is a story of Polycrates, the tyrant ruler of Samos, who lived more than five hundred years before Christ. Polycrates seemed to be hung with horseshoes; good luck kept knocking at his door. Amasis, King of Egypt, formed an alliance with him.

Then Amasis, fearing that Polycrates' constant good luck would make the gods jealous, urged him to throw away the thing he most valued. That happened to be a handsome ring. Polycrates amiably granted the request—though who knows with what regrets—and threw the ring into the sea.

The gods would not be placated; they refused the sacrifice. Shortly afterward, Polycrates' cook gave the ruler back his ring, which he had found in the belly of a fish. Polycrates sent the news to Amasis. For Amasis this event merely strengthened his certainty about the tyrant's impending doom, so he ended the relationship. Within a few years Polycrates had been captured by a Persian governor, Oroetes, and met his death by crucifixion.

One version has it that the handsome ring was gold set with an engraved emerald. The other version, quite as likely since in those days sardonyx was greatly prized, was that Polycrates' ring was a sardonyx, without engraving, set in a gold cornucopia.

In the period of the Hellenes (around 300–100 B.C.), signet rings with engraved stones in them took the place of those made all of metal. The chalcedonies (including sardonyx) were popular for this use. But they were soon jockeying for position with the colorful transparent precious gems newly out in trade from India.

The betrothal ring of Roman times was given not solely for the sake of sentiment, but also for a practical purpose: that of sealing objects in the home of the married couple.

It was believed that a ring dropped from one's finger was a portent of calamity. The Emperor Hadrian, when he dropped a ring bearing his own engraved image, exclaimed, "This is a sign of death."

The story is told of a wealthy man whose signet ring dropped from his finger and the engraved stone shattered into hopeless fragments. As a result, he could not transact any business for forty-five days—the length of time that passed before his new signet could be engraved. So important a verification was the seal that a businessman could not continue without one.

It was somewhat the same in social interaction, even in the time of Shakespeare's *Cymbeline*. Posthumus Leonatus, laying a bet with Iachimo over a lady's virtue, bet his ring on her, saying, "My ring I hold dear as my finger; 'tis part of it."

Seal rings were very popular from about the end of the Civil

War to 1885. The stone was often a rectangular onyx, perhaps 1¼ inches long. If the owner was well-to-do, a rose diamond monogram would be inset on the stone. If the stone was a sardonyx, the initial was cut through the white layer to the rosy brown layer below. Cameo rings of that period sometimes had the dark layer atop the white.

Queen Elizabeth I is said to have presented the earl of Essex a ring set with a sardonyx cameo on which was carved her portrait. Then Essex was sentenced to death. His queen would save him, he knew; so he attempted to send her the ring by messenger. But the treacherous messenger took it instead to the countess of Nottingham, who hated Essex. She hid the ring away so that Elizabeth did not know of it, assuring the earl's death. Finally, when the countess was on her own deathbed, she confessed her sin to the queen. Elizabeth (so one tale goes) shook the dying woman, crying, "God may forgive you, but I cannot!"

ALTERNATE BIRTHSTONE FOR AUGUST

◇

Peridot

ALTERNATE ZODIACAL STONE FOR

LEO

(July 23–August 23)

*. . . A string of perfect gems, of purest ray serene,
Strung together on a loose golden thread.*

—GEORGE DU MAURIER
TRILBY, PART 6

In numerological terms, peridot is a 6.

Initially, people with strong organizational tendencies or who prefer structure, discipline and practicality are drawn to peridot. Upon deeper inspection, those who have a quiet sensitivity are attracted to the calming green color of this gem. Such individuals may be specialists in their fields and go quietly among people, seeking harmony.

Those born to cherish its gentle allure are cooperative by nature, diplomatic, and do their best work in groups of people or in a community.

Peridot will appeal to those who have a connoisseur's taste in gems.

The aura around peridot suggests that once it is yours, the stone will remain forever within the family, cherished for its emanations of stability and enduring graciousness.

The energy encompassing this gem is one of faithfulness, fairness, and the ability to express love and affection openly with trust. It will bestow a quiet strength, an awareness of the life force, and a humanity not experienced by many. It will create harmonies parallel to the wearer's own vibrations.

✧

PHYSICAL PROPERTIES

The alternate birthstone for August is the peridot, whose color is as inviting as sun-dappled shade. It knows only shades of one color: olive green, ranging from light yellow-green to dark, nearly brown-green. As an exception to this rule, very rarely a brown peridot is discovered. This gem is also called olivine or chrysolite.

The darker olive-green stones are the olivines. The lighter ones, which vary from a yellow-green to a bottle green, are the chrysolites. The poet Shelley wrote of "the chrysolite of the sunrise."

In the days of the Romans, the word topaz indicated the chrysolite we know today.

Most used today in jewelry are two shades: the light golden-green and a gay, sparkling, grassy green. The parent mineral, olivine, is common, but fine peridot crystals are rare. Because they are frequently small and exquisite, these handsome transparent gems are often used where clusters of little green stones are needed in a jewel design.

Peridot in French is called *chrysolithe*. In Spanish it is *crisolito* or *peridoto*. In Italian it is *olivina*.

Peridot is a hard silicate gem, 6.5–7 on the Mohs scale, and medium heavy; yet it is fragile, fracturing irregularly. It has a glassy luster.

Through the centuries, chrysolite has been the birthstone for September. The Jews, the Spanish, the Arabs, the Russians, and the Italians so assigned it. From the 1400s into the early 1900s this designation prevailed. Then in 1912, The American National Retail Jewelers Association named peridot as alternate birthstone for August. Peridot is an alternate to garnet as the state stone of New Mexico.

Peridot is not a common gemstone in any locality. From about 1500 B.C. these stones have come from the island of Zebirget, or Saint John, in the western part of the Red Sea. This island, rich in certain gems, was for over thirty-five hundred years a major producer of chrysolites of great enough size and suitable quality to be desirable as gemstones.

Saint John was known in early times as the Isle of Serpents. There was a legend that numerous serpents guarded the precious gemstones against men who wished to take them from the island. Needless to say, men changed that. An Egyptian king mounted a campaign to rid the valuable island of its serpents. As late as the nineteenth century, Egyptian rulers held exclusive rights to the production of the mines on the island of Zebirget. Around the beginning of World War I, mining ceased, and no more gems were shipped from there. Today, clear crystals of a beautiful warm green color are still found in lava on that fabled island.

Peridots have come from Burma and from Arizona. Those found in Arizona are usually of the darker olivine hues. Near Hilo, Hawaii, small but fine peridot crystals have been found in a deposit of fine black sand. The parent mineral and some gemstones are also found in Norway; Eifel, West Germany; around Mount Vesuvius in Italy; and in the Ural Mountains of the USSR.

The most prolific source of peridot today is located a few miles north of Mogok, the legendary valley of rubies in Burma. Here the gemstone occurs as crystals in a weathered matrix of serpentine. The mining is comparatively easy in this sort of setting. Quarries are created by blasting; or mine shafts are sunk by hand. The fragments of serpentine rock are chipped away with hammers. The peridot crystals, some of them weighing one hundred carats each, are hauled up to the surface in baskets by miners standing on rickety-looking bamboo scaffolds.

Occasionally peridot has come to earth embedded in meteorites. One meteorite, which fell in Siberia, was discovered in 1749 to contain perfect peridot crystals. These gifts from the universe are not always of gem quality, though they are beautiful and certainly unusual. Some have been mounted in jewelry as conversation pieces.

✧

SHOPPING FOR PERIDOTS

Peridot is not an especially expensive gem; yet it has within it so much of sunlight and springtime that you'll feel gladness just being around it. Try to look at peridots unmounted, for they are sure to suggest to you the mounting in which they would be perfectly displayed. Consider them in a pendant or a delicately scaled pin or brooch, where light can bounce through the gems themselves.

The shy twinkle of peridot needs to be well matched with the color of its mounting. The more bravely colored olivines can cope well with either gold or white metal. Somehow, a chrysolite that is light in color is most beautiful set in white gold or platinum or even sterling silver. Flanked with diamonds, it is irresistible. The yellowness of its green is given a more lightweight and airy look with white metal, rather than gold, around it. The author has a one-carat brilliant-cut chrysolite set in a sterling mounting shaped like a lemniscate (a lying-down figure eight, symbol of infinity). This setting is very open and effective for the delicate hue of the stone.

✧

CHARACTERISTICS AND ATTRIBUTES

Pope Gregory the Great associated peridot with the Dominions, the fifth from highest in the ranks of angels. The Dominions carry out the will of the Thrones, another angelic rank who administer divine judgments.

Peridot has been called "green gold" and "evening emerald." It is a gem of springtime, the symbol of eloquence and persuasiveness. Its satiny gleam will bring you gladness and serenity and help you overcome timidity.

The shy green chrysolite is the gemstone of the Israelite tribe of Simeon and of the apostle Matthew. It is the gem of May's special apostle, Bartholomew, who was illustrious for his multiple virtues. Its particular hour is seven o'clock in the morning. It is the seventh stone on the first high priest's breastplate; and the second stone on the breastplate of the Second Temple. Its golden tones stand for the excellence of Christ's divine nature, and true spiritual teachings accompanied by miracles.

The clear and beautiful chrysolite, engraved with a vulture, has the power to constrain the winds. It prevents demons from gathering near the gem and its wearer. Engraved with an ass, the chrysolite will drive away darkness and the powers of darkness, and grant the ability to foresee the future.

Its qualities caused it to be known as the keeper of the sun, capable of shielding the eyesight in the presence of the subtle but harmful rays of the eclipse.

Chrysolite, if set in gold, will dispel fear of things that go bump in the night. However, a stone which is not engraved and which is to be used as protection against negative energies, should be pierced and strung on the hair of an ass and worn on the left arm.

Peridot is the gemstone associated with the angel Alair, one of the great devas or spirits, who oversees the growth of trees and woods. The chrysolite is the seventh foundation stone of the Holy City, it is attributed to the sun, the planets Mercury and Venus, and the fixed star Tortoise at 8 degrees Capricorn.

Peridot has very etheric vibrations, those of lightness and beauty, of clairvoyance and problem-solving ability.

✧

HEALING MAGIC

Peridot's healing qualities are not so much for various parts of the physical body as for specific overall treatment for it, such as regenerating tissue and aligning the subtle bodies. It gives much to the assuagement of spiritual uncertainty. It serves to protect against disorder in the mind. It is a general strengthener.

As with all gemstones, peridot's vibrations may be passed on to a person either through wearing the stone; through Ayurvedic methods, Teletherapy, or Radionics; or by taking the elixir.

Here follows a partial list of the body organs or areas, physical and emotional maladies, and psychological ailments for which peridot elixir may be used.

It may be used in detoxifying the body of harmful substances; it works with the adrenals and the liver. It stimulates self-healing and improves absorption of nutrients.

Peridot cleanses the subconscious, working to alleviate depression, anxiety, and stress and to return one's emotional balance and mental clarity.

In the spiritual realm, peridot elixir raises consciousness and attunes one to the higher self, helping bring out clairvoyant abilities. It is useful to amplify meditation and creative visualization.

This gentle yellow-green gem acts through the heart chakra and works with all subtle bodies, especially the astral body.

It is best worn at the throat. Take three drops of elixir daily in eight ounces of water.

•   •   •

✧

PERIDOT DREAMS

If the peridot you dream of is in a jewel case, it means that someone you know is hiding a secret. A peridot that has been poorly cared for indicates that you need to learn how to take a joke more gracefully. The sun sparkling off an olivine means that some rumor may have you upset; but the truth will put events back into perspective for you.

Wearing a peridot on your right hand in a dream indicates that you are an honest person who has no fear of trusting others. If you dream of turning up a peridot while spading in your garden, it is a sign of unexpected news or unannounced visitors.

Should one you love give you a chrysolite in a dream, it indicates that tenderness and harmony will be hallmark of your relationship.

✧

PERIDOTS THROUGH HISTORY

Many peridots, brought back by the Crusaders as emeralds, still decorate European churches. Not that the colors of emeralds and peridots are so much alike if one has an eye for nuances, for peridot in any shade still has that distinctive honeyed cast to its green. It was entirely likely that neither buyer nor seller knew the difference. And people returning home after such a pilgrimage as the Crusades wanted to make thanksgiving gifts of value and importance to their churches. Therefore they acquired—perhaps even "liberated"—a stone that they believed was emerald.

Peridot was often used for ecclesiastical purposes. It was very popular during the Baroque Period of the late sixteenth to early eighteenth centuries.

Juba, during the lifetime of Jesus, wrote that the procurator Philemon brought the first specimen of peridot to Berenice, mother of Ptolemy II. From this stone Ptolemy is said to have had a statue made of his wife Arsinoë.

Some of the most notable peridots known today are in the Morgan Collection at the American Museum of Natural History, New York City; in Higginbotham Hall in the Field Museum of Natural History, Chicago; and in the great Dom or Cathedral at Cologne, in the Treasury of the Three Magi. These are large crystals, some nearly two inches long.

The largest peridot was found on the volcanic island of Saint John in the Red Sea, 188 miles east of Aswan. Cut, it weighs 310 carats. It is presently in the Smithsonian Institution, in the nation's capital.

BIRTHSTONE FOR SEPTEMBER

❖

Sapphire

ZODIACAL STONE FOR

VIRGO

(September 24–October 23)

> *The wakeful nightingale*
> *She all night long her amourous descant sung;*
> *Silence was pleas'd; now glow'd the firmament*
> *With living sapphires; Hesperus, that led*
> *The starry host, rode brightest, till the moon,*
> *Rising in clouded majesty, at length*
> *Apparent queen, unveil'd her peerless light,*
> *And o'er the dark her silver mantle threw.*

—JOHN MILTON
PARADISE LOST, BOOK 4

---✧---

Numerologically, sapphire is an 11, a Master Number which reduces to a 2, giving it the dual number 11/2.

Those seeking a gem that is out of the ordinary will be drawn to sapphire. If it is your birthstone, you revel in your individuality and make no apologies for it. You want a gem that adapts to all circumstances and moods, from candlelight to tropical sunshine.

On an inner level, women and men who are humanitarian-oriented are best suited to wear this gem—people who serve others selflessly and reap much pleasure from it; people who are conscientious and fair and seek harmony in their life. Their sapphire will become a family heirloom, passed down through generations, or given as a symbol of love as a wedding or engagement gem.

Sapphire is more apt to draw women to its energy. Despite its outward appearance of distinct originality, it is a gem that vibrates to a person of deep empathy who does not shrink from emotionalism. There is a gentleness surrounding sapphire; and it requires a similar vibration in return in order to be happy.

The energy of the gem is one of eclectic and sporadic creativity and may, at times, send out a nervous, chaotic signal to its owner.

✧

PHYSICAL PROPERTIES

Sapphire is a transparent stone, one of extraordinary brilliance. Most people think of sapphire as blue, and it is . . . sometimes. Its blues range from clear pale ice blue to clear sky blue to intense, weighty-looking, nearly opaque royal blue. In the early Middle Ages (the time of Charlemagne) the best-quality sapphires available in Europe had a decidedly gray cast to them. Interestingly enough, during that period pale, misty or chalky colors were the fashion in *all* gemstones. It was not until the magnificent deep blue sapphires were found in Burma that the vibrant sapphire colors we are familiar with today became widely sought after.

Sapphire is from the mineral corundum. When corundum occurs as red, it is called ruby. Sapphire also naturally occurs in a sparkling rainbow of hues, all the vivid or gentle shades of pink, golden, violet, orange, dark green, lemon yellow, and white. A violet sapphire, when clear and properly cut, makes an amethyst look pale. But a white sapphire is a surprisingly boring stone, having neither fire nor color. So, think of the color of orange juice with a few drops of cranberry mixed in it, then envision that as a transparent, sparkling stone, and you have brought to mind the fantastic reddish-yellow sapphire, the *padparadchah*. (*Padna* means lotus; *raga* means color—that is, lotus blossom color.)

Parti-colored sapphires occur in nature. These are stones colored with different tints. Some natural sapphires are purple in daylight and red in electric light. Some sapphires "bleed"—seem less vivid in color—under artificial light.

This gemstone's less-familiar colors are of exceptional beauty and may easily be more costly than blue. However, the most beloved color is sapphire's blue, emblematic of heaven. It is said that gazing upon sapphire—particularly a large one—gives the wearer a sense of peace and infinity. Robert Burton, in *Anatomy of Melancholy*, wrote that it "frees the mind, mends manners." Of all blue gemstones, said Burton, sapphire is the fairest.

Sapphires that are choice in all respects are becoming rarer. For fifty years Kashmir, in the Himalayas of India, produced the finest quality, most desirable sapphires of an intense, rich blue which did not change in sunlight or tungsten lighting. Now Kashmir is depleted. Burma, whence came the royal blue sapphires, is finished as a source. Sri Lanka, the chief source of new sapphires today, cannot last forever. Some stones of a rather steely blue have been found in Montana; others (often too pale or too dark by some jewelers' current standards) come from near Bangkok, Thailand, and Queensland, Australia. One solution at present is to use fine old stones from estate jewelry, remounting them.

As has been mentioned in the chapters on garnet and ruby, some sapphires may have natural stars within the stone. This six-pointed star becomes visible when light shines into the stone. It is even attractively visible in white star sapphires.

Star stones are cloudy, rather than completely transparent. In poor specimens of the gem, the color may be pale and the star indistinct or irregular. The natural colors range from a definite blue to a pale gray. They can be man-made. Under scientific tests, these manufactured stones show the identical properties of the real ones, such as hardness and transparency, plus tiny, tiny bubbles resulting from the manufacturing process.

A sapphire gemstone having the star within is cut in a high cabochon, a mound shape that is polished but has no little flat spots, or facets, cut on it. This shape makes use of the incoming light so that it is reflected as a star from the gem's interior.

Muslim gem cutters came to Ceylon in the tenth century. It is unlikely that cutters in any other part of the world would have the unique understanding of sapphire that the Sri Lankans have handed down through so many generations. These people cut not for symmetry, but for color and to preserve size. In sapphire, often the deepest color appears in one part of the crystal more than in other parts. Also, seen one way the color is blue; another way, it is purple. The stone must be oriented so that when cut, it is the blue which is reflected through the table (the flat-cut top) of the stone. The section of rough gemstone bearing the most intense color must be correctly faceted to reflect up through the table.

To suit the Western criterion of symmetry, these gems are sometimes recut.

✧

SHOPPING FOR SAPPHIRES

You may find satisfaction in either a genuine sapphire or a synthetic. Especially in star stones, consider the synthetics. Not only are they less expensive than the natural stones, but they are chemically identical and structurally similar to the genuine, and have the same degree of hardness. In the synthetic asterias, the star pattern is especially sharp. The stones are produced in black, blue, white, and rose-pink; the blue in particular is the ideal deep blue. And the white asterias are subtly endearing, displaying light within light. Bear in mind that star stones, either natural or synthetic, are not clear, but tend toward an other-worldly mistiness.

Synthetic transparent sapphires can rival the natural ones in appearance and other virtues of the genuine gems. Often, what is called a synthetic sapphire may be a synthetic spinel (see page 242). Ask your jeweler which you're looking at, and have him explain the differences in the two gems. If you're shopping for sapphire, you need to know what spinel looks like.

Genuine sapphires have presence. Somehow no other word fits this spectacular gemstone so well. Even a small stone has in it the capability to beckon you to it, to recognize your relationship with it. Its magnificent blue is so deep that you can almost walk into it. Either alone in one color, or using several of its natural colors, or combined with diamonds—or emeralds or even rubies, for those whose fancy by now is soaring—this gem makes a stunning piece of jewelry, whether in a pendant, a sunburst pin or ring, or a lavish set of several pieces.

For a man, a sapphire ring in his chosen color, or a well-designed tie tack, can be a sedate yet fantastically beautiful use of this gem. Black star sapphires are popular now; they can be a serene but rich understatement in men's jewelry.

✧

CHARACTERISTICS AND ATTRIBUTES

Sapphire, the birthstone for September, is the emblem of chastity. It also represents the height of celestial hope. Because its most familiar natural color is blue, the ancient Persians believed that the earth rested upon a great sapphire which lent its color to light the sky.

Sapphire has always been a talismanic stone, an object imbued with magical powers. In the making of talismans or amulets, a thirteenth-century book denotes specific figures to be engraved on particular gemstones for fullest magical effect. On a sapphire, the figure of a bearded man or a ram has the power to cure or prevent infirmities, to preserve one from poisons and protect from all demons. This image confers honors and exalts the wearer. Among jewels still preserved from the Greek and Roman periods is a sapphire cameo, light blue-gray in color, exquisitely carved with the head of a bearded man.

Actually, the ancient Greeks and Romans used sapphire sparingly, as its rarity made it prohibitively expensive. The regalia (royal jewels) of nearly every European country included sapphire among the gemstones. Kings wore sapphire about their necks to preserve them from envy or deception, and to attract divine favor.

An odd use for sapphire was recorded in 1495. It was written that if one puts a spider in a box and then holds a sapphire at the mouth of the box, the power of the gem kills the spider.

In medieval times, sapphire was worn by priests to reduce their sexual appetites and (in case that failed to work) to guard against insanity. As early as the sixth century, the Pope decreed that every cardinal was to wear a sapphire ring on his right, or "blessing," hand. In the twelfth century, the Bishop of Rheims spoke glowingly of the beauty and nobility of the sapphire. By the fourteenth century, every bishop as he took office was presented with a sapphire ring. The stone symbolized the divine powers vested in him which gave him the secular and sacred rights of dispensing judgments or blessings.

The Englishman Sir Richard Burton, the nineteenth-century explorer, translator, author, and Oriental scholar, owned a large star sapphire which brought him prompt attention and good horses wherever he traveled. Only those who served him well were rewarded with a view of the fabulous stone. The Orientals regarded a star stone as a guiding gem, guarding against witchcraft, warding off evil, bringing good fortune to its first wearer even after the stone left his possession.

Burton called his star sapphire his talisman. We don't know exactly what Burton believed, but he did carry the stone with him at all times; and as he rode away on a fresh horse, it was evident that the stone had at least brought *him* good fortune!

In the twelfth century, sapphire was a favorite stone of soothsayers and necromancers, who said that it enabled them to talk with the dead and to make predictions. An author writing in the 1700s assigned it the number 6. However, modern numerology gives the word sapphire an 11 designation. Eleven is a Master Number of high tension and great power, signifying selfless service to mankind.

The second stone in the second row of the High Priest's breast-plate was a sapphire. It is a Foundation Stone of the Holy City.

Pope Gregory identified sapphire with the Virtues, third from highest in the angelic hierarchy. These are the angels who are present to work miracles and deliver God's grace.

The sapphire signifies truth and constancy, and the secret message from the Almighty. Worn by a man, it stands for wisdom and lofty and altruistic thoughts. It is the symbol of the apostles Paul and Andrew. It is a tradition among the Jews that the Ten Commandments were engraved upon a mighty sapphire.

Sapphire is associated with childhood, autumn, the planets Venus, Jupiter, and Mercury, and the fixed star the Goat at 15 degrees Gemini. The Hindus attributed it to July. Its hour is ten in the morning. It is a gem for Thursday and Friday; the star sapphire is for Tuesday.

The ancients believed that sapphire was the gem of the guardian angel Ashmodei. Ashmodei is a messenger of God, a protecting household spirit, "the prince of sheddim," and "the great philosopher."

The word sapphire occurs in the Hebrew and Persian languages, and is derived from a Sanskrit word meaning "Beloved of Saturn." The Persian word is *saffir*. In French or Arabic it is *safir*; in Greek, *sapphiros*. The Spanish call it *zafiro*; in German it is *saphir*. Pliny called it *sappirus* or *sapphirus*. Mystical Jews use the similar word *sefiroth* to denote the emanations of God in the universe.

The dazzling brilliance of the sapphire has been the inspiration for insightful passages of the world's great poetry. The English poet and prose writer John Milton, who composed his famous epic poem, *Paradise Lost*, in 1667 after he went blind, referred to the stars as "living sapphires."

Thomas Gray, an English romantic poet of the 1700s, wrote of Milton's loss of vision. Gray seems to present the possibility that Milton, traveling in meditation or out of body, had gazed upon the forbidden sight of the Throne of God and became blind from that. Consider Gray's words from "The Progress of Poesy" and see what you think:

He pass'd the flaming bounds of place and time,
[He saw] the living throne, the sapphire-blaze

Where angels tremble while they gaze
. . . but, blasted with excess of light
Closed his eyes in endless night.

The poet Shelley referred to "the sapphire ocean." Sapphire was the gemstone of Neptune, god of the sea. This brilliant gem is the symbol for the natural sciences, for astronomy and astrology. The contemplation of the sky, the sun, moon, stars and planets, and the study of planetary influences on human events, may be intensified by wearing a sapphire.

✧

HEALING MAGIC

It is only to be expected that a gemstone with the intense energies of sapphire would also wield colossal power in healing. Sapphire was used in early Atlantis, when humankind first began eating heavy proteins, in order to adjust the body to this diet. The gemstone's activities are centered on the solar plexus and pituitary chakras. This stimulates regeneration of the intestinal tract, stomach, and pituitary gland. Heart and kidney action are improved, and disorders in these parts are alleviated.

As with all gemstones, the vibrations of sapphires and star sapphire may be passed on to a person either through wearing the stone; through Ayurvedic methods, Teletherapy, or Radionics; or by taking the elixir.

Here follows a partial list of the body organs or areas, physical and emotional maladies, and psychological ailments for which sapphire elixir may be used.

It is useful in detoxifying the body of harmful substances or from exposure to radiation. It improves the action of the muscle system.

Sapphire is beneficial in treating mental imbalances, depression, stress, or hyperactivity. It helps the nursing mother to have sufficient milk. It eases pain, and helps the body to assimilate all nutrients and protein.

In the metaphysical and spiritual realms, the use of sapphire aids in astral projection, psychokinesis, channeling, telepathy, and clairvoyance. It raises the consciousness and helps attune one to the higher self. It works with mind, body, and spirit to bring inner peace. It is beneficial to all the chakras, as well as the astral and emotional bodies; it cleanses the aura.

Sapphire or star sapphire can be worn anywhere on the body; next to the skin is best.

Dosage of sapphire elixir is three to seven drops per dose on an empty stomach, three or four times each day for two weeks. Then stop for a week to observe changes. Resume taking on the same on-off cycle until the condition is improved.

Gurudas's book on gem elixirs suggests that with star sapphire, one might fast for seven days per month, using mango or papaya juice. Each day drink one quart of the juice, plus one ounce of distilled water containing seven drops of star sapphire elixir.

Gem elixirs are truly effective, so follow directions.

✧

SAPPHIRE DREAMS

If you dream of wearing sapphires, it's a warning about your impulsive behavior, so take a look at your performance and get your act together like a thinking person. If the sapphires you dreamed of were set in a ring or a brooch, you'll suffer with regret for some all-too-spontaneous act. But if you dream of sapphires worn by others, or in a window display, the influence of powerful friends will soon help you up a few rungs on the social ladder. You may meet a captain of industry, a Beautiful Person, a bank president, a prince or princess, or some other person of power and authority.

The sapphire's blue seen in a dream is an indication of relief from worry through the intervention of outside sources.

If you have taken a lover, and question whether you've made a wise selection, a dream of sapphires gives a good prediction for your affair: your lover will be there for you when needed. In business matters, dreaming of sapphires forecasts gain and good fortune. If it's your friend wearing this lovely blue gem in your dream, he or she will have good luck.

◆

SAPPHIRES THROUGH HISTORY

Sapphire is identified with the Divine Law of Order which equals Truth. The gem represents the pure illumined state.

A Biblical legend is that before the Flood, God sent the Archangel Raphael to Noah with a book, and the message that this holy book contained all the secrets and mysteries of the universe. The book was made of sapphire. During the grim, gray days of the Flood, the marvelous sapphire lighted the dim ark for Noah as he imbibed of the wisdom of the stone. In the following generations, the sapphire descended through Shem, Abraham, and Jacob to Levi, Moses, and Joshua. From Joshua it passed to Solomon, who learned from it the soundness of his judgment, all his healing skills, and his mastery over demons.

Edward the Confessor, the saint who reigned as king Edward I of England from 1041 to 1066, is said to have had a sapphire talisman which, for greatest effectiveness, he always wore next to his flesh. A second sapphire belonging to Edward is still in existence. It is mounted in the uppermost cross of the Imperial State Crown which the English sovereign wears when appearing in state, as at a ceremonial opening of Parliament.

Edward was canonized in 1161. This second "sapphire of Saint Edward" was originally set in the coronation ring worn by Edward I at his crowning in 1042. He was buried at Westminster Abbey wearing the ring, and it was left untouched on his hand for two hundred years. In the time of Henry III, Edward's tomb was opened, and the saint's remains were transferred to a new and splendid shrine behind the high altar. Robes and ornaments buried with him were removed for preservation.

Nearly 570 years later, at the coronation of Queen Victoria, she wore the newly made Imperial State Crown with Edward's sapphire in it. It is the longest-owned of the English Crown Jewels.

The Star of India, a perfect blue star sapphire weighing 563.35 carats, is the largest known star sapphire. It is remarkable also for the size and perfection of the natural star within the stone. It is known to be nearly four centuries old. John Pierpont Morgan, a wealthy nineteenth-century American industrialist and banker, purchased the stone and presented it to the American Museum of

Natural History in New York City. In October 1964, it was among the jewels in the American Museum's Morgan Gem Collection. Three daring beach boy/thieves, led by "Murph the Surf," stole it right out of the museum.

For months the fabulous gem was supposed lost; then in April 1965 the New York City Police Department recovered it and returned it to the Museum. It is now displayed in a special electric safe case together with a rich blue Burma star sapphire of 94 carats, the deep purple Midnight Star Sapphire of 116 carats, and the DeLong Star Ruby, weighing 100.32 carats.

The great leader Charlemagne was King of the Franks from A.D. 768 to 800 and then Holy Roman Emperor of the West for another fourteen years. He was a patron of education, the arts, and science. He possessed a sapphire talisman of great power. It was said to have belonged first to his wife. As he had several wives, mistresses, and concubines, it's hard to say now just which one of the lot she might have been. Her purpose in owning such a talisman was to keep Charlemagne's affections constant to herself.

The jewel was made by the Magi in the train of Harun-al-Rashid, Caliph of Baghdad and Ruler of the East at the same time Charlemagne was King and Emperor. Though the two strong men may have disagreed on religious principles, they cooperated as rulers, exchanging gifts, among which was an elephant given to Charlemagne by Harun-al-Rashid. (And possibly a wife, mistress, or concubine as well.)

The talisman has two sapphires, each a cabochon (half-sphere) with the flat sides together. Mounted between the sapphires is a bit of wood from the True Cross. The elaborate mounting is gold, with several other small stones surrounding the two large ones in a regular pattern. The talisman reportedly worked so well that Charlemagne's love for his wife endured even after her death. When he was on his own deathbed in agony, the talisman was brought to him and its powers of love enabled him to complete peacefully the transition from this life to the next.

This 1,100-year-old jewel is in existence today and is on display in the Cathedral Treasury in Rheims, France.

BIRTHSTONE FOR OCTOBER

◆

ZODIACAL STONE FOR

LIBRA

(September 24–October 23)

. . . Follow the Romany patteran
East where the silence broods
By a purple wave on an opal beach
In the hush of the Mahim woods.

. . . The heart of a man to the heart of a maid—
Light of my tents, be fleet;
Morning waits at the end of the world,
And the world is all at our feet!

—RUDYARD KIPLING
"THE GIPSY TRAIL"

The numeral of opal is 8.

Initially, you are drawn to this gem because there is no other stone like it in the world. If it is your birthstone, you are self-confident and ambitious; you know your own mind. You'll delight in opal's flashing now-you-see-me-now-you-don't colors. You'll buy it because it is, indeed, unique. No other gem—not even another opal—is exactly like the one you choose.

Opal is for those in positions of power. The position may be in finance, development, government, or education—but it carries heavy responsibility. You who find opal a calming, harmonious, and even mystical energy should wear it all the time. A person of discernment, refinement, and acuteness of judgment will choose opal.

But opal may not choose you. Opal is picky about the one who wears it. If you aren't that one, pay the consequences. Opal's strong vibrations promise the wearer that he will get exactly what he deserves—not more, not less. This is why it is said that if the wrong person wears opal, bad luck will attend him. No wonder; for the energy of this fine gem demands the wearer's purity of heart and motive in every situation. An individual who harbors constant negative intent or feelings cannot wear opal without that negativity turning back on him and wreaking havoc.

So let opal choose you. It is a discerning gem for the chosen few.

Opal stands for ideals and their manifestation, for creativity and mystical inspiration. Its vibrations open the door of the psyche to higher consciousness.

· · ·

✧

PHYSICAL PROPERTIES

The birthstone for October is a translucent silica gel which occurs not in crystals but in blobs, and which is 5 to 10 percent water. Within the blobs are tightly packed rows and blocks made up of microscopically visible silica spheres. These spheres and the spaces between them break up and reflect light waves coming into them, splitting it up into prismatic colors. The colorful opal actually has no color within. It is the play of light among the many spheres and spaces in the mass which causes flashes of crimson, violet, blue, and green as the stone is turned. And the more uniform the packing of the little spheres, the more vivid the colors.

Opal is never found in alluvial gem gravels. Opal occurs from five to thirty-five yards below the earth's surface. It is always a secondary mineral, deposited in seams and cavities in the surrounding rocks long after they were formed. It is mined in the most casual-seeming way by digging a shaft, widening it, and then digging down until one comes to the level of opal. There tunnels are dug in every direction, following the opal seam. Once the site plays out, the miner moves on to another likely place.

The word opal is credited with more than one origin. It may come from the Sanskrit *upala*, meaning precious stone. Or it may be derived from the Greek *opallios*, meaning change of color. The Indonesian name for it is based on the Sanskrit *maya* (illusion) and the Javanese *kali*, or river. Hence the highly descriptive Indonesian term *kalumaya*, meaning river of illusion.

Opals today are found primarily in Australia, Czechoslovakia, and Mexico. Guatemala, Honduras, Nevada, and Idaho produce some also.

Possibly the most precarious opals are those found at Rainbow Ridge and Virgin Valley in Nevada. When removed from the ground, these opals are quite cold, and glowing with color. But they fragment readily, particularly if exposed to heat or sunlight immediately after being unearthed. It is as if these gems cringe away from heat and light, and in so doing destroy themselves. A more scientific explanation may be that they are comparatively newly formed, and simply are not yet ready to be taken from Mother Earth.

Generally the luster of an opal is more brilliant on a warm day, or when the stone is warmed in the hand before being examined. This may explain some loss of life in the stone when it is away from its owner.

✧

SHOPPING FOR OPALS

If you're ready to buy an opal, it is especially important to look at lots of them first. As you will see in this section, there are so many things to consider about opal that—unless *your stone* comes along right away—you'll need to make some discoveries about the characteristics of this ever-changing gem.

A connoisseur judging the quality of opal must recognize three things: the stone's background color; the pattern in which the colors are distributed; and the character of the color. There are four basic types of opal: white, black, transparent, and common. These types have several alternate names we'll mention as we go along.

Background colors. White opals are white or milky. Black opals may be black, or shades of blue or gray. Black opals and white opals are the most sought after. Even their beauty depends on the pattern and the depth of the play of color. The most desired colors for black opal are red, violet, orange, yellow, green, and blue. A black opal with a harlequin pattern in the first three colors would be most sought after.

The *transparent opals* tend to be either fire opals or water opals, and are often called Mexican opals because they are found only in Mexico. Fire opals are yellow to orangy-red, and may or may not show a play of colors. Some gorgeous opals have great brilliance but no iridescence at all. The water opal has little color or iridescence.

Common opal shows a milky opalescence. It has no play of color because it lacks the rows of tiny spheres and spaces which distinguish other opal. It is commercially desirable only when it has an attractive color and fire; then it may be faceted.

The *hydrophane opal* is huddled and lifeless, almost opaque when dry, but becomes transparent when wet. In it lurks a spot of color, which it displays when it is wetted.

Wood opal has been found, in which opal replaced wood in the petrification process. There the play of color swirls with the grain.

Patterns. The fires of opal are called harlequin, flash, flame, or pin-fire. The most desirable iridescence is harlequin, where the mosaic pattern appears in spangled patches of equal size.

Character of the Color. Sometimes the pattern within a black or white opal will have a flash-like quality; or it may have a streaked effect resembling flames in a fireplace. In the pin-fire pattern, the colors stay in the same place.

✧

CHARACTERISTICS AND ATTRIBUTES

Opal, for all its ancient associations with the glory of Greece and Rome, is not among the gemstones of Biblical fame. It is not a Foundation Stone of the Holy City, nor is it mentioned in connection with the first High Priest's breastplate, or the Breastplate of the Second Temple, or any of the Twelve Tribes of Israel, or with any of the apostles. Perhaps its very evanescence, the hide-and-seek quality that makes it unique, has kept opal from being named for any eternal use.

For opal dies. It is unusually susceptible to changes in its water content or its temperature. Sometimes fine cracks will craze the surface of a lovely gem opal, diminishing its value and its display of colors. For this reason, jewelers have recommended that owners give their opals an occasional overnight soak in room-temperature edible oil, clean them with mild detergent solution, then rinse and dry them with a cloth.

Sixteenth-century gem cutters feared opal for a completely practical reason. Because of its peculiar internal structure, an opal which was being cut or polished might simply fall apart on the workbench. And the hapless gem cutters had to replace any stone they broke.

Opal is an aid in controlling one's temper and properly using anger. The Orientals consider opal to be the anchor of hope and symbol of purity; and its wearer is protected from all ills, for he or she is held in the hand of God. If you receive an opal as a gift, the giving of it removes any possible tinge of misfortune and assures the recipient only good.

Yet, according to three independent contemporary psychics, the opal brings justice. Evidently basing their statements on the principle of the individual's responsibility for his own actions, the psychics agree that the opal you wear acts according to the universal law of cause and effect: whatever energies you send out (negative or positive) return to you in one way or another until you have learned your lesson. So perhaps the great lesson that opal has to teach us is to think and act in a positive, wise, and loving manner.

The fire opal is a gem of summer, of six o'clock in the evening. Opal has been associated with the sun and with the planet Mercury.

Opal is the gem of the angel Nibra Ha-Rishon, one of the emanations of God. Along with Metatron and Logos, Makon and Sophia, Nibra Ha-Rishon is ranked among the highest of angelic beings.

During Roman and then medieval times opal was used as an eye stone, curing eye troubles, rendering its wearer (like Gyges, of whom we speak later) invisible. Its reputation could have been endangered then, for people lived in daily fear of the Evil Eye. Surely a stone whose color did not stay in one place, but magically scurried about here and there, must have evil powers!

At the turn of the twentieth century, if a Russian peasant saw an opal among goods for sale, she or he would buy nothing more that day, for it was still believed that opal was the embodiment of the Evil Eye.

✧

HEALING MAGIC

As with all gemstones, opal's vibrations may be passed on to a person either through wearing the stone; through Ayurvedic methods, Teletherapy, or Radionics; or by taking the elixir.

Here follows a partial list of the body organs or areas, physical and emotional maladies, and psychological ailments for which opal elixir may be used.

In healing, the effects of opal vary a bit depending on the background color of the gemstone.

The *colorless or transparent water opal* restores the rejuvenative capacities of the spleen and abdominal region. It calms down mood swings, amplifies thoughts, and enhances meditation. It works with the etheric, mental, and emotional bodies.

It should be worn over the abdomen.

The *common opal* (white, yellow, or pink background) treats autism, dyslexia, and epilepsy, problems of physical coordination, and problems of vision. It enhances the work of the pineal and pituitary glands. Working with the crown, third eye and solar plexus chakras, it increases intuition and balances the feminine qualities in one.

Wear common opal at the throat.

Red or orange fire opal alleviates leukemia, improves sight and eases eye diseases. It increases mental clarity, intuition, and other psychic gifts. It calms the nerves and eases depression and apathy. Fire opal works with the red corpuscles and their tissue regenerative capabilities and aids in all disorders of the blood.

Use fire opal elixir in a bath this way: seven drops opal, seven drops of tincture of rosewater and chamomile, one fluid ounce of distilled water, plus a small amount of pure grain alcohol. Add this mixture to your bathwater.

The *black opal* (ranging in color from gold-brown to black background) is associated with the lower astral planes and the desires and difficulties of that region. Black opal was used in Lemuria when the race, at first genderless, was divided into sexes. Diseases of the reproductive system began to develop because the emotions were either suppressed or not attuned to higher levels. Opal helped balance the base emotions with higher realizations.

Black opal affects the testicles, ovaries, pancreas, and spleen; it helps with liver diseases and all diseases associated with the genital area. It treats those who are depressed, particularly by sexual issues, by transforming the responses from the desire level to the higher sensitivity level.

As has been stated, opal amplifies the thought force, so think positive!

Wear black opal at the throat or on the ring finger.

✧
OPAL DREAMS

If you dream that you are given an opal or wear one, you will know misunderstanding, but will not be at fault. Seeing opals in a dream foretells a season of unexpected good luck. This fine omen is intensified if the opals seen were fire opals. One cannot look into opal without seeing the rainbow, symbol of fortune's smile.

If opals flash all around you in a dream, you will enjoy a delightful vacation. If you dream of a sky that is like opal, it means you'll hug and make up with someone you are fond of.

Three opals set in a ring or brooch indicate that your life will begin to be smoother and more harmonious. A dream of wearing many opals signifies that you care not for the opinions of others— you merrily do your own thing.

Dreaming of losing an opal means that someone or something of value to you will be temporarily lost.

✧
OPALS THROUGH HISTORY

Plato told a legend of a mystical ring, set with an opal. It came into the possession of Gyges, a shepherd employed by the king of Lydia. One day when Gyges was tending his flock, there came a hard storm, followed by an earthquake which opened up a deep valley in the earth nearby. Gyges began to explore the valley. He found there a hollow horse made of brass, with convenient apertures at its sides. Looking through these apertures, he beheld within the horse the body of a very large man, on whose finger was a golden ring.

Gyges, certain that the ring had been meant for him, took it and speedily climbed up out of the valley. Within a few days he met with the other shepherds, who were preparing their monthly reports for the king. While they sat together, Gyges twisted his newfound treasure on his finger. Suddenly, as the opal turned toward his palm, he realized that he had become invisible. He heard the others talking excitedly about him, wondering where he had gone. He continued to twist the ring—and reappeared when the opal was on the top of his finger. He tested the powers of the ring again and again. Then, realizing the extraordinary opportunities that lay within his grasp, he requested that he be the one to carry the shepherds' reports to the king.

Once at court with his useful selective invisibility, Gyges was able to enlist the aid of the queen in slaying the king and becoming the new sovereign of the kingdom.

Probably the most curious thing about opal is that for most of its twenty centuries of use as a jewel, up until a certain event in literary history, this phenomenal gemstone was considered the best of good luck. Since it seemed to combine in its sparkling interior all the colors found in the rainbow, opal was credited with all the virtues of all the gems combined. Its fantastic play of lights was the very symbol of hope and good fortune. And for those born in October, its magic worked overtime.

Opal was among the gems the Church found suitable for setting into episcopal rings. The stone protected its wearer from disease. Blonde women wore opal to help preserve the light color of their hair. The individual who wore opal was healthy, wealthy, and preternaturally blonde.

Pliny called opal "most precious," second only to emerald itself. The Romans and Greeks of his day dearly prized opal. The stone's popularity continued even through the Dark Ages into the Renaissance. An American collector owns a handsomely designed gold ring of the period A.D. 550–750, bearing a red opal surrounded by delicate gold scrollwork. This is incalculably valuable as an artifact, since opals tend not to live to such a ripe old age in good condition.

Opal mines at Czernowitz in Hungary (now known as Chernovtsy in present-day U.S.S.R.) were operated for centuries. At the beginning of the fifteenth century, more than three hundred men worked there.

In Renaissance England, the opal was high on the must list of gemstones. Members of the nobility, led by Queen Elizabeth I, wore lavish parures of opal. Parures (sets of jewelry) were apt to include earrings, brooches, bracelets, necklets, and stomachers. On New Year's Day in 1584, Sir Christopher Hatton presented to Her Majesty a magnificent opal parure made up of stones bought in Constantinople and Czernowitz.

Then came the literary event whose result probably dismayed its author as much as it did the gem merchants of the day. In 1829 the popular and admired writer, Sir Walter Scott, published his book *Anne of Geierstein*. Anne's grandmother was the Lady Hermione, daughter of a Persian shaman, who always wore in her hair a clasp set with a mysterious opal. The opal seemed to typify Hermione's moods. When she was animated, the sparkle of the gem became more pronounced, its "little tongue of flame" increasing in vivacity. When the lady spoke excitedly, the jewel became more brilliant, emitting a twinkling and flashing gleam from itself, rather than merely reflecting light. But let Lady Hermione lose her temper, and the opal in her hair flashed broodingly red as though in empathy.

The mystic gemstone held a fascination for Hermione's personal maids. They observed that she never removed this jewel except when her hair was being dressed; and that she seemed listless until it was restored to its place. If any liquid came near the gem, she got nervous.

Hermione married a baron and bore him a daughter. At the baby's christening, a spiteful old biddy accused Hermione of being a witch who was afraid of the holy water from the baptismal font. The baron, hasty in his anxiety to prove otherwise, accidentally splashed a drop of water on the opal. The opal shot forth a brilliant spark like a falling star—and lost all its color and life. The Lady Hermione sighed with pain and fainted. Quickly she was carried to her bedchamber, where she and the baron spoke privately for a time. He sent for a doctor, then returned to the chapel to pray.

Two hours after the opal had been touched by the holy water, the doctor opened the bedchamber door—and found in her bed the only trace of Lady Hermione: a pile of light grey ash.

It is not known now what prompted the eminent author to choose opal as the device of the lady's downfall. Perhaps he had the intuition that the changeable gem held more secrets than it would ever tell. Perhaps his book was only a story of one individual and one opal; but all Scott's work was accepted enthusiastically. His readers took this story literally. Their reaction was immediate and widespread. People began to believe that opals were bad luck, they were dangerous, they should be locked up. Sales fell off sharply. The price of opals dropped to less than half their former figure.

Opals did not recover their popularity for about sixty years. Then, toward the end of Queen Victoria's reign, black opals were found at Lightning Ridge in Australia. The doughty little queen was enchanted with the discovery. Opals unlucky? Pish-tosh! said Victoria, who had as good an eye for commerce as the next queen. She revived the centuries-old fashion for them. She began to wear opals, she gave them to her daughters, friends, and relatives. She even had an immense parure designed to show them off, plus a few dozen diamonds for emphasis.

Then Queen Victoria died. Edward VII ascended the throne; and his beautiful Danish wife Queen Alexandra reverted to orthodoxy in the regalia. She had the opals in the parure removed and rubies set in their place. The beautiful black opals of Queen Victoria's time rose with her favor, and fell without it. They have never been reset.

The Spanish royal family had an unlucky opal which was reputed to have caused the death of five of its princes or princesses. The gemstone was retired from family service and hung around the neck of the statue of the Virgin of Almudena, where, it was felt, the gem's ways might be mended.

In 1909, in the opal fields of Australia, a beautiful and unusual object came to light. It was the skeleton of a small serpent, which evidently had become opalized by natural processes. It was perfectly detailed, fantastic in its play of colors. As an amulet, it would be of outstanding value even today.

In the thirteenth century, Albertus Magnus wrote of a stone that was set in the Imperial Crown of the Holy Roman Empire, and guarded the regal honor. The stone was an opal of grand characteristics. Albertus called it the Orphanus, because none like it had ever been seen. "It is of a subtle vinous tinge," he said, "and its hue is as though pure white snow flashed and sparkled with the color of bright, ruddy wine, and was overcome with this radiance." In an earlier era, the stone shone at night; but by Albertus's time it no longer did.

The Belgian princess Stephanie owned an extensive parure—bracelets, earrings, pins for her hair, necklaces, and girdle—set with opals.

Among the French crown jewels are several handsome opals. A most remarkable fire opal had belonged to the Empress Josephine. Because of its many flame-red flashes, the stone was named the Burning of Troy.

Romans called opal *opthalmos* from the Greek *ophthalmos*, meaning eye; they used it as a curative stone for eye diseases and mishaps. Roman generals carried staves topped with opal so that they would have good fortune in military campaigns. Pliny, in a marvelous flight of fancy, wrote that in opal was the living fire of the ruby, the glorious purple of the amethyst, the sea green of the emerald, all glittering together in an incredible mixture of light.

The wealthy Roman senator Nonius owned an opal "large as a hazel nut," of which he was quite fond. Marc Antony, greedily desiring the stone as a gift for Cleopatra, demanded it. Nonius, rather than give up his precious gem, fled Rome to live in exile. Of all his great wealth, he was said to have taken with him only the opal. Evidently he believed that it would continue to cause fortune to smile on him.

Then in the 1700s, in some ancient ruins at Alexandria, Egypt, a peasant found a ring set with a precious stone. The stone was an opal about as large as a hazelnut, cut cabochon. After some time the ring reached Constantinople. There it was appraised at "several thousand ducats." The antiquity of the gemstone, its size and description, led many people of the time to believe it was the famed "opal of Nonius."

ALTERNATE BIRTHSTONE FOR OCTOBER

Tourmaline

ALTERNATE ZODIACAL STONE FOR

LIBRA

(September 24–October 23)

. . . She hangs upon the cheek of night
Like a rich jewel in an Ethiop's ear;
Beauty too rich for use,
For earth too dear.

—WILLIAM SHAKESPEARE
ROMEO AND JULIET, I.V.

—————————————————— ✧ ——————————————————

Numerologically, tourmaline is a Master Number 11, which reduces to a 2, giving it the dual number 11/2.

Initially, those who are adaptive, flexible, love to travel and find life one big adventure are drawn to the diverse shades and colors of tourmaline. This kind of person likes it because it's different: one-of-a-kind, many-in-one. On a deeper level, those with a high degree of discernment, compassion, adaptability, and ability to compromise find tourmaline right for them.

Just as this gemstone comes from a fragile, breakable source, those born to this stone also possess a similar fragile and gentle inward nature. Tourmaline will never be worn by many, but mostly by those who have a strong streak of high emotionalism and sensitivity within them. Women will be more drawn to this stone than will men, because of the intrinsically gentle vibration surrounding it. A man who finds tourmaline attractive will know himself well, and not be at all embarrassed by his own capability for gentility and tenderness.

The energy surrounding tourmaline draws people who crave a quiet harmony within and outside themselves. Once this marriage of individual and gemstone is joined, tourmaline bestows an otherworldly serenity, wisdom, and intuitive abilities. It is a gem for the person who values his or her emotional balance first and foremost.

✧

PHYSICAL PROPERTIES

In tourmaline, as in the playful and flashing opal, are the diversity of shades and colors of the autumn season: blue, yellow, red, pink, green, and brown. Black tourmaline is found in the Tyrol, though this is not gem quality. Unlike the opal, tourmaline is transparent, and forms in crystals. These crystals have small parallel channels or threadlike lines along their sides which are an identifying feature of the mineral.

Tourmaline, alternate birthstone for October, is a stunningly complex aluminum silicate containing a great variety of chemical elements which vary from one crystal to the next and sometimes within a single crystal. Even the two ends of the crystal can be different in color. A crystal may have a red end and a blue end, with brown and orange and yellow in its center to keep things stirred up; or it may be red inside and green outside (watermelon), or vice versa. It has more hues, shades, and tints than any other gemstone, plus a lovely fire.

Viewed from one end, the crystal may be transparent while from the opposite end it appears opaque.

Tourmaline has been used as a gemstone for centuries, but not until the early 1700s was it recognized as a distinct species. It had been popularly confused with topaz, zircon, amethyst, ruby, and sapphire.

The name tourmaline comes from an ancient Singhalese word, *turmali*, meaning a mixture of precious stones. Red and pink tourmalines are called *rubellites*. The black stones are *schorls*. Blue tourmalines—quite rare—are called *indicolites*; they may shade from light to dark, masking as aquamarine or sapphire. The violet reds are *siberites*. The yellow to yellow greens used to be called *Ceylonese peridot* or *Ceylonese chrysolite*, though because of the resulting confusion with genuine peridots those names are not used much now. The brown tourmaline *(dravite)* ranges from yellow into brown. The colorless tourmaline, known as *achroite*, is seldom used for gems.

A bright-dark peacock blue, a strange and mystical color, is found in Africa. This shade has no fire, but set with diamonds it is outstanding. Incredibly, this unique shade is sometimes heat-treated to turn it emerald green.

Rarely, tourmalines will reveal a usable chatoyancy, a cat's-eye effect that hovers over the stone, in green or pink.

It is a highly durable stone, with a gentle luster, very low cleavage, and a hardness of 7 to 7.5 on the Mohs scale. Synthetic tourmalines are manufactured for industrial and gem use.

The most important source of tourmalines is Brazil. All the colors are found there, often in a single vein. Tourmaline occurs in extensively weathered rock that can be readily broken up. Therefore, mining equipment is of the utmost simplicity: a pick and shovel. Hundred of itinerant miners mark out a claim and begin digging either a shaft or a tunnel. When they reach the gem concentration, they clean it out, then go on to another site.

In the United States, tourmalines have been found in Connecticut, Maine, New York, Texas, and California.

When cutting the rough stone, the cutter must consider its power of revealing two different colors so that the most attractive color is revealed. Neither table cut nor cabochon is suitable for the highly transparent tourmaline. Faceted all over, step cut or brilliant cut, its beauty surges forward. In the company of gold and diamonds, its allure becomes magical.

Because of the centuries-long confusion about the identity of tourmaline, any part it may have played in history has been under a different name.

✧

SHOPPING FOR TOURMALINES

Shopping for tourmaline should be quite a pleasure, as almost any desired color is available. Stones are also cut so that they are half one color and half another, or three colors. Ask to see the stone under magnification, so that you'll know that the color runs true within your stone. Be aware that the stone is dichroic, and will show one color from one view and different color from another view. As has been mentioned, it's a good precaution to know your jeweler. Before buying, find out if the tourmaline you like is natural or synthetic.

Color and purity are criteria for tourmaline. The potential for sparkle is in the hardness, but the cut determines this. A fine tourmaline is highly transparent, so this stone loses appeal if the table is too large or if it is cut cabochon. Brilliant or emerald cuts show off tourmaline's characteristics best.

• • •

✧
CHARACTERISTICS AND ATTRIBUTES

In glorious Roman times, tourmaline was credited with the capability of dispersing fears and melancholic passions, of attracting favors and friends. It is the gemstone of the Muses, bringing great inspiration to writers.

Carry a tourmaline in your pocket to promote understanding with those you see every day. Worn on the hand, the gem brings you beauty and peace, and helps you progress in brotherhood, patience, and harmony. Used in meditation, it is an aid to focusing on your direction in earth life. When mounted as a pendant or a charm, tourmaline give you a sense of underlying purpose in new undertakings.

In the rough, tourmaline is a nurturing stone, quieting the mind and bringing compassion into love so that the two equal wisdom.

Green tourmaline is the gem for May. In the yellow shades, it is a gem of autumn, and the sixth hour of the morning. Brown tourmaline is the stone associated with New York; the other colors are associated with Maine, New England, Texas, and California.

Tourmaline is the gemstone of the angel Tadhiel, "righteousness of God." Tadhiel is credited with preventing the Biblical Abraham from sacrificing Isaac, the much beloved son of his old age. Prepared to slay Isaac, as God had commanded, for a burnt-offering, Abraham was relieved of this dread duty by the angel's voice saying, "Do not lay your hand on the lad . . . for now I know that you fear [love] God."

Industrially, tourmaline has several applications. It is widely used in the optical industry. In submarines it is used to measure pressure variations and the intensity of radiation emanations. It is the only substance which, in World War II, could measure the pressure developed by the explosion of atomic bombs.

Tourmaline is pyroelectric: when the stone is slightly warmed, it becomes electrically charged, one end being positive, the other end negative. Cool the stone, and reverse the charge. The Dutch call it *Aschentrekker*, from its habit of attracting or repelling ashes. They used to use a tourmaline to draw the ashes from the bowls of their long-stemmed tobacco pipes.

Benjamin Franklin's friend, Dr. Haberden, sent him tourmalines from London. Franklin was delighted at their performance, and had one set in a pivot ring. Heat from his finger was enough to charge the stone, making it attract dust, feathers, cat hair, dandruff, and bits of paper.

In Brazil, the green variety of tourmaline is often called Brazilian emerald. There, for a long time, it has been employed as the gemstone mounted in episcopal rings. Frequently a blue stone—preferably sapphire—has been put into bishops' rings. However, in the early days of the Church—about A.D. 520—Avitus, archbishop of Vienna, wrote a letter proposing the design for his own episcopal ring. The ring itself represented two dolphins facing each other at the setting, with their tails forming the bottom side of the hoop. The ring was to be made of electrum (an alloy of gold and silver), which has the tawny hue of gold and the whiteness of silver, and set with an emerald.

✧

HEALING MAGIC

In a book by William Thomas Fernie, M.D., first published in 1907, the doctor named the chemical constituents of tourmaline: silica, alumina, magnesia, oxide of iron, boracic acid, soda, and fluorine. (Dr. Fernie did not say—possibly did not know—that tourmaline is the only common rock-forming mineral that contains boron; and that it also contains trace amounts of lithium, potassium, cobalt, manganese, gallium, tin, nickel, bismuth, lead, and zinc.) He spoke of scientific processes such as trituration, distillation, "poudering," and prescribed infinitesimally minimal doses ("the millionth of a grain, and no more") to be taken at stated intervals.

Silica, he said, has the unique virtue of controlling excessive perspiration of the feet. It also has the power to cure kidney stones. Alumina seems to affect chiefly the sexual system and the mucous membranes, easing all medical problems that occur because of lack of internal secretions, and being especially suitable for "old, dry and thin" persons. Magnesia, being a constituent of sea water, is good for treating swelling of the lymph glands, and affects the entire system beneficially. A boracic acid mixture was used against sore throat. Soda, said Dr. Fernie, has little action on the human system.

What he most sincerely recommended in regard to the use of chemicals contained in gemstones was, first of all, the tiniest possible doses. (A startling exception to this rule was his prescription, for consumption and for strengthening the heart, of powdered pearl in ten-grain doses.) Second, he suggested instead that wearing the gemstone containing the chemicals would give a better result than taking the chemicals as medication.

Dr. Fernie did not specifically mention the vibrations of gemstones and their chemicals; his way of putting it was that the needed chemical constituents of the gemstones would make themselves available to the wearer.

So, through careful medical investigation and observation, Dr. Fernie came to a conclusion similar to that accepted for centuries: Wear or use the right gems and they will help make you well again.

The vibrations of tourmaline regulate the endocrine system, balancing hormone levels and secretions.

As Dr. Fernie suggested, some of the minerals contained in tourmaline are effective in restoring the balance of internal lubrication. From Lenora Huett comes the channeled information that the amateur or beginning healer should not use tourmaline casually for healing, as it has a great variety of uses and its effect differs from one individual to another.

As with all gemstones, tourmaline's vibrations may be passed on to a person either through wearing the stone; through Ayurvedic methods, Teletherapy, or Radionics; or by taking the elixir.

Here follows a partial list of the body organs or areas, physical and emotional maladies, and psychological ailments for which tourmaline elixir may be used.

Tourmaline has special affinity for the intestinal tract, and is capable of either binding action or loosening action there. It also affects emotions and vibrations, raising or lowering them. Plainly, this is not a healing stone to fool with. It should first be studied and its properties well learned before using it on anyone.

Tourmaline's major work is with the seven primary chakras.

There are eight different tourmalines to consider when wearing the gemstone or using its vibrations in healing. Watermelon tourmaline elixir must be used with each of them in order to stimulate the piezoelectric* capabilities and crystalline structure of the other tourmalines. All tourmaline stimulates the biomagnetic, electrical, and crystalline properties within the human body.

Each tourmaline elixir activates a particular chakra, treating diseases associated with it and amplifying the attributes of that chakra. Each elixir also stimulates interaction among the subtle bodies and strengthens the body meridians and energy lines.

Tourmaline elixir can be applied externally in an ointment containing equal amounts of the watermelon elixir and the specific color, plus oils of clove, coconut, castor, and jojoba. Use the correct color tourmaline (with watermelon elixir) for each chakra.

Black, or schorl, elixir acts through the first (base) chakra. It offers protection against negativity and the earth's radiation. It stimulates the reflex points associated with the coccyx; and alleviates arthritis, dyslexia, heart disease, and adrenal disorders. It helps with anxiety and disorientation and awakens altruism.

Red, or rubellite, elixir works with the second (spleen) chakra to stimulate creativity or fertility and to alleviate gonorrhea and syphilis. It balances the passive and the aggressive in one.

White, or uvite, elixir activates the third (solar plexus) chakra. Digestion, emotional problems, and ulcers are eased. It also works to improve the action of the spleen and the white corpuscles.

Green tourmaline elixir opens the fourth (heart) chakra. It can completely regenerate the heart, thymus, ductless gland system, and immune system. A masculine influence, this elixir helps with father-image problems.

Blue, or indicolite, elixir opens the fifth (throat) chakra to improve communication. It strengthens the lungs, larynx, and thyroid. Gurudas also recommends using this with green tourmaline.

Cat's-eye tourmaline elixir works on a broad basis with the sixth (third eye) chakra. It stimulates the entire endocrine system, activates visions, and helps the individual to advance spiritually.

---

* Industrially, piezoelectric power is produced by squeezing or pressing crystals to reduce the force necessary for a task such as riveting, concrete mixing, taking X rays, and so on.

Achroite, or clear, tourmaline elixir opens the seventh (crown) chakra. This elixir is another powerful tool to be used in spiritual growth, aligning all the subtle bodies and chakras, attuning one more to the higher self and increasing spiritual understanding. Once this process has begun, it will be easier to rid the body of toxicity, and all vibrational remedies of gems and flowers will work more advantageously.

✧

TOURMALINE DREAMS

Dreams of tourmaline all seem to be connected with color. The black tourmaline is the most mysterious, for it draws to itself the other elements of time, place, persons, and actions in the dream, and invites you to interpret the combination the way it "feels" to you.

The yellow tourmaline indicates a relaxed, fun-tastic day with a friend. If the gem you dream of is pink, you will know tenderness and delight in a close relationship. A blue tourmaline seen in a dream stands for an honest, open talk with a wise counselor.

Colors of brown or a brown tourmaline in a dream show that you are well grounded and have a definite goal in all that you do. Red or green tourmaline stands for healing, renewal, building, and fresh vitality in your life.

✧

TOURMALINES THROUGH HISTORY

There is a unique fact about tourmaline: it has no history. It has been recognized as a distinct gemstone only since the eighteenth century. Its range of colors has caused it to be mistaken for emerald, sapphire, topaz, carnelian, and zircon. Perhaps some of the legends about emeralds or sapphires are really about tourmaline. We don't know.

BIRTHSTONE FOR NOVEMBER

◇

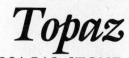

ZODIACAL STONE FOR

SCORPIO

(October 24–November 22)

I look upon you as a gem of the old rock.

—SIR THOMAS BROWNE

$\diamond$

Topaz is a numeral 6.

The powerful are drawn to this gem, first as an investment value and second, for its obvious quality in the world of precious stones. People who have executive careers in business or government, the leaders and administrators of the world, feel the lure of topaz. Those who are achieving success and/or material wealth will appreciate this stone.

If it is your birthstone, you are seeking deeper truths to satisfy your inner needs; you prefer that feeling of being centered, of staying within the flow while you pursue your goals. For you, topaz will create that mystical atmosphere in a powerful way.

Topaz creates compassion, harmony, outward awareness in the wearer. Those who are family oriented, patriotic, and concerned for the welfare of others will keep this gem forever. Its aura bestows an equilibrium in self and inspires altruistic efforts for others.

$\diamond$

PHYSICAL PROPERTIES

Topaz alone has always been the birthstone for November. Through at least fourteen centuries, until 1912 when the American National Retail Jewelers Association selected an alternate, no other gemstone was designated for this month. It was found pleasing and appropriate by not only the Jews and Romans, but also the Spanish, Arabs, Italians, Poles, and Russians, through the present century.

Like the opal for October, topaz seems a singularly appropriate gem for November. Generally thought of as a transparent golden brown the color of sherry wine, it might be light green or sky blue, reddish violet or brownish yellow, all the hues of late autumn.

There are also the colorless topazes which the Portugese call *pingos d'agoa*, or drops of water. These stones, often quite immense and flawless, are in some countries called slaves' diamonds. However, moisture dulls them, and they lack the fire of genuine diamond.

The brownish yellow topaz of Brazil can be changed by gradual heating and cooling to a delightful rose pink which occurs only rarely in nature. The stones to be heat-treated are packed in an inert substance, for example magnesia. Then they are slowly heated under controlled conditions, and in the presence of oxygen, until they become red. An orangey pink may result if the heat is not high enough; but get it too high, and certain stones crack. When the stones are cool, the resulting pink shade is permanent. Properly cut then, the topaz smiles and dazzles in a manner exquisitely feminine.

The topaz which has been laser-treated is a beautiful, haunting, unearthly Maxfield Parrish blue.

As a mineral, topaz is an aluminum fluorosilicate. It occurs in cavities of rocks which have been formed by intense heat. Topaz gem crystals are caused by the action of hot acid vapors rich in fluorine upon the aluminum silicates in the surrounding rock. It also concentrates in alluvial or glacial deposits, especially in the form of round translucent pebbles.

Topaz contains some water. It is one of the few gemstones in which is found the element fluorine. Flaws and minute cavities are not uncommon. The flaws take the form of a teardrop, or feathering. In the cavities may be found either gaseous liquids or tiny crystals of other minerals such as hematite, ilmenite, or rutile.

Rough topaz crystals usually have sharp edges and well defined faces, with a high, natural surface polish. Topaz has a fondness for rock crystal, often forming twin crystals in which the two occur together. This gentle autumn gemstone is easily cleaved. Though a very hard stone (8 on the Mohs' scale), it has no toughness and could fracture if struck on a hard object.

Topaz crystals are found in all sizes, from the tiniest on up to more than one hundred pounds. In 1902, a topaz from Brazil, weighing four pounds, was given to Pope Leo XIII upon the celebration of his silver jubilee.

In ancient times topaz was mined on the island of Zebirget, in Egypt, and in Saxony. Around the turn of the twentieth century it was mined in Maine. Today it is found in Utah and California, as well as in Brazil, the Ural Mountains, Japan, Sri Lanka, Madagascar, Siberia, Australia, and Mexico.

✧

SHOPPING FOR TOPAZ

When you're searching for genuine topaz, there are a few things you can be aware of to test the genuineness of the stone (as opposed to the completely respectable but more abundant citrine). Topaz has an unusual velvety body appearance, a soft beauty despite its dazzle. To the feel, it is more slippery than other gemstones. It has the rare attribute of being pyroelectric, which means that rubbing it against cloth or applying gentle heat will strongly charge the stone with electricity that attracts bits of paper or fluff. Some stones, under the same treatment, will glow phosphorescently in the dark.

It will be to your advantage to ask to see both topaz and citrine at one time, for comparison purposes.

For use in a ring, topaz will most likely be step cut. The cushion brilliant cut is also used to good effect.

✧

CHARACTERISTICS AND ATTRIBUTES

Genuine topaz was one of the powerful stones of antiquity, ranking high with amethyst, lapis lazuli, turquoise, zircon, peridot, and emerald. This gem, especially in its warm yellow, orange, and pink shades, represents the creative energies; it works through the law of attraction and manifestation. Through its atomic structure it speeds up the unfoldment of thoughts into concrete forms.

The light blue or white topaz crystals are an aid in developing higher inner awareness.

Also in the deeper spiritual sense topaz portrays uprightness, as well as the ardent contemplation of the prophecies. It was the ninth foundation stone of the Holy City. Engraved with the Israelite tribal name of Dan, it was the second stone on the Breastplate of the High Priest.

Topaz stood for the apostle James the Less. It is also the gemstone of Matthew, the special apostle for the month of July; and of Apollo, the Roman god of love. As a talismanic gemstone, it cheerfully serves on Tuesday, and also signifies Ashmodel, who is April's guardian angel and ruler of the zodiacal sign Taurus. Ashmodel was formerly one of the chiefs of the order of Cherubim.

Pope Gregory linked topaz with the Cherubim, second from bottom in the hierarchy of Heavenly Hosts. The Cherubim's duties are to contemplate the wisdom of God and emanate that wisdom to stir every living thing toward renewed growth.

The wine-gold topaz symbolizes the autumn season; the pink topaz stands for both spring and summer. The Hindus considered it the gemstone for December. Its favored day and time is Sunday, at four in the afternoon.

In earlier times topaz represented Sagittarius, the Archer. Another belief system attributed it to the planets Mercury, Neptune, Saturn and Mars. Along with sardonyx, it is the gemstone of the left and right wing of the fixed star Raven at 8 degrees Libra. A topaz engraved with a falcon helps the wearer to attract the favors of kings, princes, and distinguished personages.

✦

HEALING MAGIC

Saint Hildegard, the twelfth-century mystic and Abbess of Bingen, recommended topaz to cure diminishing vision. The topaz was to be soaked in wine for three days and nights. Just before gong to sleep, the sufferer was to rub his eyes with the moistened gemstone so that the moisture touched the eyeball itself. As an additional benefit, after using topaz the patient would sleep better than usual.

During the plague epidemics of the Middle Ages, an especially wonderful topaz was successfully used to treat the boils caused by the disease. The stone was simply rubbed over and around the fevered abscesses, and many were cured by it. Perhaps the patients' awareness of its previous owners worked its own benefits. This gem, then in the possession of a Roman physician, had belonged to both Pope Clement VI and Pope Gregory II.

Topaz, through creating lightness in the spirit and raising hope, has the faculty of smoothing the sharp edges from the personality. Great strength of love emanates from this stone. These gentle qualities are advantageous in ridding a person of headache, causing the nerves and muscles to relax so that the ache simply ceases to be.

In modern-day Gem Therapy, topaz is the single gem used to treat adenoids, cough, croup, deafness, goiter, swollen glands, mumps, obesity, pancreatitis, quinsy, tonsillitis, and whooping cough.

As with all gemstones, the vibrations of topaz may be passed on to a person either through wearing the stone; through Ayurvedic methods, Teletherapy, or Radionics, or by taking the elixir.

Here follows a partial list of the body organs or areas, physical and emotional maladies, and psychological ailments for which topaz elixir may be used.

Topaz has the amazing capacity for general tissue regeneration. This means that by meditating on topaz the aging process can be reversed, and that diseases of aging can be treated with topaz. Spiritually this gemstone influences rebirth of the self, rejuvenates the etheric body, and aligns it with the physical body.

The vibrations of topaz are good for treating poor circulation, hemorrhage, gout, and maladies of the nervous system. It helps to correct emotional imbalance, easing stress, depression, and worry. It controls anger, envy, and jealousy. It aids the sense of taste (another thing that goes wrong in aging) and is an excellent general strengthener. Topaz works with the brow and the solar plexus chakras, and the etheric body.

It can be worn anywhere on the body.

Take as an elixir; or apply it externally, mixed with such oils as peanut, coconut, or jojoba.

✧
TOPAZ DREAMS

If you dream of being presented with jewelry set with topaz, it indicates that someone loves you more than he or she can say. If that someone is not a relative, an interesting love affair will soon occupy your attention. Dream that you own a topaz, and it foretells that fortune will be liberal in her favors, and that you'll have pleasing companions along your pathway. Should your dreamed-of topaz be pink, it forecasts a happy marriage.

In your dream, should you lose a topaz, you may be hurt by the jealousy of a friend who seeks your position in life and love. Dream of holding a beautiful topaz, and no harm shall befall you.

Should you dream you are buying a topaz, it means that you are working to accommodate perspective in your affairs. A topaz crystal, seen among other crystals you own, indicates that you are efficient and well organized.

✧
TOPAZ THROUGH HISTORY

There's something romantically adventurous about topazes. First found on a desert isle shrouded in fog, the untouchable property of kings, guarded by serpents and dug out of the earth by slaves—even the very name of the gem and of its birthplace huddle in mystery. The Sanskrit word *topaz* means fire, but even that interesting explanation seems too wan to serve this fabled gem of ancient history.

The name topaz might have come from the island Topazion (or Topazius or Topazos), where it was first found thousands of years ago. The word could have been derived from the Greek *topazion*, meaning to seek; sailors gave the island its name because it was frequently surrounded with fog and they wasted a lot of time sailing around trying to find it. One early writer (no doubt brain-fogged) even located it in the Arabian Sea. This barren desert island of many names lies in the Red Sea about thirty-five miles off the coast of Egypt. Nowadays known as Saint John, it has been called Zebirget, Zebirged, and the Serpent Isle.

The land—and its jewels—was sacred to the Egyptian kings fifteen hundred years before Christ's birth. One of the island's legends was that anyone landing there without proper authorization was killed. Another legend was that the gems shone at night, to reveal their location, but because of the snakes they had to be mined by day. Many a pharoah preened himself wearing his gemstones from the tightly guarded little island before one of them thought to order all the serpents destroyed.

Through the centuries that gemstones have been used, and worn, and praised, and even glorified, some of the most popular have been known by several names. Topaz, for example, was a Biblical name for peridot or chrysolite. Even this is subject to some debate, for the Hebrew *Pitdah*, the name for the second stone on the breastplate, probably comes from the Sanskrit *pita*, meaning yellow. *Pita* describes topaz better than it does peridot.

Amulets made of various materials have been worn since earliest times. Those of metals, wood, and stones have been thought especially efficacious because the materials come from earth. An amulet is generally used to protect the wearer from injuries and ill health, to bring happiness and wealth, and to lengthen life.

An amulet used by the Chinese combined five stones: diamond, ruby (or topaz or yellow sapphire), emerald, pearl, and coral. The five substances (or their vibrations) were thought to combine the protecting influences of the different deities presiding over them, and to assure long life.

It would be hard to find a people who, as a whole, have revered and employed gemstones in higher ways than the Hindus. One of the oldest known talismanic jewels is the "nine-gem" jewel, the Hindu *naoratna*. Described in an old Hindu manuscript on gems, this jewel was designed to combine all the powerful astrological influences. It was made as a ring. The jewels formed an eight-point mandala, whose points represented the planets, around a central "sun." The sun was represented by a ruby. In the east was Venus, the diamond. In the southeast was the moon, shown by a pearl. To the south was Mars, a coral. Southwest was Rahu, a jacinth. In the west was Saturn, represented by sapphire. In the northeast was Jupiter, topaz. In the north, cat's-eye stood for the descending node. Northwest was Mercury, signified by emerald.

Probably not many were rich enough to own a *naoratna* of flawless genuine gems; but those who did found their riches increased, their health and happiness bountiful.

Also important in Hindu belief was the Kalpa Tree, a symbolical offering to the gods. It glowed with precious stones: pearls hung from its boughs and emeralds from its twigs. The leaves were coral and zircons. Its roots were sapphire, the base of its trunk diamonds, the trunk itself topaz, the upper branches cat's-eye.

In modern times topaz has lent its name—and inadvertently, its reputation—to the quartz stones which are known as Brazilian topaz, citrine topaz, Scotch topaz, smoky topaz, quartz topaz, Spanish topaz. The yellow quartz stones have been called Palmyra topaz, the browner shades Madeira topaz. The gemstone has been so misidentified that the word topaz sounds suspicious now.

The yellow sapphire is called oriental topaz. On the other hand, in Sri Lanka the colorless topaz is called water sapphire. Yellow stones there, whether topaz or something else, are called king topaz. Yellowish garnets are called topazolite. Blue-green topaz is sometimes sold as aquamarine. And to turn one's head completely backward, genuine topaz is sometimes called Brazilian topaz, the same as the quartz stone.

In order to distinguish the real thing from its many namesakes and look-alikes, genuine topaz is often called precious topaz. Such lavish and inexact use of the word leads one to wonder if it's all because *topaz* (whisper it!) has such an exotic Far Eastern sound reminiscent of camel bells and hot desert winds and muezzins in their minarets calling the faithful to prayer.

One spectacular case of bewildered identity concerns a huge gemstone, the 1,680-carat Braganza in the Portugese crown jewels. Boasted for years to be one of the world's largest diamonds, the Braganza is no longer seen or spoken of. For it is now believed to be a colorless topaz. And although topazes have been found whose single crystals weigh over one hundred pounds, the Braganza is still a gem to brag about.

ALTERNATE BIRTHSTONE FOR NOVEMBER

◆

ALTERNATE ZODIACAL STONE FOR

SCORPIO

(October 24–November 22)

. . . And the light that was left from making the sun
God gathered it up in a shining ball
And flung it against the darkness,
Spangling the night with the moon and stars. . . .

—JAMES WELDON JOHNSON
"THE CREATION: A NEGRO SERMON"

Numerologically speaking, citrine is a 6.

On first contact, this stone invites rugged individualists to buy and wear it. The gem prefers those go-getters of the world who are confident, pioneering in some effort, who enjoy pushing back frontiers.

Citrine draws those who like their gemstones off the beaten path, something perhaps a bit flashy or large. It likes being worn in a thoughtfully designed setting that is imaginative, outreaching, and far from mundane. This gem favors someone of courage, someone strong willed and original. Its vibration is high for those who dare . . . in any way.

It is the birthstone of those with a sense of loyalty to humanity. It's a gem of unselfish energy, giving out lovingly and willingly to others. It vibrates well with any form of artistic expression. The emanations surrounding citrine are those of intense creativity and a flair for the original. Worn by the wrong person, citrine can make its wearer feel nervous and uneasy. On the right person, the gem provides brilliant flashes of insight for artistic perfection.

This gleaming yellow stone holds a high degree of emotionalism. In a crisis or trauma, even though the wearer may not be feeling particularly brave, she or he can draw a great deal of strength from this gem. Citrine will spread over its wearer a cloak of peace and stability.

✧

PHYSICAL PROPERTIES

Citrine, November's alternate birthstone, is a crystalline quartz gem of the general class known as smoky quartz. Probably through no wish of its own, this attractive stone has an identity problem. Very popular during Victorian times, it was then simply referred to as topaz. The Spanish label it *topacio falso*, almost as though the stone had been caught trying to assume some other personality. Sometimes it is dignified as golden quartz, but most often it has to answer to a great variety of other names, all ending with the word topaz. It is not topaz, it doesn't want to be topaz, it is tougher and more durable than topaz; it is a competent and lovely stone, proud to be just what it is: quartz.

Citrine is a French word, meaning lemon-colored. Strictly speaking then, citrines are yellow. They also have an internal structure peculiar to them, and when viewed from different angles will show two different colors. But there is no strongly held line of demarcation between citrine and smoky quartz, and so the name varies from one jeweler to another. Sometimes color alone decides what name shall be used. (Which brings us back full circle to the word topaz!)

But in practice, many of the citrines we see in jewelry stores began as some other color of smoky quartz, or even poorly colored amethysts, and, through heat-treating, their colors were permanently changed into the light and cheerful gemstones called citrine.

The crystals of citrine grow to large size, with flawless specimens frequently found. Much of the citrine used in jewelry today comes from Brazil.

The colors of smoky quartz shade from yellow to red-orange to a pleasant brown. Its shades all have the dreaminess of smoke-grey in them. This does not interfere with their transparency; it is a distinctive characteristic of this gemstone. When it is a sparrow brown or smoky yellow and comes from the Cairngorm Mountains in Scotland, it is called by the hauntingly beautiful name cairngorm.

There is also a black, a color that has proved undesirable for a gemstone. The smoky black stones are called morion. If subjected to high heat, morion becomes colorless; but at a moderate temperature it changes color to a luxurious brown. Surrounded with plentiful accents of yellow-gold, especially if the gemstone is good-sized, this makes a stunning jewel.

· · ·

✧
SHOPPING FOR CITRINES

If you like big gemstones, the quartz gems (of which citrine is only one) provide a wonderful array to choose from at reasonable prices. Citrine's browns, smoky browns, yellow-greens, orange-flushed yellows, and pure yellows are never precisely the same in any two gems. They do not have the velvety look of topaz, nor its pyroelectric properties, but they do have wonderful sparkle, brilliance, and depth of color.

As citrine dazzles equally well in natural or artificial light, it is highly suitable for evening wear. Imagine a big, cheerful sunny yellow citrine in a ring mounted with yellow gold and paired with a pendant citrine on a gold chain. Think of it against a white or cream-colored blouse for your business day and with dressier clothing for a night on the town.

Citrine set in gold bracelets, earrings, or a brooch will provide that extra look of elegance in any setting. The stones will usually be cut as oval brilliants or cushion brilliants, or in a modified step cut.

Citrine jewelry for men would probably be already mounted in rings or heavy and masculine-looking wrist chains. With this beautiful gemstone (for which synthetics are not manufactured) it's easy to choose well and be satisfied with your choice.

✧
CHARACTERISTICS AND ATTRIBUTES

The traditions of healing properties and the legends that apply to citrine have in the past been attributed to true topaz. But newly channeled information tells us more about this beautiful gemstone.

Citrine is associated with the angel Caneloas, a most holy angel invoked in magical rites.

Cairngorm is a gem belonging to autumn.

Worn as a gemstone, especially over the heart, citrine opens your being to the certainty of universal abundance. Citrine's is a transformative energy. It helps you establish your own belief system, which may include—or be independent of—familiar religious creeds or philosophical teachings.

The presence of citrine in a room where you work can lend you positive energies, strength, and clarity of purpose. As a meditational stone, citrine brings healing humor to outer or inner turmoil, enabling you to analyze the possible solutions and through this synthesize the answer you need.

Being able to look at citrine from time to time can promote calmness and stability. Frequently holding or handling a citrine enables you to distinguish the true inner messages from the false. It gives you strength to perform the actions that spiritual advancement demands, especially in cases where your own desires conflict with higher inner directives. There is a serenity in citrine which can be tapped into and made a part of your own strengths. Association with this quietly lovely stone will help you achieve balance, understanding, and peace of mind.

✦
HEALING MAGIC

As with all gemstones, citrine's vibrations may be passed on to a person either through wearing the stone; through Ayurvedic methods, Teletherapy, or Radionics; or by taking the elixir.

Here follows a partial list of the body organs or areas, physical and emotional maladies, and psychological ailments for which citrine elixir may be used.

Citrine, as we have stated, is associated with activating and clarifying the mental powers and turning negative thoughts to positive ones. Like topaz but perhaps not as strongly, it stimulates regeneration of the tissues. Citrine is powerful in treating blood poisoning resulting from massive infections such as appendicitis or gangrene. It is also effective in disorders of the immune system and intestinal upsets.

It works with the heart, kidneys, liver, and muscle system to bring new vitality to the body on the cellular level. It is a general strengthener.

Citrine works with the base, heart, and throat chakras, and the astral and emotional bodies, as well as the mental body.

Wear it anywhere on the physical body. Citrine elixir can be applied externally with an atomizer.

✧
CITRINE DREAMS

If you dream of a tree whose fruits are citrines, a situation that puzzles you will become clear. A large yellow citrine, held in the palm of the hand in a dream, indicates that one will know both peace and delight in newfound freedom.

A dream of a brown citrine, lying alone on a table, is a prediction that you'll learn something in a new way, which will permit you to forgive yourself for some action which is long past.

If someone gives you a citrine pendant in a dream, this person is asking for your trust. Give that trust, for as you believe, so shall it be for you. Dream of wearing a citrine on your finger or wrist, and it means you'll be able to release old narrow attitudes and adopt different ones which will light your way along a higher path.

✧
CITRINES THROUGH HISTORY

During the times of the Scottish clan wars, and the wars between England and Scotland, the Scots warriors always wore an amulet into battle. The practical Scotsmen even got multiple duty from their amulets. These were created in the form of a large brooch or pin. Not only were they expected to serve as protective devices, but they were also used at the shoulder to fasten the great piece of heavy wool fabric, called a plaid, which served Scots men and women as cape, robe, raincoat, and bedding.

The amulet/brooch was a jewel of value. It was made of silver, often set with stones or gems. A favored stone for this use was cairngorm, smoky quartz from the granitic Cairngorm Mountains in the eastern highlands of Scotland. If, despite the power of his amulet, a warrior's time should come to die, the person who found his body was expected to give him decent burial. Payment for this final service would be the brooch, performing its last duty to its owner.

BIRTHSTONE FOR DECEMBER

ZODIACAL STONE FOR

SAGITTARIUS

(November 23–December 21)

'Tis not the weight of jewel or plate
Or the fondle of silk and fur
'Tis the spirit in which the gift is rich,
As the gifts of the wise ones were;
And we are not told whose gift was gold
Or whose was the gift of myrrh.

—EDMUND VANCE COOKE
"THE SPIRIT OF THE GIFT"

Numerologically, turquoise is a 1, the number of beginnings, the number of power and pure will.

Initially, more women than men are enchanted by this gem. Men will like it only if they are highly sensitive and in touch with their emotions. There is a living warmth that exudes from this soft blue gemstone; and when it is held, it feels almost like soft velvet, appealing to the gentle core of the individual.

On a deeper level, those whose birthstone is turquoise, or those who purchase it, will be powerful in some way. Either in the present or in the future they will possess and exert control: over finances, over events, over people.

Turquoise enjoys those who are assertive, well directed, or independent thinkers. The gem's energy enhances a sturdy individualism, a confident will, and a pioneering spirit. It is a gem for the adventurous who enjoy wearing a bold stone in a distinctive setting.

✧

PHYSICAL PROPERTIES

We mostly think of turquoise as though it were only blue, waxy-smooth, and free from inclusions. Yet this most appealing of the opaque gemstones ranges from yellow-green to apple green to greenish blue to purest sky blue to darker sky blue. In Egypt, for example, in fourteenth-century Europe, and in some particular cultures even today, the greenish turquoise was the most favored. This may be more the result of the availability of a given color; that is, you've got green, you like green.

In Iran, where the national symbol is turquoise, a darker sky blue is most favored, without any of the accompanying matrix included. Medium quality there is sky blue to green-blue with little matrix. The lowest quality is poor in color and more plentiful in matrix. In the United States, while the pure turquoise is possibly more prized, the gem with part of its reticulated matrix is also appreciated for its greater appearance of liveliness and action.

The best form of matrix turquoise is called spider web, because the lines are thin and delicate, letting the color burst through. The stone seems stifled and overwhelmed when the matrix is heavy.

Turquoise has always been thought to be amorphous, that is to say forming in blobs. It occurs as veins, nodules, stalactite masses, and encrustations. But recently some turquoise was found in the United States in triclinic crystal forms.

All turquoise contains some water. It is the only phosphate gem; it will burn to powder. Because it is an extremely porous stone, its heavenly blue can become dingy and green-tinged through damage from dirt, soap, air, grease, liquids, or age.

At the turn of the twentieth century, it was a popular scam to dye ivory, or the teeth of fossil animals, with phosphate of iron, and sell the resulting product for turquoise. It was said that the color lasted well; however, as it was also said to be genuine turquoise, one might entertain doubts.

This gemstone seldom lies deeper than a hundred feet down into the earth. More frequently it is found either on or close to the surface. It forms in cracks and cavities in volcanic rocks, and is often found in weathered masses, talus debris, and sedimentary gravels.

Splendid sky-blue specimens come from Neyshābūr in Iran, and fabled Samarkand in Turkestan. Greener-hued stones come from Nevada and Los Arillos, New Mexico.

Traditional techniques for cutting turquoise were developed centuries ago in Persia, and are the same there today. The master cutter buys the rough stones from the mine owner. His apprentices work on the less valuable stones. Only the master cutter handles the finest quality, trimming them to their optimum size and shape and polishing them. A sixteenth-century writer related that the finest turquoise was polished with bamboo, and that the lesser qualities were polished with fine sand and then with "the polisher of turquoise.'' Whatever its shape, it must be cut cabochon, for the vaulting curve brings out its beauty.

The happy-looking turquoise enchances its setting, whether it be copper, silver, or gold; whether worn by a rosy-cheeked English girl, a brawny Navajo chief, or a plum-black African tribesman. In all its long history, it has been associated with the good in life.

✧

SHOPPING FOR TURQUOISE

It's easy to get fooled on turquoise, since the stone is porous and will accept dyes and wax readily. A ragamuffin specimen of this lovely stone can be dressed up to look like a fine lady, and it will only be after you know her a while that the truth leaks out. We suggest that you take the advice of a reputable jeweler when you're shopping for turquoise.

If you travel in the American Southwest, you'll find ample opportunities to buy handmade Indian jewelry—silver or copper set with turquoise. These pieces are exquisite—and often unique. The craftsman puts into each piece of jewelry his creative energies, his feelings for that particular day, the phase of the moon, and myriad other considerations that don't go into factory-assembled stuff. Indian jewelry is amuletic, so use that property to its greatest extent.

While most jewelry that you find in the West is handmade, some is not. The quickest way to tell is to look for symmetry. Any piece which is precisely symmetrical is probably not handmade. What you're checking for here is tiny details. Is the engraving almost but not quite exactly the same on each side? It's probably handmade. Are the tiny balls of silver in the mounting exactly the same size and placed on in exactly the same way? If they're not, it's probably handmade.

Turquoise jewelry is perfect for anyone, male or female, of any age. It is usually cut cabochon. For American tastes, it includes some of the matrix. Too much matrix gives a sad and heavy look to the stone. The finest matrix is delicate and understated.

· · ·

✧

CHARACTERISTICS AND ATTRIBUTES

Turquoise, the sky-blue birthstone for December, engenders wisdom and brings greater depth to understanding. Those wearing turquoise will know nature and the earth; they will be the ones who can be depended on in times of need. A closeness forms between the turquoise and the wearer, opening up the wearer to the simple yet intrinsic truths of life.

It is a stone of great vitality, one that helps to bring the physical body into balance. Meditation upon turquoise can soothe and calm the inner person.

For centuries the usual virtues ascribed to blue stones were also attributed to this one. But in the thirteenth century, through association with the Turks, it became known as *Turkis* and was then Frenchified into *turquoise*. From the Turks came a new and unique capability, that of preventing its wearer from injuries in falls. This protection especially applied to falls from an animal while riding. Later the stone came to grant equal protection against falls from a building or a precipice, or even from having a building or wall fall on the wearer.

This is a stone that has the capability of securing cordial regard. Wear turquoise and your friends will always stand by you. It protects the innocent; it is a pledge of true affection. Further, by cheering the soul, it conciliates quarrels and restores broken relationships.

A seventeenth-century authority on the curative and healing powers of gemstones states that for the promptest effect, the turquoise should be worn on the hand, either the index finger or the little finger. Suspended by a string within a glass, turquoise will tell the hour by the number of strokes against the glass.

It is a gem of Persia, of winter, of the planets Jupiter, Venus and Mercury. It is the stone for Saturday, and the talismanic gem for Wednesday. It is the eleventh stone on the breastplate of the first High Priest of the Jews. Its best hour is five in the morning, when the sky needs the gem's blueness.

Turquoise is the gemstone associated with the angel Verchiel. He is one of the rulers of the order of Powers. Verchiel is angel of July, ruler of the zodiacal sign Leo. He is governor of the sun.

Turquoise is always on your side; but it works better for you if you receive it as a gift rather than purchase it. The story is told of a seventeenth-century man who always wore a stunningly beautiful turquoise ring. It was at its height of color when he was in best health; but when he felt ill, the stone paled with him. Upon his death, the color left the stone altogether. A friend who had known him all his life purchased the ring despite the sad change in its appearance.

The purchaser gave his son the turquoise, asking him to wear it so that they could see if it were true that the giving of the stone could revitalize it. The son was Anselmus de Boot, court physician to Emperor Rudolph II of Bohemia. Not caring for the look of the stone in its poor state, he had it engraved as a signet and began wearing it. Within a few weeks the turquoise had regained its former high color and luster.

The many powers of gemstones were common knowledge in earlier days. Charles V of France asked his court jester what was the property of the turquoise, and the jester, slyly mangling the belief, replied, "Why, if you should happen to fall from a high tower whilst you were wearing a turquoise on your finger, the turquoise would remain unbroken."

De Boot related an incident involving the turquoise his father had given him, which served to prove the belief. While de Boot was traveling at night, his horse stumbled and threw him. Neither man nor horse was hurt. But next morning de Boot observed that his turquoise ring, taking the injury upon itself, had a quarter of it broken off.

✧

HEALING MAGIC

As with all gemstones, turquoise's vibrations may be passed on to a person either through wearing the stone; through Ayurvedic methods, Teletherapy, or Radionics; or by taking the elixir.

Here follows a partial list of the body organs or areas, physical and emotional maladies, and psychological ailments for which turquoise elixir may be used.

Turquoise is a profound master healer. The blues and greens of the stone are master enhancers in the color spectrum. Turquoise strengthens the entire anatomy, stimulates overall tissue regeneration, and is an aid in all diseases. It strengthens and aligns all the chakras, body meridians, force lines, and subtle bodies. It improves the absorption of nutrients and increases circulation. Working with the subtle bodies, it promotes higher consciousness.

Turquoise is helpful in anorexia or bulimia, and in detoxifying the body of harmful substances, either taken into the body or manufactured by it. It treats eye problems, the nasal passages, and the mucous membranes.

The wearing of turquoise (such as on the bridle) strengthens work animals. It protects against environmental pollutants, and improves meditation. Those who are naturally peaceable will find that turquoise works with them readily, providing great energies and a new and welcome sense of purpose and balance.

Especially when muscular tissue is involved, such as torn tendons or ligaments, or when the muscles are stressed, infected, or suffer lack of oxygen, turquoise improves the circulation in these tissues.

This master healing gemstone can be worn anywhere on the body; the area near the stone automatically improves. It is especially effective when worn in a ring or set in silver in a bracelet worn on the left arm.

Turquoise elixir can be used in the bath, or externally (combined with oils) as an ointment.

✧

DREAMS OF TURQUOISE

If you dream of a display of American Indian jewelry set with turquoise, it indicates that you'll come to a clearer understanding in an important relationship. If you are allowed to choose one of the pieces for your own, it signifies that an inner purification will bring healing to yourself or someone dear.

Dreaming of an oval turquoise set in silver means that you are capable and willing in a job situation. A cut and polished turquoise of deep blue stands for the positive energies that you set free in others through your grasp of their problems.

A turquoise pendant, worn over someone's heart in a dream, shows that that person has great self-confidence.

✧
TURQUOISE THROUGH HISTORY

Turquoise has been used in jewelry for at least seventy-five hundred years. The Chaldeans called it *torkeja*. Probably the world's oldest known turquoise jewelry is a set of four turquoise and gold bracelets made seventy-five hundred years ago for Queen Zer of the First Egyptian Dynasty.

Early Egyptian goldsmith-jewelers set it into household ornaments and even chariots. They wrought gold and turquoise into falcons, lotus blossoms, deities, and scarabs, to exert magic for the wearer.

In the Egyptian Museum in Cairo is a gorget from the tomb of Tutankhamen, who reigned in Egypt around 1358 B.C. This amuletic neck ornament, shaped like a vulture with upspread wings, is the symbol of the goddess Nekhebet. Intricately crafted, the jewel is made of gold, turquoise, and other precious stones in a fantastic design of gold and red and blue. In the body alone the author was able to count sixty-seven pieces of turquoise, each one shaped exactly to fit its space.

The Aztecs had a type of turquoise they called *teuxivitl*, which meant turquoise of the gods. These were extremely fine, clear stones, of which there was a limited number. They had been brought from some distant land. Some specimens appeared to be half-spheres; others were flat. No one was permitted to wear these stones, for they had been dedicated to the gods.

Tibetans, Persians, and Turks attached turquoise to their horses' bridles, for they believed that the stones not only made their mounts more sure-footed, but also protected them from the ill effects of drinking cold water when overheated from exertion.

In the Far East, turquoise is frequently engraved with inscriptions from the Koran, in Persian or Arabic, then the lettering is filled with gold. These jewels are used in amulets.

In A.D. 410, while Alaric and his Visigoths were sacking Rome, the Pueblo Indians of the American Southwest were mining turquoise. Turquoise beads, dating from A.D. 900–1100, were found in the excavations of Pueblo Bonito, New Mexico. This sacred stone appears in many American Indian legends.

In a Navajo sand painting of their religious ceremonies in the early twentieth century, the four rain-making gods are shown wearing turquoise and coral necklaces. The four gods represent the cardinal points of east, south, west, and north. From the right wrist of each god was suspended a tobacco pouch decorated with the representation of a stone pipe. The Navajos believed that within this pouch the god places a ray of sunlight with which to light his pipe. When he smokes, clouds form in the sky and it rains.

Another Navajo sand painting, the God of the Whirlwind, shows this deity wearing turquoise ear pendants and necklace. The Navajos—who also have mined turquoise on and off for centuries— wear it in quantity.

Turquoise occurs only in extremely dry climates. The oldest known turquoise mines in the world were in the rugged, extraordinary colorful Sinai Peninsula, which forms the border between Palestine and Egypt. Haroeris, a military captain, led an expedition for Amenemhet II into the Sinai to search for turquoise—in the twentieth century before Christ. He and his train endured blast-furnace heat for months, searching the dry sandy ground, and questioning natives. At last, in Serabit el-Khadem, two-thousand feet above sea level in the granite mountains whose peaks rose eight-thousand feet, Haroeris found "turquoise for eternity."

The mines were guarded by Egyptian soldiers, controlled by the Egyptian kings. Soon there were more than two-thousand laborers, mostly Semitic captives or slaves in bondage, in the Sinai turquoise mines. Heavy traffic began on the route out of the mountains back toward civilization, for in the same locality were found additional natural resources—copper and malachite, peridot and other precious stones. Today the peninsula is yielding oil and manganese.

Judging by the surviving jewelry from that area, the turquoise found there was on the green side, and spotty. Yet during the Third Egyptian Dynasty, the Twelfth Dynasty, the Eighteenth Dynasty and the Nineteenth, all of which were several centuries before Christ, these mines yielded turquoise for jewelry, amulets, ornamented palace furnishings, and funerary jewelry.

After 1100 B.C. there were no traces of further work in the Sinai mines, until they were rediscovered by a Major McDonald in 1845.

A bit after the original opening of the Sinai mines, in the Kuh-i-Binalud Mountains northwest of then Nishapur in Persia, deposits discovered were of stunningly beautiful light-blue to medium-blue turquoises with a fine waxy luster. As early as the thirteenth century, the gemstone was sold by Turkish merchants. The French called it *pierre turquoise*, stone of the Turks, whence came the name we use today. Now it is found in Turkestan, Arabia, Australia, South Africa, Arizona, Nevada, New Mexico, and California. Just recently turquoise has been found in northeast Tanzania.

The mines near Neyshābūr, Iran (formerly Persia), have been worked for several thousand years. As had been the case throughout the millennia, the most beautiful turquoises available today are still coming from that area. The Persian word for the gem is *ferozah*, meaning victorious. And indeed it is.

Jean Baptiste Tavernier, the traveler and gem dealer, visited the Persian mines in 1661. He reported that turquoise was found only in Persia, where there were two mines, the Old Rock and the New. The Old Rock (the mine near Neyshābūr) produced the most beautiful stones, which the king of Persia reserved only for himself. At the New Rock, five days' travel from the Old, the stones were more greenish blue, shading to white. These stones could be bought at trifling cost.

Surviving examples of Islamic rings containing gems from the old and the new mines show that the old mine turquoise, taken from the ground in the eleventh century, was much deeper blue than the new mine material, which was dug in the twelfth.

Turquoise has been used in jewelry throughout all periods of history. The Aztecs wore it; so did the Incas. It was important in Biblical times. It is recorded that turquoise was being used in jewelry five centuries before Christ. An inscription at Susa, dating from the time of Darius I (fifth century B.C.), refers to this splendid gemstone. Other writings of the ninth and tenth centuries also speak of turquoise mines.

In 1604 Boris Godunov, Tsar of Russia, received a present from the powerful Persian Shah Abbas: a throne set with turquoise, rubies, and pearls. There were 824 turquoises of good size, plus one that was enormous. Of rubies there were 552, and 127 pearls. Among the Russian crown jewels is a lovely diadem made of fine Persian turquoises surrounded with major diamonds. Napoleon's empress, Josephine, had an entire parure of turquoises and diamonds.

The apple-green shade of turquoise was popular in the fourteenth century. During the late Georgian and the Edwardian periods, the gem was set with diamonds, in tiaras or necklaces. Turquoise was popularly used with coral in the 1920s; and today it is often seen, set in silver, in the company of carnelian and mother of pearl.

Among American Indian tribes of the Southwest where the gemstone occurs, turquoise has traditional significance. The Zuni, the Navajo, and the Hopi Indians are three of the tribes who use it themselves and make jewelry for non-Indians to wear. The Navajo jewelry is energetically styled, the silver mounting fitted around the stone to emphasize the gem's beauty. The Zuni work is much more delicate, with the turquoise cut to fit into the silver mounting. The Zunis say that their craftsmen can work an entire lifetime with only the scraps left by the Navajos.

With both, the turquoise jewelry represents the expression of the wearer's soul. The designs are ancient. Much of the jewelry has amuletic symbolism.

In Chaco Canyon, New Mexico, in 1897, an archaeological expedition found more than fifty-thousand turquoise objects—mosaic pendants, beads, carved birds. Pots at the site were dated, and from that it has been concluded that the turquoise artifacts were made in the period A.D. 950–1150.

ALTERNATE BIRTHSTONE FOR DECEMBER

◇

Zircon

ALTERNATE ZODIACAL STONE FOR

SAGITTARIUS

(November 23–December 21)

*Good name in man and woman, dear mylord,
Is the immediate jewel of their souls.*

—WILLIAM SHAKESPEARE
OTHELLO, III. iii.

Zircon is a numeral 4.

Zircon will attract primarily the connoisseur who appreciates the beauty and honesty of the stone for what it is. Its brilliance rivals that of diamond and, because of this, can be passed off as diamond by a nonreputable dealer; the consonant number 7 warns that fakery can take place.*

If zircon is your birthstone, it will have a mystical allure for you. There is peace and harmony within the stone, peace and harmony within your inner being. The vibrations of the stone respond to your unselfishness, your need to be of service in the world.

This is a gemstone for a calm, passive individual, not one with a flamboyant personality.

Zircon's aura is one of a grounding of energies, helping the wearer remain organized and consistent, and emphasizing his or her integrity. Zircon, its energy steady and unwavering, will stabilize the personality.

✧

PHYSICAL PROPERTIES

The alternate birthstone for December is zircon. Zircon (from the mineral zirconium silicate) has four extra names: jacinth (hyacinth) and jargon (jargoon). The word zircon comes from the Persian *zargoon*, meaning gold-colored; or the Arabic *zarquin*,

---

* For explanation of consonant numbers, see introductory section "The Importance of Numerology."

meaning vermilion. Commonly *jacinth* refers to the reddish and brownish varieties; *jargon* refers to the white, honey-colored, or smoky stones. A colorless zircon that crops up near Matara, Sri Lanka, is called a Matara diamond. The brown zircon sometimes goes by the name malacon.

In nature zircons occur in colorless to yellow, red, orange, reddish brown, yellow green to darkish green, and—rarely—blue or violet. The most wanted gem zircons are the colorless, the golden brown, and the sky blue. These colors are achieved through heat-treating red-brown stones for up to two hours. When the stones are heated at almost 1,800 degrees Fahrenheit in a vacuum, the result is blue or colorless gems. The bright blues are sometimes called starlites. The blue in particular becomes clear and lively, surpassing the natural in color and fire.

If oxygen is sent through the crucible while the stones are heating, they become colorless, red, or golden yellow. The color remains stable in most of the treated stones; however, after a time the blues may become paler and the whites may take on green or amber tinges.

Natural zircon also may fade or cloud with the passage of time. The reason for this is that zircon contains small amounts of the radioactive elements uranium and thorium; and heat or light may act on these elements.

In Thailand the stones are heated in a crude charcoal oven or in a ball of fireclay, the proper temperatures being achieved by experience, or possibly by divination. Even when the procedure is approached more scientifically, the stones have minds of their own. Some turn out gray and yucky, some crackle beyond redemption— and some are glorious blue or golden or clear.

When being cut on the cutting wheel, many zircons fluoresce with a brilliant orange light. Their hardness may be as low as 6 or as high as 7½ on the Mohs' scale. They possess a high adamantine (diamondlike) luster and a vibrant fire.

The brilliance of zircon (the sparkle, the glitter, the amount of light reflected back from the stone) is exceeded only by that of diamond. When well cut, the transparent zircon blazes with warm light.

Zircon is brittle; after long wear, the cut stones will chip on the facet edges. In shipping cut zircons, each one is packed in a separate paper to avoid possible scratching or chipping damage, called paper wear.

Zircon is found in all kinds of rocks and deposits throughout the world. The richest sources are alluvial deposits in Sri Lanka, Burma, Thailand, Kampuchea, Laos, and Vietnam; and gold gravels in the USSR. No matter where they occur, zircons are always in the company of other precious stones.

Those found in Sri Lanka have the most breathtaking range of colors. Blue does not occur there, but it does in the Mogok Valley in Burma, where there are also red, brown, and green. In Laos, Thailand, and Vietnam the brown, reddish brown, and yellow gemstones are mined.

It is zircon which makes it possible to determine the age of a gemstone deposit. The thorium or uranium in the stones bombards the atomic structure of the crystal, which then collapses into a blob of zirconia and silica. The zircons become greenish and cloudy. Other physical changes occur, including the alteration of the two radioactive elements to lead. By measuring the remaining amounts of uranium and thorium against that of lead, the age of the zircon and its deposit may be calculated. In this way it has been determined that the gem gravels of Sri Lanka are about 550 million years old.

✧

SHOPPING FOR ZIRCONS

The most striking characteristics of zircon are its fire and brilliance. You may set out wanting a colorless zircon because most people will think it is a diamond; but once you see the colors and their radiance, you could change your mind. This brilliant gemstone (or, say, a group of small ones artfully mounted) would make a dazzling cocktail ring. Imagine your stone or stones dramatically mounted in earrings, a pin or brooch, or in a bracelet.

Need an extraordinary gift for that special man in your life? Why not a zircon set in a little-finger ring?

With this gem, it is advisable to consult a reputable jeweler. If you buy the stone and then have it mounted, your jeweler will be able to give you an appraisal. This will include the stone's cutting pattern and carat weight, plus similar information on any additional stones in the mounting; the type of metal in the mounting; and the value of the entire piece when it is completed.

✧

CHARACTERISTICS AND ATTRIBUTES

The violet or purple jacinth is an emblem of royal stateliness. It symbolized Simon Zelotes, the Zealot; also "the celestial rapture of the learned and their high thoughts and their humble descent to human things out of regard for the weak." Jacinth is the seventh stone in Aaron's breastplate, the eleventh stone in the foundation of the Holy City.

Zircon in Sanskrit is *gomeda*. In Burmese it is *gomok*; in Canton Chinese it is *pi-si*. The Arabic word for zircon is *hajar yamani*.

One of the Sanskrit words for hyacinth is *rahuratna*, meaning that the gem was dedicated to the dragon who caused eclipses of the sun and of the moon. Because the stone was sacred to this malevolent entity of great power, it was believed to intervene to avert the wearer's misfortune, in a case of the major evil overcoming the minor.

Jacinth is one of the precious gemstones in the *naoratna*, the Hindu nine-gem jewel combining all the powerful astrological influences. The jacinth is placed in the position of the southwest, Rahu.

The wonderful glowing Kalpa Tree, the symbolic Hindu offering to the gods, was created entirely of precious gems. Zircons and coral made its foliage.

Zircon is a serene stone that enables man to be at peace with himself. It is helpful in healing the spirit. Individuals of a quiet nature will readily relate to zircon and be able to use it to restore inner balance.

Paradoxically, jacinth stands for the adolescent period of growth, that wide-eyed and inconsistent time when we are most vulnerable to internal and external influences, and would most need the gemstone's calming capability.

Zircon, worn during the times when Mercury is retrograde, counteracts the negative effects of that planet.

Zircon is a gem of summer; the talismanic stone of Tsuriel, the guardian angel of September. Tsuriel, "my rock is God," is a prince of the order of Principalities. He is ruler of the zodiacal sign Libra; one of seventy childbed amulet angels; he cures stupidity.

As jacinth, zircon is at its best at one in the afternoon. The Chaldeans associated it with the planet Jupiter. It is influenced by the fixed star Shoulder of Equus Major at 18 degrees Pisces. Of the Seven Heavens of Mohammedanism, the sixth was made of jacinth.

✧

HEALING MAGIC

The following procedure in the use of the jacinth was recommended in the twelfth century by Saint Hildegard, the Abbess of Bingen: "If anyone is bewitched by phantoms or by magical spells, so that he has lost his wits, take a hot loaf of pure wheaten bread and cut the upper crust in the form of a cross—not, however, cutting it quite through—and then pass the stone along the cutting, reciting these words: 'May God, who cast away all precious stones from the devil . . . cast away from thee, [name], all phantoms and all magic spells, and free thee from the pain of this madness.' "

The patient was then to eat of the bread. All other solid food given to the sick person was to be treated similarly.

To relieve a pain in one's heart, the sign of the cross should be made over the heart with a jacinth while the above prayer is recited.

A jacinth was also used as an aid to slumber, although one sixteenth-century owner of a large jacinth complained that his didn't help him much.

In 1602 a recipe was published for "the most noble electuary of jacinth." An electuary was a pasty mess containing honey or syrup and combined with gemstones and other ingredients, to be used medicinally. This one consisted of jacinth, sapphire, pearl, ruby, emerald, topaz, garnet, amber, white and red coral, plus animal and vegetable substances—a total of thirty-four ingredients.

Another remedy, this one for fevers, combined powdered jacinth with an equal quantity of "poppy syrup," or laudanum. In this case, modern patients who have never tried powdered-gemstone mixtures might feel that laudanum was the thingamabob that did the job.

As with all gemstones, zircon's vibrations may be passed on to a person either through wearing the stone; through Ayurvedic methods, Teletherapy, Radionics; or by taking the elixir.

Here follows a partial list of the body organs or areas, physical and emotional maladies, and psychological ailments for which zircon elixir may be used.

Zircon opens and balances the pineal and pituitary glands on the physical level, realigning the astral, emotional, and spiritual bodies. It is very helpful in instilling caution, in dealing with guilt or insomnia, or in getting the temper under control.

Zircon treats disorders of the liver and the metabolism. It raises the consciousness and increases psychic abilities. It works through the base and brow chakras, and helps to clarify visions.

The elixir of zircon can be taken in the usual doses of three to seven drops, three to four times daily, for two weeks on, one week off; or it can be used in the bath.

✦

ZIRCON DREAMS

If you dream of a jewel case full of zircon jewelry, it means that you're a loving, romantic person who needs to float back down to earth now and then. If someone gives you a zircon in a dream, it's a prediction that a recently started venture will work out well. You may suffer initial losses, but time will show you how the gains outweigh them.

A beautiful room decorated with zircon indicates that a handsome, well-known professional man will open new doors for you. You and he may have friendship ties that go back several years—or lives.

If you dream of buying a zircon, it's saying that a successful career in management lies ahead of you. Dreams of wearing a zircon anywhere on the body means that you'll travel for pleasure, and at the end of the journey one who loves you waits for you.

✦

ZIRCON THROUGH HISTORY

Zircon as a gemstone has been known longer than Christianity. Theophrastus, one of Aristotle's pupils, described it accurately in the fourth century B.C. Four centuries later, in Pliny's *Natural History*, the amber-colored stones were called *lyncurium*, or lynx-stones. Pliny explained that the stones had been formed from the urine of lynxes. Perhaps he got this notion from Sophocles, who postulated that amber originated in the tears of grief shed by certain birds upon the death of Jesus.

In the earlier Hellenistic period (ca. 300 to 100 B.C.) gold signet rings began to incorporate stones. The favorite stone of that time was jacinth, cut in a high convex shape to accentuate the clear, sparkling, ruddy hues.

Zircon is the gemstone belonging to Diana, Roman goddess of chastity, hunting, and the moon. It was believed to prevent the plague and other dreadful diseases. Gazing on zircon was a remedy for insomnia. In Catholic tradition, the stone is a symbol of humility. In the heyday of the Greeks and Romans it was a favorite gemstone.

Jacinth in ancient times was recommended as an amulet for travelers because it guaranteed the wearer a cordial reception at any hostelry he chanced upon. One who wore a jacinth could expect business matters to go his way, and to be rewarded thereby with riches. The stone was protective against poisons, wounds, injuries, and wasting diseases. It was especially powerful against being struck by lightning. Jacinth was said to grow pale and dull as a warning if the wearer or anyone near him became ill of the plague.

Giacinto Gimma, in 1730, said that when worn by men, the yellow jacinth denotes secrecy. Worn by a woman, it indicated generosity. It is symbolic of Sunday, of grandeur and nobility. This jewel of the sun bestows kingly dignity. It also rejoices and calms the eyes and the heart. Its accompanying animal is the king of beasts, the lion.

Magic
in
Other Gems

Besides the officially designated birthstones and zodiacal stones, there are many other gems that are fascinating simply as themselves. Those which have been known as gemstones for centuries have all sorts of legends told about them, and magical properties attributed to them. These properties and legends cannot spring up overnight, but rather, like the life of a saint, must be lived and evaluated before being thought worthy of the mantle of greatness.

One gem that is not now on any special list, but has been revered and used for six thousand years, is lapis lazuli, a deep blue opaque stone with golden-veined inclusions. Another is kunzite, discovered only a hundred years ago and too young to have many traditions formed about it. However, valuable information, presented here, regarding its properties and capabilities has been channeled psychically.

Amber, jet, and coral have also been worn and loved for centuries, though they aren't fashionable at present. Jade and carnelian have their illustrious history. Spinel has unintentionally operated behind a mask most of its long career. One of the most recent gemstone discoveries is tanzanite, found, as you might guess, in Tanzania only twenty-one years ago.

All these stones have something to recommend them as jewelry, amulets, or talismans. The magical qualities of some gems are largely untapped; the most that can be said of them is that they are beautiful, which is a magic that's uncommon enough for most of us.

✧

AMBER

The most fascinating thing about amber is not merely its great antiquity, but its insect and plant inclusions which are of another world long ago and far away. A bit of wing from an extinct butterfly, mosquitoes from the nearby swamp, ants, flies caught copulating and forever stuck in position, bubbles of air, needles fallen from the parent tree—all are captured in amber, an exact journal of climate and flora and fauna; and all are the subject of scientific curiosity and study.

Though it is used as a gem material, amber is not a mineral but a fossilized resin. It forms in globs and is soft, light, and fairly fragile. It floats on water. When burned, amber gives off a strong smell like incense. When fractured, amber splinters. Unlike jade, it is easy to carve. Its colors are an orange-yellow to dark brown; occasionally pieces will be violet, green, or black.

Amber was recovered from the sea at low tide by men and women who used spears as crowbars to pry the boulders loose from the sea floor. They scooped it up in nets. The boulders were then cut with a bow drill.

Amber also occurred in Rumania, Sicily, Burma, and Persia. The Rumanian materials tends toward a translucent yellow and brown. Sicilian amber occurs in reddish brown, greenish, and sometimes blue; it fluoresces intensely in sunlight. Amber from Burma tends to be honey brown or a much-sought-after red. Persian amber is orange-brown and opaque. A charcoal-brown amber comes today from the Dominican Republic.

Theories of the origin of amber include the belief that it was the tears of a sea bird, or was exuded from the summer earth, or that it was honey melted by the sun and solidified by the sea. Another proposition was that it was the petrified urine of a lynx, dark for male and light for female. Perhaps the loveliest tradition is the Greek one that amber formed from the tears that the Electrides shed for the death of their brother Phaëthon. These sisters were turned into poplar trees, which continued to shed tears that became amber.

Pliny recorded the use of amber necklaces on children to protect them from sorcery. The Shah of Persia possessed a cube of amber traditionally believed to have fallen from the sky in the time of Mohammed, which when worn around his neck, kept him safe from injury. Amber is the gem of the sun.

A dream of finding amber indicates that a promise will be kept.

To give or receive this in a dream is a prediction of an unexpected financial windfall, or recovery of a loss.

In other times, it was believed to drive away adders. Medicinally it was used to treat asthma and edema. For a "falling fundament" (hemorrhoids?) the sufferer was advised to put live charcoal in a chamber pot, scattering bits of amber into the coals, and sit over this to receive the fumes. Amber mixed with honey and rose oil was a cure for deafness. Mixed only with honey from Attica, it brightened eyesight.

Amber elixir amplifies thoughts and spiritualizes the intellect. It strengthens the thyroid, inner ear, and neurological tissue.

The Etruscans of the sixth century B.C. were fascinated with death and life after death. In their tombs has been found costly amber tomb jewelry for both men and women. To these people amber, which was ancient even to them, proved that life did indeed exist after death. They imported the gentle gem from the Baltic Sea, over two-thousand miles away, and carved out beads for funerary jewelry. (As Baltic amber has a particular chemical composition, it was archaeologically identified.) The so-called Amber Road, from the Baltic to Rome, was an important early trade route, with the Romans bartering manufactured goods for amber boulders.

Nero, Emperor of Rome, loved amber because it was the color of his wife's hair. And because the ladies of his court colored their hair to suit him, there were a lot of other amber-haired Roman women around.

Genuine amber was, up to perhaps World War II, used as mouthpieces for tobacco pipes. In India the pipe was lit by a servant, who had to put the mouthpiece in his mouth. Amber was deemed incapable of transmitting infection from servant to master.

After the death of Queen Victoria's Prince Albert, amber was popular for memorial jewelry. There was not enough of the gem material to go around, so substitutes were provided, including copal, a look-alike resin. During this period before 1900, plastics were invented mainly to simulate amber; then other uses were discovered for the new invention.

· · ·

✧
ANDALUSITE AND CHIASTOLITE

Andalusite grows in stubby square-sectioned crystals, in colors from flesh red to brown, red, or dark olive green. One variety of this stone, chiastolite, grows a fine inclusion in the shape of a cross, so the stone is used as an amulet. Chiastolite, if worn touching the skin, is said to stanch the flow of blood from any part of the body. In nursing mothers the stone increases the flow of milk. It also drives away evil spirits, and cures fevers. The transparent andalusite crystals, used as gemstones, are admired for their pink-green iridescence.

Andalusite is a talismanic gemstone for the names Adelaide and Adrian.

✧
BENITOITE

Benitoite was first discovered in 1907, in San Benito, California, still the only place where it is found. It has the quality of fluorescing under ultraviolet light. Because of its blues and violets, the gem was at first thought to be sapphire. Its crystals of various shades of blue look like tiny flat gift boxes. The deep sapphire-blue stones are used in rings and other jewelry.

✧
CARNELIAN, GEM OF THE BIBLE

Carnelian has had a busy career. It was the sixth Foundation Stone of the New Jerusalem, and the gemstone of Philip, the special apostle for April. It has been the birthstone for May, July, and August; and the zodiacal stone for Virgo. It was the first stone in the breastplate of the Second Temple. It is the gemstone for Thursday, and for Norway and Sweden. It has been attributed to the planets Jupiter, Mars, and Venus.

Carnelian is a chalcedony, opaque, whose colors range from a rich clear red to a brownish red. Because wax will not stick to it, it was used for seals and signets in early times. It was popular among the ancient Egyptians for beads and amulets. The wearing of carnelian is especially beneficial for those who have a weak voice, as the red stone has an enlivening effect.

Engraved with a man richly dressed and holding in his hand a beautiful object, carnelian stanches the flow of blood and bestows honors. Bearing the image of a man with a sword in his hand, carnelian preserves the homestead from lightning and storm, and guards its wearer from "the evil of the envious." To women in childbirth, it keeps the birth going but also brings comfort from pain. It brings cheer, good luck, and courage to men.

Among the Jews and Arabs it was an important preventive of illness, particularly the plague. It defends against poisons. Powdered and drunk in a potion, carnelian was powerful as a homeopathic remedy to stop the flow of blood. Carried or worn, it restrains anger, expels fear, and prevents injury from falls.

If you dream you are polishing a carnelian, you will become rich through your own intellectual efforts. If you dream of someone wearing a carnelian, it indicates a person of unconquerable spirit.

In healing, carnelian is useful in raising the level of vitality. It causes a divine restlessness, a searching for the things of intrinsic importance.

Among Mohammedans carnelian is popular as a talisman. It is said that Mohammed wore, on the little finger of his right hand, a silver ring set with a carnelian engraved for use as a seal.

In early Christian times carnelian was also a popular talismanic stone. Christians at first dared not reveal themselves for fear of persecution; but they wanted some object that would declare their faith to fellow believers. Certain symbols, such as the ship, the fish, the palm branch, the hand and cross, and the wheel cross, were engraved on carnelian and other gemstones and, even after Christianity was established, worn as symbols of belief in Christ.

✧

CORAL

Corals are found in all the warm shallow seas, particularly the Mediterranean. Coral is the skeleton of sea animals which are similar to sea anemones and jellyfish. These animals cling together in colonies to form reefs. There are numerous varieties of coral, which have differing skeletal forms and colors. Precious coral, whose colors range from flesh white to deep red, grows in branchlike masses up to a half-inch in diameter.

Probably ever since its discovery, coral has been used in medicine and magic. Since Roman times, it has been worn by children to protect them from the Evil Eye and witchcraft. It is worn as an amulet against sterility. It is used for rosaries, and as beads it is made into necklaces and bracelets.

The Gauls used coral as ornament on their helmets and weapons. Engraved with certain Latin words mentioning Hecate, coral will preserve the individual from thunderbolts, lightning, poison, and defeat in battle. Bound to the masthead of a ship with the skin of a seal, coral will avert wind and tempests. Wearing coral counteracts the negative effects of the planet Mars retrograde.

In ancient times it was used against skin troubles, sore eyes, and tuberculosis (called blood-spitting then). The Japanese made a tincture of red coral, which was taken as a syrup to cleanse the blood.

The method of preparing coral was to grind it in an iron mortar to a fine powder, then add rosewater drop by drop, forming the mixture into balls for use. In 1696 this was a specific remedy for whooping cough and croup. It was said also to "restore the decays of nature."

If you dream of seeing coral growing, it means that you'll take a journey by water. Should you dream of owning coral jewelry, it's a sign of the loveliness and beauty you put into your everyday life.

It has long been esteemed in India as a substance endowed with occult and medicinal properties. In Gem Therapy, coral is the single gem used to treat the curses of the digestive process: colic, gallstones, hemorrhoids, hepatitis, and jaundice. It is also considered effective against warts.

Coral elixir strengthens the heart and circulatory system. It acts to halt senility and aids concentration. It balances the entire character.

A portrait of the Maharani of Sikkim, painted in 1908, shows her wearing many jewels, including a gold ring set with coral, a large crown set with pearls, turquoise, and coral, and a triple bracelet of coral. A book written in Sanskrit describes a ring in which the nine most precious gemstones have been set. They are diamond, ruby, cat's-eye, pearl, zircon, emerald, topaz, sapphire, and coral.

✧

HEMATITE

Hematite is a red oxide of iron, which shows a red streak; the name comes from the word *haima*, meaning blood. Red or black hematite is used for intaglio-cut settings for rings and necklaces. The black has a subtle steely-green iridescence. Around 60 B.C., Azchalias of Babylon wrote that the wearer of a talisman of hematite could expect an advantageous outcome of lawsuits and judgments, and that kings hearing his petition would rule in his favor. On the battlefield, warriors who rubbed themselves all over with a hematite stone were invulnerable.

If you dream of a polished hematite, it means that you will have the power to see yourself objectively, without distortion. A ring set with a hematite predicts a promotion or achievement in some vital area of your life.

Hematite elixir treats all blood disorders and cleanses the kidneys.

✧

JADE

Jade is actually two unrelated minerals, jadeite and nephrite, spoken of as one. Jadeite occurs in a soft mauve, gray, a happy orange hue, and green, of which only one shade is called spinach jade.

To connoisseurs, the finest shade of jade is imperial green, the true green of emerald, with a touch-me texture so deep that one's finger ought to sink into it. Imperial green was named for the last empress of China, whose collection of this particular color jade numbered in the hundreds of thousands of pieces.

Nephrite, which is $6\frac{1}{2}$ as compared with jadeite's 7, on the Mohs scale, is just as tough and desirable. Its most precious color—particularly appreciated in the Orient—is mutton fat, a creamy white shading to beige in its creases. It also occurs in dark gray, yellow, and black. All jade is apt to be a bit mottled: perhaps a pale green with drifts of mauve, or white with light green streamers.

To the Chinese, jade embodies the five cardinal virtues: charity, modesty, courage, justice, and wisdom. Contemplation of jade will bring to mind the best attainments of humanity. In its smoothness there is suggested benevolence; in its polish, knowledge; in the stone's firmness, righteousness; its harmlessness suggests virtuous action. In the spotlessness of jade, purity is implied; in its imperishable character is endurance; in its revelation of its own flaws, frankness. Its ability to be passed from hand to hand without being sullied suggests moral conduct; when struck, it rings, suggesting music.

Jade has the quality of being able to sound the depth of a problem and to bring tranquillity to it. It is a warm, tender stone that soothes the one gazing on it or holding it. Its greens speak to the emotions, purifying them. Lavender jade is helpful in healing mental problems. Red jade rouses anger and clarifies the source so that answers will be found. The mauve jade has a delicate vibration, subtle and spiritual in its nature and development. Jade helps one draw strength and resources from past lives.

Dreams of green jade point out a need for more quiet and time alone in your busy life. If you dream of white jade it signifies that something you thought worthless will prove of unusual value. Red jade in a dream stands for a problem that is very troublesome at this time; the answer to it will be found through a cooperative endeavor.

Indians during the Spanish Conquest used it for all disorders of the kidney, including kidney stones, and as an aid in childbirth. A Chinese encyclopedia of 1596 refers to the medicinal "divine liquor of jade." Equal parts of jade, rice, and dew water were boiled in a copper pot, then filtered and drunk. Its effects were to strengthen the muscles and give them suppleness, harden the bones, calm the mind, enrich the flesh and purify the blood.

Not surprisingly, modern gem elixir made with jade treats the heart, kidneys, liver, and spleen, and cleanses the blood. It is an aid in astral projection.

Jade was used in the New Stone Age, beginning about 10,000 B.C. In ancient Egypt, it is known to have been used as early as 5000 B.C. It was used in Switzerland by the Lake Dwellers until

1500 B.C. It was introduced in China in the early 1700s, and at once assumed its proper place of veneration and value.

Though it is respected now for its beauty in ornaments, its first uses were utilitarian. Jade was carved into adzes, axheads, knives, spear tips, and other weapons, prayer gongs, vases, cups, figurines, tools, ritual objects and fingering pieces, as well as amulets. It is hard, and as tough as old boots—pure hell to carve—but in the hands of an expert that poses no problem except time. Many exquisite jade *objets d'art* have taken months in the carving.

In 1176 the "Illustrated Description of Ancient Jade" was published in China; this seven-hundred-book catalog listed the superlative collection of jade objects belonging to the first emperor of the Southern Sung Dynasty. The most remarkable piece in this enormous treasury was a four-sided plaque of pure white jade over two feet tall and wide, whose design had been miraculously engraved on it. There was a figure of the Buddhist saint Samantabahadra seated on a mat with a vase on its left and an alms bowl on the right, surrounded by rocks enveloped in clouds. The plaque was said to have been washed out of a sacred cave by a violent, mysterious current in 1068.

In Egypt, a celt (a prehistoric axelike tool) of nephrite was found, both faces of which were engraved with mystical inscriptions in Greek. Other such implements exist with Chaldean inscriptions and Mithraic scenes. (Mithraism was a Persian religious cult that rivaled Christianity in the late Roman Empire. The celt with Mithraic scenes was found in Great Britain.)

✧

JET

Jet is black, black, or black. It's of vegetable origin, having fossilized from the wood of cone-bearing plants. Actually it is a variety of extremely hard coal. It is tough and durable, warm to the touch, and able to take a high polish. It is much softer than minerals used for gems, being only about 3.75. During its polishing with tripoli and oil, jet must be kept cooled with water or it will fly apart under the heat. Yet it has a toughness that makes it suitable for jewelry.

The ancient Greeks dedicated jet to Cybele, the goddess of nature. It is associated with the planet Saturn. When worn by a traveler, jet will protect her or him from accident and inconvenience. As an amulet it was used by numerous religions to ward off the effects of the Evil Eye. Since it was thought to give spiritual strength, rosaries and bracelets were made from it and worn by Christian monks and nuns.

Dreams of jet indicate a negative, materialistic approach to life. If someone gives you a jet object in a dream, it's a prediction of disappointment. If, however, you give away a jet ornament, it means that you're able to drop old grudges and move forward serenely.

Jet is said to have healing powers in treating headaches, epilepsy, and tumors. The powder mixed with wine may be taken to ease toothaches. Jet has often been made into an ointment with beeswax and is used in treating toothaches and tumors. A pungent oil can be made from it which, when held to the nose, "ripens wounds" and is effective in treating gout, cramps, and palsy.

Jet is said to ease anxiety and depression. It is good for colds, epilepsy, fever, and premenstrual syndrome.

Paleolithic man used jet for talismanic purposes. Jet ornaments, shaped by flint implements, have been found among Paleolithic remains in the caves of the Kesserloch in Switzerland. They were also found in Paleolithic cave deposits in Belgium, where the jet pieces had been rounded and pierced as if for use in necklaces or pendants. The jet in Switzerland was identified as having come from deposits near Württemberg; that in Belgium from Lorraine; so even those eons ago there was trade.

The Pueblo Indians used jet (among other materials) for making amulets. A fine figure of a frog was found at Pueblo Bonito in 1896. The craftsman gave the jet frog turquoise eyes and a turquoise collar.

The finest variety known is Whitby jet, found by the monks at Whitby Abbey in Yorkshire, before the Reformation. After Queen Victoria's husband, Prince Albert, died, the entire nation was drawn with the Queen into prolonged mourning, during which period jet jewelry was immensely popular.

· · ·

✦

KUNZITE

Kunzite was discovered in Connecticut in 1879, and just before 1900 in Pala, California. The stone was named for George Frederick Kunz, the eminent gemologist at Tiffany's. Kunzite is an orchid pink of various shades, or a lilac blue. It is a particularly clean and brilliant stone. To retain as much of the richness of color as possible, it is always cut deep. Kunzite can be colorless, violet, or strong rose-violet, depending on which side of the crystal you look through.

Another power of kunzite is that of absorbing sunlight or artificial light and then glowing in the dark. Kunzite contains lithium and some radioactive uranium. Its parent mineral, spodumene, is an important industrial source of lithium and lithium salts.

Recent divination associates this lovely gemstone with the angel Atar, a Zoroastrian genius of fire, and a chief of the celestial beings called Yazatas. Under the leadership of the archangels, the Yazatas guard the interests of humankind.

If you dream of a kunzite ring, it's an indication that you'll be very happy with one you love. Dreams of buying an unmounted kunzite mean that it will be a long time before you marry. Seeing someone wearing a kunzite on the lapel or near the collarbone signifies that the person is more important than he seems to be.

In healing, it is most useful for relieving shoulder muscle tension and for causing the blood to flow within the body more easily. When used, the stone should be kept moving so as not to draw further blockages to the area under treatment.

Kunzite elixir balances the entire cardiovascular system on the physical and cellular levels, and generally regenerates tissue. It is valuable in treating blood disorders.

There is a singing nature to this stone, a happy and sociable feeling. Kunzite has a flowing, orderly quality about it; its gentle but firm impact on the wearer is to make him become steadier, more disciplined.

• • •

✧

LAPIS LAZULI

Catherine II of Russia, a woman who truly loved luxury, knew how to make the eyes of even Russian nobles widen: she had the walls of a ballroom at Tsarskoye Seloe lined with lapis lazuli. Though it has been mined for six thousand years, lapis has always been considered a rare and precious stone.

And no wonder. There is only one source of this wonderful deep-blue or violet-blue stone: the Badakhshān district of Afghanistan. There are no roads that lead there. The way is treacherous and hostile, obstructed by swift rivers, deep gorges, sharp ridges, frightening cliffs, bitter marshes, an avalanche now and then, and, toward journey's end, numbing cold. The mines are located high on a frigid, wind-scoured mountaintop. And once you arrive, you find the mines tightly guarded, as they have been from the beginning. The only way to get lapis lazuli out to the world is to carry it in twenty- to fifty-pound pieces, on foot down the terrible narrow mountain pathways.

Lapis lazuli is opaque, rather a peculiar property in a gemstone so revered. But its color, even in a small piece, seems as deep as a canyon. Frequently there are inclusions of gold-colored iron pyrite veins, which give the velvety lost-in-dreams blue a look of action and vitality. Sometimes the inclusions will be of white calcite, far less rich and important-looking than the pyrite and consequently less expensive for the piece.

Lapis was believed by the Sumerians to be the gift of the heavens to their people. The mines were a long distance from southern Mesopotamia, with the journey even harder then than now. Nevertheless, the Sumerians recognized their stone of stones. Because the way was so arduous, they carried out only the finest specimens. They associated the intense blue of lapis lazuli with the vast expanse of blue sky to be seen in Mesopotamia, and greatly revered the gem for this reason.

One of the sacred Sumerian tales concerns the Queen of Heaven, the mother-goddess Inanna's descent to the underworld, wearing a crown that was undoubtedly set with lapis beads, carrying a lapis lazuli measuring rod and line. A Sumerian cuneiform tablet carries a poem to Inanna describing plans to build for her a great shrine of lapis lazuli. Other such tablets praise the glories of the deep-blue gem.

In the early 1920s, in the tomb of Queen Puabi of the Sumerians (around 2600 B.C.) were found numerous objects of lapis lazuli: a crown of gold leaves bearing a band of lapis beads and lapis "eyes," a lapis lazuli choker for her neck, and seven or more strands of lapis roundels. Fine Sumerian seals were made of lapis lazuli; one seal, now in a British museum, delineates Inanna standing under the moon, with an eye motif and the goddess's seven-pointed rosette. The finest ring excavated from this same area is of gold, lapis lazuli, and carnelian.

Lapis is used not only for jewelry, and for veneering precious boxes and ballroom walls, but in medieval times it was the basis for the loveliest and most enduring of blue paints and dyes. A nobleman commissioning an illuminated manuscript or a painting was careful to specify that only "ultramarine"—lapis lazuli—be used. It was especially effective when the subject was of a spiritual nature, such as for the robe of the Virgin Mary or the cassock of a monk transcribing a sacred work. The ultramarine blues painted centuries ago are today as fresh as the day they were applied.

If you dream of finding lapis lazuli, it's a sign that events will at last start going your way. If the stone is set in gold, you'll be lucky financially too. If there is an argument over this gem, it's a warning to look carefully at any papers you will sign soon.

In meditational use of lapis lazuli, the stone enables the user to gain a higher insight into all things that concern him. Psychic Lenora Huett channels the advice that the stone be placed on the crown chakra, at the back top of the head, during meditation. Lapis lazuli is not a stone to be used for divination, but rather for self-realization and the development of inner discipline. It also helps in opening the throat or communications chakra.

✦

MALACHITE

Malachite is a green carbonate of copper. Its colors range from light to dark green, are variegated, and occur in ripples, knobs, whorls, eye-spots, and uneven bands. Its most spectacular effect is that of the eye of a hurricane, surrounded by swirling green winds.

Malachite amplifies the wearer's mood, whether positive or negative. It was used to ward off evil spirits. It provided physical protection, and augmented wealth. Apache Indians attached a bead of malachite to rifles to ensure shooting accuracy. It is a gem of midsummer, and of the names Mark and Martha.

It is the gem of Nadiel, angel of migration and ruler of December.

To dream of malachite in any form signifies sweeping changes in your life. Keep your eye on your goal, and those changes will be for your betterment.

Malachite should not be ground, for its dust is highly toxic. But if the stone is made into an elixir for healing, on the cellular level this gem promotes complete tissue regeneration. It is an antidote to radiation, especially that absorbed by workers at video terminals.

This strange-looking gem is a valuable decorative stone used in polished slabs for small tables, boxes, and ornaments. In Leningrad, Russia, the magnificent columns of Saint Isaac's cathedral and the hall facings of the Winter Palace are made of malachite.

Malachite was being mined in the Sinai Peninsula in 4000 B.C. It was used in jewelry and amulets; also it was crushed and used as a pigment called mountain green.

✧

MARCASITE

Marcasite is the gem mineral that is cut into tiny twinkles and set in white gold in rings your grandmother wore. Sometimes settings as big as one's fingernail were made up entirely of marcasites. Often it substituted for diamond, ornamenting red garnet or blue spinel. Marcasite is hard and heavy, but fragile because it is apt to cleave any old way. It is sometimes called white iron pyrite. It grows in the form of rosettes. As a mineral it is pale yellow with a slight greenish tinge; but as a gemstone, on its faceted surfaces there is a bright, metallic, oyster-white luster. The stones are always quite small and set close together for a sparkling effect. Its name comes from the Arabic *marqashita*.

Dreams of marcasite will always have a timeless quality about them—and this signifies that clocks and calendars don't mean much to you. If you have repeated dreams of this gem, you should look at your life-style and see if you're truly satisfied with its direction.

In healing, marcasite crystals may be used for spot cleaning of debris formed under the skin; scar tissue, arthritic calculi, kidney and bladder stones, gallstones, and minor spot-pain of unknown origin.

The crystal or crystals should be held in the hand slightly above the trouble spot and moved in a clockwise motion, starting from the center and widening the circles, nine circles in all. On the ninth circle, give your wrist a light flip as you "discard" the debris psychically removed. Do this at least three times, a few times daily.

For some people, treatment with marcasite vibrations may be helpful in skin disorders such as acne, eczema, or ringworm.

Always rinse hands and crystal in running water after each healing use.

✧

ONYX

Onyx is a cryptocrystalline quartz, meaning that the crystals are minute. It is often marked with white or colored bands. It may be white, green, brown, or black, or a combination of colors.

Onyx is the gem of Saturn, the midnight hour, and the angel Gabriel. Gabriel is one of the two highest-ranking angels. He presides over Paradise, and sits on the left-hand side of God. He is the spirit of Truth.

Dreams of onyx in colors are gateway dreams—a new life and new attitude are opening to you. If you dream of black onyx, you will resist this gradual rearrangement. But go with it; it's good.

Onyx has been used against epilepsy, melancholy, and depression. It is said to transmute negative vibrations so that they are given forth as positive. It aids in the ability to think objectively. It helps with emotional stability, calms fears of the unknown. It works through the solar plexus and stabilizes the pancreas.

It is carved and used for jewelry, figurines, book ends, and more. The Indians and Persians used onyx in necklaces and talismans against the Evil Eye. It is the eleventh stone in the breastplate of the High Priest and was also used with the ephod (the apron-like garment worn under the breastplate); and it was the fifth Foundation Stone of the Holy City.

Over a figure of the Mother Mary, on the tomb of Saint Elizabeth of Marburg, was a fine onyx engraved with the heads of Castor and Pollux, twin sons of Leda by Zeus.

✧

ORTHOCLASE

Orthoclase is a feldspar gem, handsome kissing-cousin of the elegant moonstone. Its transparent yellow or pink shade is used as a gemstone. The yellow is barely yellow, with a hint of pussy-willow grey luster down in it, so that the stone is neither yellow nor grey, but flashes pale yellow and almost grey, like the subtle colors of a winter goldfinch created of glass. In a stone of two or three carats or more, the color variations are endlessly interesting.

It is the gem for the angel Metatron, greatest of all the heavenly hierarchs. He is prince of the Divine Presence, heavenly scribe, the tallest angel in heaven. Metatron is the angel of life and death.

Dreams of unmounted orthoclase imply new openness and adaptability in your love relationships. An orthoclase worn on the wrist signifies the erasure of old restrictions.

Used in healing, an orthoclase crystal is good for treating the eyes, either diseases of the eye or vision problems. Wash the hands and the crystal with soap and water before starting treatment of each eye, and when finished. Hold the tumbled crystal, or the cut and polished gemstone, with the thumb and two fingers. Make a sweeping motion about three inches away from the closed eyelids, starting at the bridge of the nose and making an outward arc to the temple. At the end of each arc lift the crystal up slightly.

✧

QUARTZ

Naturally formed clear quartz crystals (rock crystal), though not highly suitable as gemstones, are of interest here because of the intense energies they make available to human beings. Quartz is so important in the Aquarian Age that numerous books have been published on using its energies in meditation, divination, checking Akashic records, healing, and other uses.

Clear quartz crystals are a naturally balanced energy field. Quartz can block an excessive flow of energy, calming the person. It can transmit energy from one system to another. It can store energy or focus it. It can heighten perceptions in meditation, increase the power of telepathic transmission, and vastly speed up the healing of cuts and burns.

Used in healing, a quartz crystal can revitalize and restore energy and balance to the physical body. It removes thought forms and increases psychic awareness.

Dreaming of quartz crystals is an indication that you must watch your energy levels and be more aware of your overall health.

There are numerous kinds of quartz that are all highly useful in healing. Rutilated quartz or purple or violet quartz helps reverse aging, eases depression, and quells fears. Clear quartz treats disorders of the abdominal area and the pituitary gland. Rose quartz brings increased fertility and restores balance to the emotions. Blue quartz strengthens the immune system and the metabolism. Black quartz eases heart diseases, muscular deterioration, and neurological disorders.

Quartz crystals can grow to great size. A milky quartz crystal found in Siberia weighed 13 metric tons: 28,660 pounds.

✧

RHODOCHROSITE

A rather unusual gemstone, which is fun to say, is rhodochrosite, a manganese carbonate with a hardness of 4 on the Mohs' scale. It is a rare pink crystal which is translucent and has a vitreous to pearly luster and a pale pinkish streak through it. It also occurs in banded pinks and whites. A large mass of the crystals may be polished for use as an ornamental stone. As a gem it may be faceted, or cut cabochon, and mounted in jewelry. This gem is also of interest to scientists and collectors.

In healing, rhodochrosite elixir is used to prevent mental breakdown and extreme emotional trauma. It detoxifies the kidneys and cleanses the subconscious mind. It strengthens the sense of self.

✧

SPINEL

In Spanish it is *espinela*. Its Greek term translates as "a spark." Its colors are red, blue, brown, and black. The violet stone is called almandine spinel; the orange red, rubicelle; rosy red is called balas ruby (coming from Balascia, ancient capital of the province of Badakhshān in Afghanistan); and the deep crimson is ruby spinel. Yellow and green spinels are quite rare. The violet stone has captivating hues. The deep blue spinel is exciting, with a cool aloofness in its color. It resembles sapphire, but never quite *becomes* sapphire, any more than the red ones transform into ruby. One type of spinel is a light steel blue in daylight but appears violet under artificial light.

The stone tends toward brittleness; but because it is hard and clear and takes a high polish, with a variety of compelling colors, spinel makes a fine gemstone. However, it is so often called by the names of other stones that it has a hard time just being itself.

Oddly, though spinel is available and not expensive, synthetic spinel is widely used—as a substitute for other stones. In class rings and inexpensive jewelry in general, there may be a "topaz" or a "sapphire" that is really synthetic spinel.

Spinel is the gem of Raziel, angel of proclamation. He is the angel who revealed to Adam the Divine Mysteries.

If you dream of owning a red spinel, this is a warning to evaluate very carefully any proposal that is made to you this month. Should you dream that you try to trade an object you own for a blue spinel, you will be rewarded for honesty in some waking endeavor. If someone gives you a spinel in a dream, it signifies that you must learn to accommodate yourself to changed circumstances.

It is said that the vibrations of spinel are a sporadic energy with the capability of renewing vitality and the desire to try again. It gives hope to those who thought hope was dead. It's a good starter-upper. It attracts help from others, raises the thoughts, and purifies the imagination. In healing it is a powerful general cleanser. It aligns the etheric and emotional bodies.

In 1801 a series of tests were made with various minerals upon a woman who was psychically sensitive. When spinel was held near her, she felt a force that began in her hand and moved upward along her arm. No further use was reported of this discovery.

Once a woman named Heraclis found a stork with a broken leg. These birds are encouraged to nest around houses in Europe, as it is believed they bring good luck. Though in poor health and wealth herself, Heraclis mended the bird's leg, and fed it until it was well and able to leave. Some time later the stork returned, bearing in its beak a balas ruby—a rosy red spinel—as a gift of gratitude for her kindness.

For many centuries fine rosy red spinel was thought to be ruby. Many famous rubies—such as the Côte de Bretagne, which was carved in the shape of a dragon, the Ruby of the Black Prince of England, and the Timur Ruby that once belonged to Tamerlane, the Mogul conqueror of the late fourteenth century—have proved to be spinels.

✧
STAUROLITE

Staurolite, found in Georgia, Virginia, France, and Italy, forms crystals in the shape of crosses. It is a hard (7–7.5) brown semiopaque hydrated aluminum iron silicate. Sometimes the crosses look like +, sometimes like ✕. In a book written in 1758, the staurolite was sometimes called Baseler Taufstein (baptismal stone) or *lapis crucifer*, the cross-shaped stone. In Brittany the crystal is worn as a charm because, as the legend goes, the stone was dropped from the heavens. Also known as fairy crosses or fairy tears, they are said to have formed from the tears of the fairies at the time of Jesus's crucifixion. President Theodore Roosevelt wore one as a charm on his pocket watch chain.

Staurolite is valuable for grounding one to earth energies while meditating. Used with clear or blue quartz, it can provide protection and discernment in astral travel.

✧
TANZANITE

Tanzanite, only twenty-one years old as a gemstone, had to be or do something spectacular to achieve notice in the gem world.

Discovered in northern Tanzania near Mount Kilimanjaro in 1967, it came to the attention of Henry B. Platt, then president of Tiffany's in New York. Mr. Platt knew there was a need for a gemstone of good deep blue that was less expensive than sapphire. He decided to give this hard, clear, lustrous, beautiful new stone a name and launch it as a gem.

His campaign proved successful, for tanzanite is one of the "in" stones in today's market. It compares superbly with sapphire, for in its splendid violet-blue color there is plenty of fire. Many famous people have bought tanzanite for their gem collections. A historical romance author I know has a stunning tanzanite gemstone set in an antique mounting of yellow gold, in a pleasing blend of the old and the new.

Tanzanite's spectacular trick is its property of trichroism. Turned in one direction, its color is brilliant blue; in another direction it becomes purple; in a third it is almost flesh pink. The brown, pink, yellow, or green tanzanite may be heat-treated to obtain the gem's most-wanted violet-blue color. It is found in only one location, and the supply there has become sharply limited. So, as a gem, it may always be on the rare side, and of continuing value to collectors.

Its healing abilities are narrow but potent: it strengthens the male genitals or the female cervix and increases fertility. It stimulates the base chakra, balances the individual, and increases creativity.

✧

TITANITE

Titanite, or sphene, varies from white to rose red, yellow green, gray, dark brown, and black. It is transparent or translucent, with a sometimes diamondlike luster. Some colors show trichroism (three different colors, depending on which section of the crystal one looks through). Transparent stones of good color are cut cabochon or faceted and make attractive and valuable gemstones.

Titanite elixir is used in healing the ethereal aspects of the individual. It aligns the mental, emotional, and spiritual bodies, and stimulates metabolism.

Moldavite:
THE GEM FROM OUTER SPACE

Now and then there comes along a discovery—or a rediscovery—which is so important that the world seems to pause for a moment as if in tribute before continuing its regular course. In Atlantis this substance was quartz crystal, still important to us thousands of years later. In the time of Pythagoras it was the relativity among numerals. Today, as we enter the Aquarian Age, a period of opening consciousness, some who are attuned to the Infinite have rediscovered moldavite.

Since moldavite is a tektite mineral, of meteoritic origin, first let's get some background on meteorites and tektites. Meteorites (debris from meteors, or "shooting stars") are extraterrestrial objects that for billions of years have been falling to earth. In your own lifetime uncounted numbers of meteorites have fallen; but most of them, once they enter earth's atmosphere, melt or disintegrate from heat and friction. Those that are large enough to survive the entry into the atmosphere crash shallowly into the land.

Tektites are meteoritic in origin. Tektite is a natural glass, black to brown to green, its particles frequently thumb-sized and rounded in shape. These blobs are composed of approximately 73 percent silica, and the remainder consists of various oxides plus other common components of rocks formed on earth.

Tektites are not especially recommended for gem use in rings, since their hardness is only about 5.5 to 6, which is that of window glass. There are fewer than ten places on earth where tektites are found: Czechoslovakia, Australia, Indonesia, the Philippines, Texas, and Georgia.

Moldavite is a tektite. Because of its origin, moldavite does not form in crystals. It most frequently occurs in a flattened egg shape. Moldavite is a charcoal green, a dark green with a definite gray in the coloration. A display box full of moldavite shards is pretty boring, looking an awful lot like broken charcoal. But when you hold a piece up to light, the wonderful secret of moldavite springs itself on you. It is transparent in spite of its darkness; it is full of wrinkles and bubbles and swirls. It has undeniable personality and immense presence.

Moldavite itself is of uncertain, though most likely meteoritic, origin. It was created somewhere in outer space, formed under conditions of extremely high temperatures and rapid cooling, and came to earth. It is found exclusively in Moravia and Bohemia, around the Moldau (Vltava) River in Czechoslovakia.

Moldavite can be cut, faceted, and polished as a gem. In this form it takes on a more olive hue, losing some of its mystery. It was used as a gemstone in France and England in the eighteenth century. Then it was popular to set brooches with gems, the first letters of which expressed a sentiment. In the word *Mizpah* ("God be with you till we meet again") either moonstone or moldavite stood for the *M*, with indicolite, zircon, peridot, asteria, hyacinth, or alternates forming the remainder.

Tektites of all colors have been objects of veneration for thousands of years. Shards of it found with other relics in a cave indicate its use twenty-five thousand years ago. In India in the second century A.D. a record was made concerning reverence for tektites which went back seven hundred years. The Sanskrit term is *agni mani*, meaning fire pearl. The *rishis* of India used tektite medicinally. In Indonesia tektites were prized for their great power and good fortune, and became a part of the inheritance a son received from his father, generation after generation. The Tibetans worshiped this stone by placing it upon their heads. They attribute to moldavite a celestial origin, believing that it came from the constellation of Orion.

This much about moldavite is recorded knowledge. But moldavite and its properties go well beyond our present investigation and understanding. Robert Simmons and his wife Kathy Warner, and Dr. Randall N. and Vicki V. Baer, are instrumental in introducing this important gem to modern use. Rob Simmons, a jeweler of Gloucester, Massachusetts, had the idea in 1984 to create jewelry to commemorate Halley's comet. Through serendipity he became acquainted with George Bruce, who had written an article on moldavite in 1958. Bruce gave Simmons some samples of moldavite. While making comet jewelry using the gemstone, Rob met Kathy, a healer and spiritual channel who had worked with crystals for more than ten years. Kathy, holding moldavite, felt drawn out of her body and into the cosmos, able to look back at Earth and feel a complete sense of oneness with all Creation. From the stone she felt not only a nurturing energy, but also a profound connection to universal intelligence and guidance.

About a year later, Rob sent a sample of moldavite and a letter to the Baers in Los Alamos, New Mexico. They are co-directors of a project to develop technologies based on light for use in healing and transformation; their book, *Windows Of Light*, deals with the use of crystals in self-transformation. The Baers phoned Rob immediately with astonishing news. Four years before, an alien master had told the Baers that they would be working with a green crystal from space. When they saw and held moldavite, they knew that was it.

From the Baer's channeling work comes the following information. Moldavite is not a stone for healing. It is a powerful tool for interdimensional communication. Its entire development was a cooperative project of alien scientists working in a distant galaxy not yet known to Earth. The stone is a combination of the meteoritic materials available there, influenced by the high-energy vibrational fields projected into and around it by the scientific entities. The meteorite in which moldavite was formed was programmed to connect with Earth.

After a journey of tens or hundreds of thousands of years, the meteorite containing moldavite landed on the target planet. There it waited, unconcerned with the passage of Earth time until its discovery. Scientists say the stone is thirteen to fifteen million years old. It therefore came to earth in the late Miocene Period when, according to Theosophical teachings, the late Lemurian-early Atlantean civilizations were in being.

Mineralogically, the crystal state (a model of order) has usually been considered superior in development to the amorphous (blob) state. The reasoning has been that if the substance itself is unordered (having formed in blobs, as tektites do), then its performance (in computers, solar technology, and so on) will also lack order. However, this has been disproved in this decade. Working

with tektites and other amorphous substances, scientists have discovered that devices can be made that are cheaper, smaller, faster,
and more durable than transistors; and these will store information
or energy, convert light and heat to electricity, harden cutting
tools, and improve optical disk memories for computers, and so
on.

In personal use, moldavite's best work is done with the third
eye and the primary mind centers. These are the centers that have
the most direct links to interdimensional communication. This is
the highest and best use of this unique stone. Other possible applications fade into insignificance.

The Baers state that moldavite must be faceted and polished in
symmetrical, geometrically balanced ways in order to activate its
tremendous capabilities and produce harmonious effects of balanced consciousness. Shapes they especially recommend are the
emerald cut or the pyramidal shape. Faceting the stone into the
same angles as the Great Pyramid gives moldavite ideal capabilities
for communicating with other dimensions.

Moldavite works best with gold, not well with silver or copper.
It works very well with quartz, particularly the Herkimer diamond, found in New York. Quartz amplifies, stabilizes, and increases the energy range of moldavite's specifically focused
capabilities. Other gems known to complement moldavite include
diamond, opal, celestite, and aquamarine.

Suggested use for a single faceted piece is to place it on hypoal-
lergenic first-aid tape and apply it to the third eye (between and
just above the brows). This can be used with meditation, and also
with various forms of interdimensional communication, with
Light-work, and during sleep.

Many other possible multiple gem applications are suggested in
the Baers' book, *The Crystal Connection.*

The Baers recommend against using salt to clear and cleanse this
gemstone, though that is a common method for clearing quartz.
They suggest using a bulk demagnetizer. Another method is to
place the moldavite in a small clear-glass bowl of water; place the
bowl in the center of the base of a pyramid. Set up a small Star of
David gridwork close around the bowl. Leave for twelve to twenty-
four hours, then wash the moldavite in running water.

You can wear your moldavite in a brooch, pendant, or in earrings. Its strange green color goes well with light, clear blues, or with the autumn shades. But be aware that this gem from outer space has capabilities and energies that you may not be familiar with. Once you are accustomed to it, you'll enjoy the journey that moldavite is ready to take you on.

———————————◇———————————

The gemstones in our lives serve us in many ways. They bring us beauty. From the cells out, they heal and balance us physically, mentally, emotionally. They ease our anxiety, improve our memory, regenerate us. They help us transcend our absorption in daily routines, by activating our chakras and enhancing our spiritual awareness. They connect us with the universe. They unite us with all that is.

Let us enjoy them then, these gifts from the earth, in the myriad ways that they are open to us. Let us use them, for the highest good.

Tables

OFFICIAL LIST OF BIRTHSTONES

◇

MONTH	BIRTHSTONE	COLORS	TRANSPARENT (T) TRANSLUCENT (Tl) OR OPAQUE (O)
January	Garnet	Red to brown to black, yellow, green, orange	T
February	Amethyst	Only purple or violet tints	T
March	Bloodstone	Bright to dark green with small red spots	Tl to O
	Aquamarine	Blue to sea green	T
April	Diamond	"Colorless," pink, brown, yellow, shades of blue	T
May	Emerald	Deep rich green	T
June	Pearl	White, pink, cream, blue-black	Tl
	Moonstone	Milky bluish opalescence	Tl
	Alexandrite	Bluish green by daylight; raspberry red by artificial light	T
July	Ruby	Deep red tinged with violet	T
August	Sardonyx	Bands of orange-red, white, and brown	Tl to O
	Peridot	Light to dark olive green	T
September	Sapphire	Blue, green, yellow, pink, violet, colorless	T
October	Opal	Background white, black, orange-red, all with vari-colored inner fires	Tl
	Tourmaline	White, all colors, black	T
November	Topaz	Golden brown, light green or blue, violet, brown, colorless	T
	Citrine	Pale yellow to smoky yellow	T
December	Turquoise	Sky blue to green	O
	Zircon	Reddish, brownish, yellow, smoky, colorless	T

MINERAL ORIGIN	RELATIVE HARDNESS MOHS' SCALE	WHERE FOUND NOW	ANCIENT BELIEFS AND USES
Garnet	6.5–7.5	South Africa, U.S.	Prevents travel accidents; fever remedy; garnet bullets made more deadly wound.
Quartz	7	South Africa, Brazil, U.S.	Inspires virtue and high ideals; symbol of justice, courage and authority; prevents drunkenness.
Quartz	7		Gives courage, strength, wisdom; heals wounds; cures impotence.
Beryl	7.5–8	Brazil, U.S.	Brings happiness, perpetual youth; tells future; power over the devil.
Carbon/ Diamond	10	South Africa, Siberia, U.S.	Softens anger; strengthens love; promotes marital accord.
Beryl	7.5–8	Colombia, S. Africa	Brings success, love, constancy; cures epilepsy.
Aragonite	3.5–4	Persian Gulf, Sri Lanka, Cultured, Japan	Brings enlightenment and courage; symbol of purity.
Feldspar	6–6.5	Brazil, U.S.	Foretells the future; acts as love charm.
Chrysoberyl	8.5	USSR	Since 1830, Russia's national gem.
Corundum	9	India, Sri Lanka, Africa, Thailand, U.S.	Brings wealth; health; wisdom; warns of enemies and dangers.
Quartz	7	Madagascar	Inspires courage; strengthens martial love.
Olivine	6.5–7	Egypt, U.S.	Overcomes timidity; brings gladness, serenity, and eloquence.
Corundum	9	Sri Lanka, U.S.	Cools the blood; guards against insanity; truth, constancy, and secret messages from the Almighty.
Silica or Quartz	5.5–6.5	Australia	Preserves blonde hair; brings luck.
Tourmaline	7–7.5	Burma, U.S.	No ancient traditions.
Topaz	8	Brazil, U.S.	Faithfulness, fruitfulness, friendship.
Quartz	7	Brazil, Sri Lanka	Same as topaz.
Turquoise	6	Iran, New Mexico, Persia	Brings prosperity; cheers the soul; prevents the wearer from falling.
Zircon	7.5	Australia, U.S.	Cures insomnia; prevents plague.

YOUR ZODIACAL STONE
◇

Capricorn	Garnet
Aquarius	Amethyst
Pisces	Aquamarine, bloodstone
Aries	Diamond
Taurus	Emerald
Gemini	Pearl, moonstone, alexandrite
Cancer	Ruby
Leo	Peridot, sardonyx
Virgo	Sapphire
Libra	Opal, tourmaline
Scorpio	Topaz, citrine
Sagittarius	Turquoise, zircon

STONES OF THE BREASTPLATE
OF AARON, FIRST HIGH PRIEST OF THE JEWS

It is instructive to see how many different interpretations can be given to a single word over the centuries. Even different versions of the Bible disagree on the exact stone used in a certain position on the breastplate. In the table below, the first gem listed seems to be the preferred one. When the breastplate is recovered from its place of centuries-old safety, as recent channelings indicate it will be, then modern gemologists, with their specialized equipment, can positively identify the stones for us.

1. Sard or carnelian, ruby, red jasper, red feldspar
2. Topaz, peridot, yellow or light-green serpentine
3. Carbuncle, emerald, rock crystal, green feldspar
4. Emerald, ruby, garnet
5. Sapphire, lapis lazuli
6. Diamond, green jasper, jade, onyx, corundum, sardonyx
7. Hyacinth, jacinth, amber, sapphire, brown, or yellow agate
8. Ruby, banded agate
9. Amethyst, dark blue or purple quartz
10. Beryl, yellow jasper, chrysolite, quartz, topaz
11. Onyx, beryl (aquamarine) malachite, turquoise
12. Jasper (green), jade

FOUNDATION STONES OF THE HOLY CITY

―――――――――◇―――――――――

It was the custom in Old Testament times to build deposits of gems and precious metals into the foundations of temples and palaces, as at Ephesus, Idfu, and Persepolis. We follow a similar tradition today in placing memorabilia in the cornerstones of new buildings.

In the foundation walls of the Holy City were set precious stones engraved with the names of the twelve apostles.

It is nearly impossible to identify these stones in modern terms, for the several versions of the Bible have used different words for the stones. The table below illustrates the radical change from older versions of the Bible to the Jerusalem Bible.

AUTHORIZED VERSION REVISED STANDARD VERSION	JERUSALEM BIBLE
1. Jasper	1. Diamond
2. Sapphire	2. Lapis lazuli
3. Agate or chalcedony	3. Turquoise
4. Emerald	4. Crystal
5. Onyx or sardonyx	5. Agate
6. Carnelian or sard	6. Ruby
7. Chrysolite	7. Gold quartz
8. Beryl	8. Malachite
9. Topaz	9. Topaz
10. Chrysoprase	10. Emerald
11. Jacinth	11. Sapphire
12. Amethyst	12. Amethyst

STONES ASSOCIATED WITH THE APOSTLES
------------------------◇------------------------

As with the Foundation Stones, it is difficult to be exact about these associations. Various sources over the centuries have added information, and the names of stones have changed or been confused. This is a compilation.

Amethyst	Judas Iscariot, Matthias
Beryl or aquamarine	Thomas
Carbuncle (garnet or ruby)	Andrew, Simon Peter
Carnelian	Philip
Chalcedony	James, son of Zebedee; Philip
Chrysolite or peridot	Matthew, Bartholomew
Chrysoprase	Jude, Lebbeus Thaddeus
Emerald	John the Baptist, James, son of Zebedee
Hyacinth, jacinth, or zircon	Simon Zelotes
Jasper	Simon Peter
Sapphire	Andrew, Paul
Sard	Bartholomew, Philip
Sardonyx	Philip; James ("the Less"), son of Alpheus
Topaz	James the Less, Matthew

STONES ASSOCIATED WITH THE ANGEL HIERARCHY

◇

The Seraphim	Sard
The Cherubim	Topaz
The Thrones	Jasper
The Dominions	Chrysolite
The Principalities	Onyx
The Powers	Beryl
The Virtues	Sapphire
The Archangels	Carbuncle
The Angel Princes	Emerald

STONES ASSOCIATED WITH SPECIFIC ANGELS

❖

It is understood that the angels are without gender, though to mortals to whom they appear, they may seem male or female. In the text of this book, they are usually given gender.

GEMSTONE	ANGEL'S NAME
Agate	Bariel
Alexandrite	Geburathiel
Amethyst	Adnachiel
Aquamarine/beryl	Humiel
Citrine	Caneloas
Diamond	Israfel, Hamatiel
Emerald	Muriel
Garnet	Amriel
Jasper	Barchiel
Kunzite	Atar
Malachite	Nadiel
Moonstone	Ofaniel
Onyx	Gabriel
Opal	Nibra Ha-Rishon
Orthoclase	Metatron
Pearl	Nelle
Peridot	Alair
Ruby	Malchadiel
Sapphire	Ashmodei, Verchiel
Sardonyx	Derdekea
Spinel	Raziel
Topaz	Ashmodel, Matthew
Tourmaline	Tadhiel
Turquoise	Verchiel
Zircon or jacinth	Tsuriel

GEMSTONES OF THE HOURS

—————————— ◇ ——————————

GEM	A.M. HOUR	GEM	P.M. HOUR
Morion	1:00	Jacinth	1:00
Hematite	2:00	Emerald	2:00
Malachite	3:00	Beryl	3:00
Lapis lazuli	4:00	Topaz	4:00
Turquoise	5:00	Ruby	5:00
Tourmaline	6:00	Opal	6:00
Chrysolite	7:00	Sardonyx	7:00
Amethyst	8:00	Chalcedony	8:00
Kunzite	9:00	Jade	9:00
Sapphire	10:00	Jasper	10:00
Garnet	11:00	Loadstone	11:00
Diamond	12:00 Noon	Onyx	12:00 Midnight

CORRESPONDENCE OF GEMS TO
METALS AND PLANETS
———————————— ◇ ————————————

PLANET	METAL	GEMSTONES
Sun	Gold	Diamond, ruby, chrysolite, hyacinth, opal
Moon	Silver	Emerald, opal, aquamarine, moonstone
Mercury	Mercury	Topaz, chrysolite, carnelian, agate, emerald, opal, turquoise, bloodstone
Venus	Copper	Light blue sapphire, agate, white pearl, chrysolite, coral, emerald, turquoise
Mars	Iron	Ruby, diamond, jasper, topaz
Jupiter	Zinc	Amethyst, turquoise, dark blue sapphire, jacinth, bloodstone
Saturn	Lead	Onyx, black pearl, chalcedony, topaz, bloodstone
Uranus	Platinum	Amber, amethyst
Neptune	Aluminum	Topaz and all iridescent stones

Bibliography

Anderson, Mary. *Numerology, the Secret Power of Numbers*. Wellingboro, Northamptonshire, Eng.: The Aquarian Press, 1981.

Attwater, Donald. *The Avenel Dictionary of Saints*. New York: Avenel Books, 1965.

Baer, Randall N. and Vicki V. *Windows of Light*. San Francisco: Harper and Row, 1984.

Bhattacharyya, Benoytosh and A. K. *Gem Therapy*. Calcutta: Firma KLM Private Ltd, 1981.

Buess, Lynn. *Numerology for the New Age*. Marina del Rey, Calif.: DeVorss and Company, 1978.

A truly awakened metaphysician, Lynn Buess shows his deep dedication to the spiritual path in all his works. His outlook comes from esoteric knowledge; he has a superior ability to transmit this to the reader.

Comay, Joan, and Ronald Brownrigg. *Who's Who in the Bible*. New York: Bonanza Books, 1980.

Crow, W. B. *Precious Stones*. Wellingboro, Northamptonshire, Eng.: The Aquarian Press 1968, 1980.

A really great small paperback book, rich with legends and knowledge of gemstones. Dates, exact details; pleasant manner of story telling.

Cudlipp, Edythe. *Jewelry*. New York: E. P. Dutton, 1980.

Dael. *The Crystal Book*. Sunol, Calif.: The Crystal Company, 1983.

Davidson, Gustav. *A Dictionary of Angels*. New York: The Free Press, Macmillan Publishing Company, 1967.
Written with humor and awe, this book, with its staggering load of research and cross-referencing, is the definitive book on angels, their origins, and their duties.

Desautels, Paul E. *The Gem Collections of the Smithsonian*. Washington, D.C.: Smithsonian Institution Press, 1979.

Dickinson, Joan Younger. *The Book of Pearls*. New York: Crown Publishers, Inc., 1968.

Evans, Joan. *Magical Jewels of the Middle Ages and the Renaissance*. New York: Dover Publications, Inc., 1976.
Good information here; but the author, a librarian at Oxford, assumed that her readers would know other languages as she did; so some valuable information gets lost within the Latin or French quotes.

Fernie, William T., M.D. *The Occult and Curative Powers of Precious Stones*. San Francisco: Harper and Row, 1973.

Finch, Elizabeth. *The Psychic Values of Gemstones*. Jerome, Ariz.: Luminary Press, 1980.
A friendly, very readable book, with plenty of research showing.

Frazer, Sir James G. *The Golden Bough*. New York: The Macmillan Company, 1958.
A collection of ancient religions and unusual stories. The definitive work of its time (1890) and still a valuable reference today.

Gregorietti, Guido. *Jewelry: History and Technique From the Egyptians to the Present*. Secaucus, N. J.: Chartwell Books, 1978.

Gubelin, Dr. Edward. *The Color Treasury of Gemstones*. New York: Thomas Y. Crowell Co., 1975.

Gurudas (channeled by Kevin Ryerson). *Gem Elixirs and Vibrational Healing. Vol. I*. Boulder, Colo.: Cassandra Press, 1985.
This is the pioneer book on the use of gem elixirs in healing. Well organized; the gemstones are given alphabetically; with fifty-five pages of tables, and clear instructions.

Kunz, George Frederick. *The Curious Lore of Precious Stones*. New York: Dover Publications, Inc., 1971.
The definitive book of books, the very Bible of information about gemstones. Absolutely loaded with legend, superstition, and information going back to the most ancient days. Frederick Kunz was gemologist at Tiffany's about the turn of the twentieth century. His library on gemstones was the world's largest. Truly a scholar, Mr. Kunz's writing is clear, vivid, forceful, and fascinating.

Kunz, George Frederick. *Rings for the Finger*. New York: Dover Publications, Inc., 1973.

Lewis, Lionel Smithett. *Saint Joseph of Arimathea at Glastonbury*. Cambridge, Eng.: James Clarke & Company, Ltd., 1982.

Lorusso, Julia, and Joel Glick. *Stratagems: a Mineral Perspective*. Albuquerque, N. M.: Brotherhood of Life, Inc., 1984.

Magill, Frank N., ed. *Great Events From History*. Englewood Cliffs, N. J.: Salem Press, Inc., 1972.

Manguel, Alberto, and Gianni Guadalupi. *The Dictionary of Imaginary Places*. New York: Macmillan Publishing Company, Inc., 1980.
Unique, beautifully written and illustrated, and exactly what the title implies.

Miller, Madeleine S., and J. Lane. *The New Harper's Bible Dictionary*. New York: Harper and Row, 1973.
Highly recommended for the Bible scholar for names, places, objects, and a thoroughgoing history of the biblical period.

Newhouse, Flower A. *Natives of Eternity*. Escondido, Calif.: The Christward Ministry, 1937, 1965.

Newhouse, Flower A. *Rediscovering the Angels*. Escondido, Calif.: The Christward Ministry, 1950, 1976.
Both Mrs. Newhouse's books mentioned here take the gentle approach to a somewhat touchy subject. Recommended for those just beginning to learn about angels.

Prinz, Martin, George Harlow, and Joseph Peters, eds. *Simon and Schuster's Guide to Rocks and Minerals*. New York: Simon and Schuster, 1977, 1978.

Richardson, Wally and Jenny, and Lenora Huett. *Spiritual Value of Gem Stones*. Marina del Rey, Calif.: Devorss and Company, Publishers, 1980.

Roberts, Brian. *The Diamond Magnates*. New York: Charles Scribner's Sons, 1972.

Robinson, Lady Stearn, and Tom Corbett. *The Dreamer's Dictionary*. New York: Warner Paperback Library, 1975.
The most thorough, most positive book available on interpretation of dreams.

Rutland, E. H. *An Introduction to the World's Gemstones*. Garden City, N. Y.: Doubleday, 1974.

Scott, Sir Walter. *Anne of Geierstein*. New York, Chicago: Dumont Publishing Co.

Shaub, Benjamin M. *Treasures From the Earth: The World of Rocks and Minerals*. New York: Crown Publishing Company, 1975.

Smith, Michael G. *Crystal Power*. Saint Paul, Minn.: Llewellyn Publications, 1985.

Thomas, William, and Kate Pavitt. *The Book of Talismans, Amulets and Zodiacal Gems*. North Hollywood, Calif.: Wilshire Book Company, 1970.

Wallace, Amy, and Bill Henkin. *The Psychic Healing Book*. Berkeley, Calif.: Wingbow Press, 1978.
Excellent introduction to methods of psychic healing. Exercises for increasing psychic awareness.

Weinstein, Michael. *The World of Jewel Stones*. New York: Sheridan House, Inc., 1958.

Wilson, Mab. *Gems*. New York: The Viking Press, 1967.
The author really loves gemstones; her work sparkles like diamond.

Wyndham, Robert Utley. *Enjoying Gems*. Brattleboro, Vt.: Stephen Greene Press, 1971.

Zim, Herbert S., and Paul R. Shaffer. *Rocks and Minerals*. New York: Golden Press, 1964.
An innocent little Golden Nature Guide; but beautifully concise, amply illustrated. A fine reference book for the layman.

Zucker, Benjamin. *A Connoisseur's Guide to Gems and Jewels*. New York: Thames & Hudson, 1984.
Wonderful for history and legends; this book has the feel of a hands-on experience.

zu Windisch-Graetz, Stephanie and Ghislaine. *Himalayan Kingdoms*. New Delhi: Roli Books International, 1981.
Beautiful photographs, excellent on-the-spot research.

Index

About the Author

Cornelia Parkinson, a professional writer since 1966, has published articles, stories, booklets, and nine books including several town histories.

Connie is a Libra, a Reiki healer, Tarot reader, mother of three adult daughters. She uses meditation, ESP, affirmations, dreams and visions daily. Her interest in gemstones, crystals, and precious metals goes back many years; she always wears or carries them. *Gem Magic* is the first of her numerous planned books on metaphysics. Her next book is about affirmations as a way of life and growth.

She now lives in Plymouth, Massachusetts.